Diagnosis and Rehabilitation
in
Clinical Neuropsychology

Diagnosis and Rehabilitation
in
Clinical Neuropsychology

By

CHARLES J. GOLDEN, Ph.D.

Assistant Professor of Psychology
The University of South Dakota
Vermillion, South Dakota

CHARLES C THOMAS · PUBLISHER
Springfield · Illinois · U.S.A.

Published and Distributed Throughout the World by
CHARLES C THOMAS • PUBLISHER
Bannerstone House
301-327 East Lawrence Avenue, Springfield, Illinois, U.S.A.

© *1978, by* CHARLES C THOMAS • PUBLISHER
ISBN 0-398-03678-0
Library of Congress Catalog Card Number: 77-4888

*With THOMAS BOOKS careful attention is given to all details of
manufacturing and design. It is the Publisher's desire to present books that are
satisfactory as to their physical qualities and artistic possibilities and
appropriate for their particular use. THOMAS BOOKS will be true to those
laws of quality that assure a good name and good will.*

Library of Congress Cataloging in Publication Data

Golden, Charles J.   1949-
    Diagnosis and rehabilitation in clinical neuro-
psychology.

    Bibliography. p.
    Includes indexes.
    1. Brain damage—Diagnosis. 2. Psychological
tests. 3. Brain—Localization of functions.
4. Neuropsychology. I. Title. [DNLM: 1. Brain
damage, Chronic—Diagnosis. 2. Brain damage,
Chronic—Rehabilitation. 3. Neurophysiology.
4. Psychophysiology. WL102 G618d]
RC386.2.G64   616.8   77-4888

Printed in the United States of America
C-1

To Ellenda

PREFACE

Human clinical neuropsychology has emerged in the last decade as one of the fastest growing subspecialties within clinical psychology. Interest in the area has been aroused by important research efforts demonstrating the utility of psychological testing in the diagnosis and assessment of brain injuries, as well as in the design and evaluation of rehabilitation programs for neurologically impaired clients.

The research relevant to clinical neuropsychology has taken several forms. One major approach has attempted a "behavioral mapping," relating behavioral functions to specific structures and pathways in the human brain. Researchers in this area have investigated the behavior of patients with well-defined brain lesions, associating these lesions with performance on numerous test procedures. Research on "split brain" individuals, whose right and left hemisphere have been separated by congenital error, injury, or surgical intervention, has added immeasurably to our knowledge about brain function.

A second major area of research has attempted to develop clinical tests and procedures that can reliably differentiate between brain-injured and neurologically intact individuals. A third line of research has attempted to develop batteries of tests and clinical procedures that cannot only diagnose the presence of brain injury but also identify such factors as the location, cause, and time of onset. Finally, some researchers have attempted to relate neuropsychological measures to the prognosis of an individual patient and to the design of rehabilitation programs that can maximally restore function to the impaired patient.

All of these areas are closely interrelated and of great importance to the clinical neuropsychologist, who needs to be familiar with each research area in order to most effectively provide clinical services to a neurologically impaired population. Unfortunately, there has yet to appear a unified review of the basic findings in each of these areas and their relationship to the clinical process. Literature involved with the practical aspects of clinical neuropsychology has been especially rare.

The lack of a unified approach has limited the growth and effectiveness of clinical neuropsychology. Often, basic information is not available to practitioners involved in the assessment and treatment of brain-injured patients. Advances in one area of research may not be communicated to other researchers and to clinical practitioners. Often this occurs because there is a failure to appreciate the relevance of the information to other areas. The lack of a central source for basic information in the field has led to the inadequate training of many clinical psychologists working with the brain-injured patient in hospital and outpatient settings. All of these conditions have made it difficult for maximally effective services to be offered to a significant number of clients. This state of affairs has also hindered the interaction of neuropsychology with other professions treating and assessing the brain-injured patient.

This volume brings together the relevant research, clinical procedures, and decision-making rules used by the clinical neuropsychologist. It is intended to serve both the professional psychologist who wishes to increase his/her knowledge in this important area, the student first learning clinical neuropsychology, and the professional in other related fields. In order to achieve this goal, this book surveys the scientific research and theory forming the foundation of clinical neuropsychology. It also covers the major clinical tests, procedures, rules of inference, and neurological data relevant to diagnosis and assessment in neuropsychology. Finally, the use of neuropsychological test procedures, evaluations, and theory for the design and evaluation of rehabilitation programs are discussed.

The first two chapters cover the theories and research linking brain structures to overt behavior. These chapters include a historical review of the development of concepts of brain function, as well as a short introduction to the physiology of the brain to acquaint the reader with the terminology used in this book. Information for these sections has been drawn from physiological psychology, neuropsychology, neurology, physiology, and anatomy. They are written so that the individual with little background in brain anatomy and physiology can follow the text with few problems.

Chapters 3 through 8 deal with clinical test procedures and the manner in which psychological testing may be used to identify a brain disorder, localize the area of a lesion, and identify the underlying neurological cause. In these chapters, the basic procedures and decision-making rules used by the neuropsychologist are presented. The ways in which neurological aspects of disorders interact with the neuropsychological test results are discussed. Chapter 7 demonstrates some of the differences and similarities in the diagnosis of children, as compared to adults. Chapter 8 illustrates the diagnostic process with the presentation of a number of actual cases.

The last two chapters identify the emotional, neurological, environmental, and neuropsychological factors that determine the recovery of a patient from brain injury. Chapter 9 details the use of neuropsychological evaluation in designing rehabilitation programs that maximally aid a patient's recovery. Chapter 10 presents a number of specific rehabilitation techniques used with neurological disorders. In each of the chapters, the emphasis is on the unique contribution that neuropsychology can make to the overall rehabilitation process.

The material in each chapter has been chosen for its utility and interest to the clinical neuropsychologist and other professionals in this area. As a result, a great deal of research, especially that involving complex physiological processes, has been largely ignored. It is recognized that the areas omitted may one day provide us with the keys to fully understanding the brain and behavior. At present, however, such research is of little clinical value. Similarly, clinical tests of little or limited proven utility have been only briefly mentioned or omitted altogether. In each case, the decisions made were in an attempt to make this volume a more practical and efficient source of information for the reader.

Clearly, one cannot become a clinical neuropsychologist simply by reading a book like this. There exist too many complicating factors and too many clinical settings and problems for this volume to do full justice to all of them. However, it is hoped that the book will provide the information and procedures that will enable the professional or student to maximally benefit from contact with brain-injured patients and clinical neuropsychologists. It is also hoped that the book will provide the professional in an allied area the information necessary to use the neuropsychologist and neuropsychological results in a way that maximizes the treatment and other aid given the brain-injured client.

CHARLES J. GOLDEN, Ph.D.

ACKNOWLEDGMENTS

I WISH TO ACKNOWLEDGE the help of many people in the preparation of this volume. I am indebted to the insights and ideas gained from Doctor Howard Gudeman and Doctor James Craine of Hawaii State Hospital, whose work is especially reflected in the chapters on rehabilitation. I would also like to acknowledge the help of Doctors Gil French and Josephine Moore, who helped me over the rough passages in the early drafts of this book. Doctor Moore has also provided the basic drawings and information from which the figures in this book were made. I would also like to extend my thanks to Doctors Arthur Canter, Charles Matthews, Charles Cleeland, and Preston Harley, who were very cooperative and helpful during the period I was gathering the information for this book.

Finally, I wish to acknowledge the help of my students who not only suffered through the reading of many of the earlier drafts but who provided enormously helpful feedback on the content and style of the manuscript. They also provided help with the many time-consuming tasks attending the writing of a book such as this. I am also very grateful to my wife, Ellen, who provided many critical evaluations of the manuscript, as well as support when it was needed.

C. J. G.

CONTENTS

Diagnosis and Rehabilitation
in
Clinical Neuropsychology

Chapter 1

THE DEVELOPMENT OF THEORIES OF BRAIN FUNCTION

Throughout history, there has been continual interest in the relationship of the brain to behavior. This interest has led to the formation of many theories of brain function. This chapter will present a short history of the development of thought on brain and behavior relationships, followed by sections on the major theories of brain function now existent.

Ancient Theories

As early as 3500 B.C., man had written on the relationship of the brain and behavior. Some evidence suggests that this relationship had been recognized as early as the Upper Paleolithic period (Chapman and Wolff, 1959). By 500 B.C., Pythagoras had identified the brain as the site of human reasoning.

Hippocrates (circa 400 B.C.) believed that the brain controlled the senses and movement. He was the first person to recognize that paralysis occurred on the side of the body opposite the side of a head injury. Herophilus of Chalcedon (300 B.C.) and Erasistratur (280 B.C.) theorized that the ventricular cavities of the brain were responsible for mental abilities and movement.

Galen (131-201 A.D.), the first experimental physiologist and physician, identified many major brain structures. Galen felt that the frontal lobes were the seat of the soul. Early Christian scholars disagreed with this idea, locating mental abilities in the ventricles. The views of these Christian scholars, led by St. Augustine, were predominant in the Western world for nearly 1000 years (Chapman and Wolff, 1959), although Arabic physicians carried on the work of Galen.

During the thirteenth century, scientists began to break away from the ventricular theory. For example, Albertus Magnus theorized that behavior was the result of a combination of structures, including the frontal lobes, midbrain, cerebellum, and ventricles.

3

By the seventeenth century, investigators were looking for a single cerebral organ as the site of mental processes (Luria, 1966). Descartes theorized that mental processes were located in the *pineal gland.* He reasoned that, since the pineal gland was in the center of the brain, it was the logical area for mental abilities to reside. Willis, in 1664, located mental faculties in the *corpus striatum,* a structure deep within the cerebral hemispheres. Vieussens theorized that mental faculties were in the white matter of the cerebral hemispheres. Lancisi chose the *corpus callosum,* a band of fibers which join the left and right cerebral hemispheres, as the seat of mental functions (Luria, 1966).

Localizationist Theory

It was not until the nineteenth century that current views on brain function began to evolve. Early in the century, Gall (1758-1828) postulated that the brain consisted of a number of separate organs. Each organ, he felt, was responsible for a basic psychological trait, such as "courage" or "wit." Gall attempted to describe differences in individuals by differences in the size of individual brain areas (Krech, 1962). Since Gall's localizations of psychological abilities rested on speculation rather than evidence, most scientists of the time rejected Gall's theories.

Despite their rejection by the scientific community, Gall's theories were very popular with the public. This resulted in the development of the "science" of phrenology. Phrenology involved, in its most popular form, the reading of cranial bumps to ascertain which of the cerebral areas were largest. This was based on the erroneous concept that the brain area under a bump was larger than other brain areas. Once it was inferred which areas of the brain were larger, predictions were made about a subject's abilities and personality.

Scientific evidence supporting a localizationist position was not available until 1861, when Paul Broca announced that motor speech was located in the left posterior frontal lobe. Broca presented two clinical cases to support his contention. Both had fairly extensive injuries, lesions in the left posterior frontal lobe, and motor speech deficits. Broca's announcement, hailed by many as a major breakthrough, led to numerous investigations into the localization of higher cognitive functions.

Wernicke (1874, reprinted 1970) announced a decade later that the understanding of speech was located in the posterior temporal lobe, although he did not indicate in which hemisphere (Wilkins and Brody, 1970). Wernicke noted that this loss of speech understanding was not accompanied by any motor deficit; only the ability to understand speech was disrupted (Geschwind, 1967).

Many other studies confirming a localizationist theory also appeared. Fritsch and Hitzig (1870) found that the major sensory and motor strips were located on either side of the central sulcus separating the parietal and frontal lobes. Kliessmaul in 1877 localized *word blindness*, an inability to read words, in the posterior left brain; others localized such functions as ideation, writing, and memory (Luria, 1966). By the mid-twentieth century, several maps had been published localizing both complex and basic psychological functions in separate parts of the brain (Kleist, 1933; Luria, 1966; Nielsen, 1946). Kleist's (1934) map indicates specific areas for such functions as reading, writing, walking, and memory.

Equipotential Theory

Many scientists found the localizationist theories unacceptable. They observed that the localizationists were unable to explain findings reported by numerous physicians: Lesions in widely disparate parts of the brain were reported to destroy such skills as writing. The localizationists said these skills were controlled by a circumscribed part of the brain. Moreover, patients with lesions in a particular area were still able to carry out a skill that had been assigned exclusively to that area.

Flourens, in the 1840s, was the foremost early advocate of an alternative to localizationist theories (Krech, 1962). Through an extensive number of experiments, logical arguments, and sometimes even practical jokes, Flourens attempted to disprove Gall's localizationist theories. In order to prove his beliefs, Flourens developed the *ablation experiment*, removing parts of the brains of pigeons and hens. He reported that excision of any part of the brain in these birds leads to generalized disorders of behavior. From his experiments, he reached three general conclusions: (1) sensory input at an elementary level is localized, but the process of perception involves the whole brain; (2) loss of function is dependent on the extent of damage, not on the location; and (3) all cerebral material is equipotential (Krech, 1962). By *equipotential,* Flourens meant that if sufficient cortical material is intact, the remaining material will take over the functions of any missing brain tissue.

Flourens, however, can be criticized on a number of different points. First, he used animals with brains so small that any ablation would invade more than one functional area. Second, he observed only motor behavior, whereas the localizationists were interested in faculties such as friendship or intellect (Krech, 1962). Despite these scientific problems, Flourens was accepted by many as having disproved localizationist theory.

However, as the work of Broca and others became known, the scientific community came to accept a localizationist approach (Luria, 1966). Consequently, little was done to support Flourens' work until the early 1900s. At this time, the equipotentialists began to again develop evidence and research to support their theory. Marie (1906) examined the preserved brain of one of the patients Broca had used to support his hypothesis of localization. Marie found that the patient had widespread damage. Marie attacked Broca's theory, indicating that the patient could not speak because the extensive lesion had caused a general loss of intellect, rather than a specific inability to speak.

Other researchers soon expressed support for the equipotentialist position (Goldstein, 1927, 1944, 1948; Gooddy, 1956; Gooddy and Reinhold, 1954; Head, 1926; Monakow, 1914). In general, these researchers held that, while basic sensorimotor functions may be localized in the brain, higher cortical processes were too complex to be confined to any one area. Head (1926) indicated that symbolic functions were mediated by the brain as a whole. He also discussed the role of the brain as a whole in such processes as vigilance (Brain, 1961; Critchley, 1961; Henson, 1961).

Although he was a prominent equipotentialist, Goldstein acknowledged the localization of many functions (Goldstein, 1927, 1939, 1944, 1948; Goldstein, Neuringer, and Olson, 1968; Quadfasel, 1968). Goldstein (1927) discussed the relationship of specific aphasic disorders to local brain lesions. However, Goldstein insisted that the higher mental functions included under his term *abstract attitude* were properties of the brain as a whole. He postulated a basic impairment of abstract attitude in all brain-injured individuals. These individuals tend to think more concretely than normal persons. He noted that the significance of a deficit depended on its relationship to the nervous system as a whole. He also encouraged consideration of a patient's reaction to an injury, as well as the direct effects of the injury itself.

Lashley also accepted the localization of basic sensory and motor skills (Lashley, 1929, 1937; Luria, 1966, 1973; Roofe, 1970). Lashley supported his equipotential views with experiments on rats similar to those of Flourens's on birds. Lashley found that impairment in maze running in the rat was directly related to the amount of cortex removed. He stated that the area removed made little difference. Lashley formulated from his experiments the *law of mass action:* The extent of behavioral impairment is directly proportional to the mass of the removed tissue. Lashley also emphasized the *multipotentiality* of brain tissue: Each part of the brain participated in more than one function (*see* Teuber, Battersby, and Bender, 1960). Lashley felt that his results were highly compatible with a view that brain tissue is equipotential and can be involved in tasks other than those assigned by the localizationist.

The importance of the equipotentialist viewpoint to neuropsychology cannot be underestimated. The view that all brain damage may produce the same kind of deficit has stimulated a great deal of research into finding a test that would identify all brain-damaged individuals. It has also led many to think that all brain-injured patients have a basic common deficit (Kaszniak, 1977).

Alternative Approach

As with the localizationist theory, the equipotentialist theory cannot encompass all the collected scientific data and clinical observations. Equipotentiality fails to account for the specific deficits often seen in the absence of general impairment in intellect, abstract attitude, perception, or other global ability. The theory also fails to account for the correspondences between sites of injury and higher cognitive deficits that have been repeatedly reported (*see* Chapter 2).

Unable to accept either the localizationist or equipotentialist models of brain function, psychologists and neurologists have searched for other models. The creation of one such model has been credited to the English neurologist, J. Hughlings Jackson, whose primary works were written during the second half of the nineteenth century (Luria, 1973), but not published in this country until 1958 (Luria, 1966). Jackson observed that the higher mental functions were not unitary abilities but made up of simpler and more basic skills. One does not have a "speech center." Rather, one has the ability to combine certain basic skills, e.g. hearing, discrimination of speech sounds, fine motor and kinesthetic control of the speech apparatus, to make more complex "higher" skills (Hebb, 1959; Ingham, 1948; Krech, 1962; Levin, 1953; Riese, 1954, 1956b).

Consequently, the loss of speech can be traced to the loss of any one of a number of basic abilities. It can be due to the loss of motor control or the loss of adequate feedback from the mouth and tongue, a defect in the understanding and use of the basic parts of speech, or the inability to decide to speak.

The loss of a specific area of the brain will cause the loss of all higher skills dependent on that area. Thus, a lesion causing the loss of speech does not indicate that we have found the area for speech. Jackson (Luria, 1966) has written that localizing damage that destroys speech and localizing speech are two different things.

Jackson also believed that behavior can exist on many different levels within the nervous system. Thus a patient may be unable to repeat the word *no*. When asked to repeat it, though, the patient is capable of saying, in exasperation, "No, Doctor, I can't say no" (Luria, 1966; Reise, 1956a, 1965). In the first instance, the patient cannot say the word voluntarily. However, when the word is given as an automatic response, the patient is able to say it. The ability to say *no* exists as two separate skills: one voluntary and one automatic. Each ability can be impaired independently of the other. Because of this, Jackson noted, behavior is rarely lost completely. There is usually an alternate way in which a task may be accomplished.

Jackson felt behavior was the result of interactions among all the areas of the brain. Even the simplest movement requires the full cooperation of all the levels of the nervous system from the peripheral nerves and the spinal cord to the cerebral hemispheres. In this regard, Jackson leaned towards a more global, nearly equipotentialist view of brain function. Jackson also felt that each area within the nervous system had a specific function it contributed to the overall system. In this regard, his views had a localizationist flavor. In fact, Jackson's views were those of neither school but reflected an integration of the significant data.

Jackson's influence can first be seen in the English neurologists of the early twentieth century. Head and others quoted liberally from Jackson. However, many missed the essential nature of what Jackson said: They interpreted his work as more supportive of an equipotentialist view for higher mental functions than it actually was. Since World War II, many major theorists have presented views compatible with Jackson's. For example, Harlow (1952) concluded from his monkey studies that, although there appeared to be some localization, no ability was completely destroyed by any limited lesion, a view entirely consistent with Jackson's ideas.

Krech (1962), after a review of much of the literature, reached two major conclusions. First, no learning process or function is entirely dependent on any one area of the cortex. Second, each area within the brain plays an unequal role in different kinds of functions. Similar conclusions have also been reached by other reviewers, such as Chapmann and Wolff (1961). These conclusions, contrary to either the localizationist or equipotentialist beliefs, are in accordance with Jackson's alternate approach.

The most detailed adaptation of the principles first suggested by Jackson has come in the work of the Russian neuropsychologist, A. R. Luria (1960-1973). Luria, building on the work of Vygotzky (1965), conceives each area in the brain as being involved in one of three basic functions: The first is regulation of the arousal level of the brain and the maintenance of proper tone. The second is the reception, integration, and analysis of sensory information from the internal and external environments. The third involves planning, executing, and verifying behavior (Luria, 1964, 1966, 1973).

All behavior requires the interaction of these basic functions. Consequently, all behavior reflects the result of the brain operating as a whole. At the same time, each area within the brain plays a specific role in each behavior. The importance of any area depends upon the behavior to be performed. For example, a simple, well-practiced act, e.g. picking up the receiver when the phone rings, requires little arousal, planning, and evaluation. Consequently, injuries to the areas involved in such acts would have little effect. However, a more complex behavior, such as telling a caller what one will be doing next Tuesday evening, does require attention and arousal, as well as planning and evaluation. An injury which would have little effect on the first behavior might be disastrous for the second.

Luria speaks of *functional systems* for each behavior. These represent the pattern of interaction among the various areas of the brain necessary to complete a behavior. A disruption at any stage is sufficient to immobilize a given functional system. However, each functional system is plastic and can change spontaneously or through retraining. For example, sensory feedback is necessary for continually knowing the location of one's fingers and arm to direct motor movement. A person who loses sensory feedback from his arm will lose an important link in doing fine motor tasks. But the functional system can be changed by using visual feedback to locate the fingers of the hand, something that was not previously needed. The patient can reestablish fine motor skills, despite the disruption of the old functional system.

Luria's hypothesis is attractive in that it can account theoretically for most observations of brain-injured patients. The effect of widely varying lesions on a single behavior is easily explained. The theory also explains the observation that certain lesions generally yield consistent deficits. The theory can account, through the concept of reorganization, for those individuals who recover from brain injury. Finally, the theory suggests ways to establish rehabilitation and treatment programs for the brain-injured patient.

Chapter 2

FUNCTIONAL LOCALIZATION IN THE BRAIN

THE MAJOR EFFORT of experimental neuropsychology has been the identification of the structural and functional aspects of the brain. Although neuropsychologists remain unable to define the mechanisms responsible for learning and memory, there have been many significant advances in recent years. Many of the areas within the brain which help determine behavior are now identified.

The first section of this chapter provides a synopsis of the major functional areas within the brain. This is intended only as a brief review to aid in the understanding of the terminology used within this book. The second section of this chapter looks at the behavioral functions of the major areas of the brain.

STRUCTURE

The largest part of the brain is made up by the right and left cerebral hemispheres. The two hemispheres form a half globe with a flat basal surface. The hemispheres are separated by a deep midline cleft, the *longitudinal fissure*. The first drawing (Fig. 2-1A) presents the appearance of the lateral surface of the left hemisphere, revealed by the removal of the skull and outer coverings of the brain. The second illustration (Fig. 2-1B) is the medial surface of the left hemisphere, seen when the hemispheres are separated along the longitudinal fissure. The third drawing (Fig. 2-1C) represents the basal (inferior) surface of the cerebral hemispheres.

The surface of the cerebral hemisphere is covered by a gray rind, or *cortex*. The gray areas of the central nervous system consist of the cell bodies of neurons serving as the brain's functional units. Underlying the cortex is white matter that links structures within the cerebral hemispheres and the central nervous system as a whole. The two hemispheres are connected, for example, by a band of white fibers, the *corpus callosum*, which

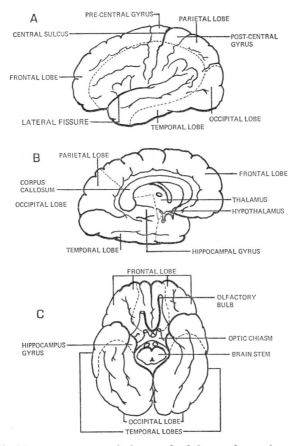

Figure 2-1. Major structures of the cerebral hemispheres from three different views: A. Lateral, B. Medial and C. Basal.

predominantly links similar areas in the two hemispheres. The white matter largely consists of fatty tissue surrounding the thin, filamentous neuronal extensions which allow communication between neurons with cell bodies located at some distance from one another. Chemical substances secreted by one neuron and received by another serve as the means of communication.

Since the two hemispheres resemble one another, though they are not identical, only the left hemisphere shall be described. Four of the major divisions within each hemisphere are the *frontal, parietal, temporal,* and *occipital lobes.* The frontal and parietal lobes are separated from the temporal lobe by the lateral fissure. The frontal and parietal lobes are separated by the central sulcus. The parietal and occipital lobes are separated by the parietoccipital fissure and its imaginary extension across the lateral surface of the hemisphere.

The surface of the hemisphere folds in upon itself in many places creating grooves along the surface named *sulci* (singular, *sulcus*). The irregularly shaped ridges between sulci are known as *gyri* (singular, *gyrus*). No two brains are identical in the size or the shape of their gyri, although the general pattern of gyri is consistent among people.

The cerebral cortex varies from place to place in the size, shape, and distribution of the cells and fibers within it. Brodmann (1909) and others have divided up the cortical surface according to these differences. Although Brodmann's *cytoarchitectural scheme* may be of questionable validity for man, it has been widely used for referring to particular parts of the cortex. The Brodmann numbers assigned to the medial and lateral aspects of the left hemisphere are presented in Figure 2-2.

LIMBIC SYSTEM: On and near the medial basal surface of the cerebral hemispheres are structures collectively called the *limbic system* (McLean, 1959; Moore, 1976; Papez, 1956). These structures are closely linked with the frontal and temporal lobes. The limbic system includes the *hippocampal gyrus*, the *cingulate gyrus*, the *olfactory lobes*, and many other structures (*see* Fig. 2-1A, B, and C). The limbic system's functioning is closely intertwined with that of another part of the brain, the *hypothalamus*.

BASAL NUCLEI: A number of major structures lie within the cerebral hemispheres. Directly beneath the cortex are white fiber tracts representing sensory projections to the cerebral hemispheres, interconnections between parts of the cortex, and outflow from the cerebral cortex to other nervous system structures. Within this white matter are gray structures, some of which are collectively known as the *basal nuclei*.

Cells originating in both the anterior (frontal) and posterior (rear) areas of the cerebral cortex send white fibers to the lower

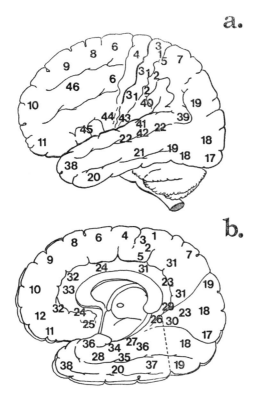

Figure 2-2. Brodmann numbers for each area on the a. lateral surface and b. medial surface. The Brodmann numbers are identical for the two hemispheres.

brain structures. As these fibers approach lower levels, they converge deep within each hemisphere to form the *internal capsule,* a broad band of white fibers making a hollow in which the *thalamus* is partially located.

The fibers of the internal capsule continue downward past the thalamus; some do not end until they reach the spinal cord. Lesions of the internal capsule may have the effect of severing major sensory and motor pathways to and from the cerebral hemispheres.

THALAMUS: Each cerebral hemisphere contains one half of the thalamus. Each half is a large, ovoid, gray mass which sits partially within the hollow made by the internal capsule. The word thalamus means *bridal chamber,* a name which reflects the deep, hidden, and secure location of the thalamus within the two hemispheres. Directly below the thalamus is the hypothalamus, which plays an important role in limbic system activities. The thalamus, hypothalamus, and a few other nearby structures form the *diencephalon* or *interbrain.* The relationship of the thalamus and hypothalamus to other brain structures can be seen in Figure 2-3.

BRAIN STEM: The brain stem consists of the *midbrain, pons,* and *medulla.* It connects the diencephalon and the cerebral hemispheres to the spinal cord (*see* Fig. 2-3).

CEREBELLUM: The cerebellum is located behind and above the pons and medulla, just under the posterior part of the cerebral hemispheres. The cerebellum consists of two large, oval hemispheres connected by a single median portion, the *vermis.* The cerebellar surface of many parallel sulci gives it a layered appearance. The cerebellum also has several deep fissures dividing each cerebellar hemisphere into separate lobes.

VENTRICLES: There are four interconnected, fluid-filled cavities

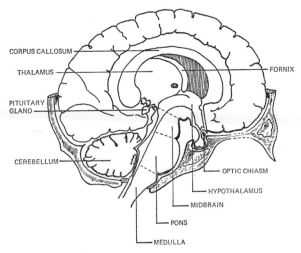

Figure 2-3. The relationship of major structures of the brain stem to the thalamus, hypothalamus, and other structures within the medial surface of the brain.

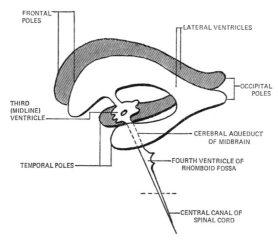

Figure 2-4. Sketch of the ventricular system. The lateral ventricles lie within the two cerebral hemispheres.

called *ventricles* within the brain. Cerebrospinal fluid is secreted by choroid plexus tissue within the ventricles and flows from the upper to the lower ventricles. A diagram of the ventricular system may be seen in Figure 2-4.

The large ventricles contained within each hemisphere are known as the *lateral ventricles*. Each is connected by a small opening to the third ventricle lying between the two lateral ventricles at the level of the thalamus and the hypothalamus. The third ventricle has a single opening which leads downward. This cerebral aqueduct courses through the midbrain and expands into the fourth ventricle, which lies in the upper pons and medulla just beneath and in front of the cerebellum.

SPINAL CORD: The spinal cord is continuous with the medulla and extends downward along the back. The spinal cord relays somatosensory information from the trunk and limbs to the brain. The cord also relays motor messages from the brain to the trunk and limbs and is responsible for some basic reflexive behavior. Within the spinal cord, the central canal is linked to the fourth ventricle.

MENINGES: The three meningeal membranes completely surround the brain and spinal cord. Outer to inner, these are the *dura mater, arachnoid membrane,* and *pia mater.* The dura mater is dense and thick, shielding the brain. The arachnoid membrane overlies the subarachnoid space, which contains cerebrospinal fluid. The thin pia mater directly adheres to the surface of the central nervous system, following its contours closely.

The cerebrospinal fluid reaches the subarachnoid space through small holes in the membranous roof of the fourth ventricle. The cerebrospinal fluid floats the central nervous system like a buoy and protects the brain. It also plays a role in the disposal of certain waste products within the brain. From its origin within the ventricles, the cerebrospinal fluid moves slowly along pressure gradients until it is absorbed into general circulation through the arachnoid villi within the subarachnoid space.

FUNCTION

The Brain Stem

The major motor and sensory tracts to and from the cerebral hemispheres pass through the brain stem. Consequently, lesions can interrupt motor and sensory pathways. Lesions at one level of the brain stem may cause decerebrate rigidity, characterized by an exaggerated contraction of skeletal muscles. There is also a decrease in general responsivity in several important reflexes (Feldmann and Sahrmann, 1971). Lesions in specific areas may result in tremor, rigidity, or loss of eye movements.

The brain stem is the site of origin of ten of the twelve cranial nerves, the nerves which are directly connected to the brain. These nerves all carry information to muscles or sensory information back to the brain. Table 2-I lists the cranial nerves and their functions.

Reticular System

Within the brain stem are scattered clusters of neurons with connections in many directions. These neuronal groups, along with interspersed fiber bundles, are the *reticular formation* (Williams and Warwick, 1975). This is the central core of the reticular system, which has both ascending and descending components. It mediates both voluntary and involuntary behavior.

TABLE 2-I

FUNCTIONS OF THE CRANIAL NERVES

Name	Function
Olfactory Nerve (I)	Sense of smell
Optic Nerve (II)	Vision
Oculomotor Nerve (III)	Eye movement; light and accommodation reactions; sensory feedback from eye muscles
Trochlear Nerve (IV)	Eye movements; sensory feedback from eye muscles
Trigeminal Nerve (V)	Sensory fibers from skin, scalp, mouth; muscles of mastication, or chewing; visceral functions
Abducens Nerve (VI)	Lateral eye movements; sensory feedback from eye muscles
Facial Nerve (VII)	Pain and temperature from ear region; deep sensibility in the face; taste buds of the front two thirds of the tongue; muscles of facial expression
Vestibulocochlear Nerve (VIII)	Hearing; some sensory feedback from internal ear areas
Glossopharyngeal Nerve (IX)	Pain and temperature from ear region; taste from the posterior third of the tongue and sensory fibers from pharynx and posterior third of the tongue
Vagus Nerve (X)	Sensation from ear region; sensations from the pharynx, larynx, and thoracic and abdominal viscera; cardiac and smooth muscle in the trunk
Spinal Accessory Nerve (XI)	Skeletal muscles, including trapezius
Hypoglossal Nerve (XII)	Musculature of the tongue

The role of the reticular system has been described as that of nonspecific arousal (Papez, 1956), activation (Gastaut, 1958), and inducing consciousness (Masland, 1958). Lindsley (1958) has emphasized a combination of general arousal, alerting, and focused attention. The reticular system is involved in sleep, both waking and going to sleep, and in remaining alert (Chusid, 1970). Disorders may cause very low levels of arousal or even a comatose (unconscious) state.

The reticular system may be aroused by outside or by internal impulses. There are especially important and widespread connections to the cerebral cortex. Because of the system's role in arousal, it is often referred to as the reticular activating system (RAS).

Cerebellum

The cerebellum is heavily involved in basic processes necessary for general motor behavior. The oldest areas of the cerebellum are concerned with keeping an individual oriented in space. The cerebellum also aids in the control of muscles keeping one upright despite the pull of gravity. The youngest, most recently developed portion of the cerebellum is involved with monitoring the background tone of voluntary movement. Lesions of the cerebellum, depending on location, may cause a variety of disorders, including the deterioration of coordinated movement; irregular and jerky movements; intention tremor when attempting to complete a voluntary task; static tremor when resting; impairment of alternating movements; impairment of muscle tone, readiness to respond; impairment in balance; disturbances of walking; and uncontrolled nystagmic movements of the eyes (Chusid, 1970). No cognitive impairment follows lesions of the cerebellum.

Thalamus

The thalamus serves as the major pathway for sensory and motor impulses to and from the cerebral hemispheres. Each half of the thalamus sends information to and receives information from the cerebral hemisphere on the same side of the brain. Lesions of the left thalamus have been associated with depressed scores on verbal tasks (Bell, 1968; Jurko and Andy, 1973; Ojemann, 1971; Ojemann and Ward, 1971; Vilkki and Laitinen, 1974). Lesions of the right thalamus have been associated with defects in spatial ability (Jurko and Andy, 1973), facial recognition (Vilkki and Laitinen, 1974), and musical hearing (Roeser and Daly, 1974). These are deficits associated with the left and right cerebral cortex respectively. Consequently, many effects of thalamic injury are those one might expect from the interruption of essential relay elements in pathways to and from the cerebral hemispheres. In many thalamic lesions, the symptoms are short lived, indicating that alternate pathways are quickly formed (Levita, Riklan, and Cooper, 1967).

Limbic System

Extensive research has been done on several of the components of the highly interconnected limbic system. The hypothalamus has been identified in the regulation of levels of hormones affecting such functions as digestion, sexual arousal, and circulation (Papez, 1958). It has also been associated with thirst, hunger, and circadian rhythms (Neff and Goldberg, 1960; Symonds, 1966).

Bilateral removal of the amygdala has been associated with a complex of symptoms including docility, inability to recognize objects visually, and indiscriminate sexual activity in animals (Glaser and Pincus, 1969; Klüver and Bucy, 1939; Mishkin, 1954; Mishkin and Pribram, 1954; Spiegel and Wycis, 1968), as well as in humans (Terzian and Dale, 1955). In contrast, Balasubramanian and Ranamurthi (1970) reported that 100 cases of bilateral destruction of the amygdala in patients with behavior disorders caused no side effects and general remission of symptoms.

The hippocampal areas have been associated with memory acquisition (Corkin, 1965; DeJong, Itabashi, and Olson, 1969; Douglas and Pribram, 1966; Isaacson, 1972; Penfield and Milner, 1958; Scoville and Milner, 1957). The primary defect, seen after bilateral injury of the hippocampus, involves the acquisition of new long-term memories (Penfield and Mathieson, 1974; Penfield and Milner, 1958; Scoville and Milner, 1957). Such patients find themselves unable to retain newly learned information. Short-term memory remains intact, if there is no other mental activity between learning and recall and if the person has a chance to rehearse (Drachman and Arbit, 1966; Drachman and Ommaya, 1964; Luria, 1971; Milner, 1968). These effects are minimal when only one hippocampal gyrus is involved (McLardy, 1970). Lesions of the left hippocampal gyrus may cause problems with verbal memory (Russell and Espir, 1961), while lesions of the right hippocampal gyrus may cause impairment in spatial memory, including maze learning (Corkin, 1965; Milner, 1965).

There is a need to be cautious with the data from individual structures within the limbic system. In most cases, lesions were not limited to one structure. Consequently, some of the behavioral losses may be more a result of limbic system interactions than the function of any single unit within the limbic system.

Researchers investigating the actions of the limbic system as a whole have indicated that it has four primary functions: memory, smell, automatic visceral functions, and emotional behavior (Moore, 1976).

The role of the limbic system in emotion has generated a great deal of theory. Limbic system dysfunction has been associated with "behavioral problems" (Glaser and Pincus, 1969); sexual dysfunction (Rosenblum, 1974); catatonia (Roberts, 1965); delirium (Medina, Rubino, and Ross, 1974); and general psychosis (Heath, 1975). At present, most of these theories result from the interpretation of casual observational data, rather than rigorous scientific evidence.

The Basal Nuclei

The basal nuclei form part of the extrapyramidal motor system, which is responsible for stereotyped postural and reflexive motor activity (Noback and Demarest, 1975). It also acts to keep individual muscles ready to respond. The extrapyramidal system consists of three primary areas: the cerebral cortex, the basal nuclei, and the midbrain (Chusid, 1970).

The basal nuclei act as relay stations between the cerebral cortex and the thalamus, although the exact role of the basal nuclei beyond this has not been agreed upon. Two theories as to the role of the basal nuclei are currently advanced. One suggests that they integrate information from visual inputs, from the balance centers of the brain, and from the muscles and joints of the body. The other proposes that the basal nuclei are only relay stations with no integrative function (Noback and Demarest, 1975). At present, it can be concluded that the basal nuclei play an important role in motor behavior, but the definition of the extent and nature of that role cannot be fully explained (Williams and Warwick, 1975).

Corpus Callosum

The corpus callosum permits communication and exchange of information between the cerebral hemispheres. In adults, cutting the corpus callosum has little apparent effect, because most information, regardless of mode of presentation, is available to both hemispheres, unless special techniques are used to present the information. In addition, the brain develops some alternative pathways to help compensate for the loss. However, special testing situations can reveal obvious deficits (Ettlinger, Blakemore, Milner, and Wilson, 1974; Gazzaniga, 1966; Geschwind, 1965; Kreuter, Kinsbourne, and Trevarthen, 1972; Myers, 1959; Nebes and Sperry, 1971; Solursh, Margulies, Ashem, and Stasiak, 1965; Zaidel and Sperry, 1973). If the corpus callosum is cut and information is presented to only one hemisphere, that hemisphere will generally work independently of the other. The study of individuals in which the corpus callosum has been cut surgically has helped provide extensive data on the normal, independent functioning of the two cerebral hemispheres.

In cases of agenesis of the corpus callosum, that structure fails to develop, and the results are less benign. Children born without a corpus callosum are often mentally retarded (Loeser and Alvord, 1968). It is not clear whether the retardation is due to the lack of a corpus callosum or to other problems those individuals develop.

In Marchierfava-Bignami's disease, degeneration of the corpus callosum results in psychiatric symptoms, including violence, which are later followed by apathy and a lack of spontaneity. Tumors of the corpus callosum may cause apathy, an inability to concentrate, forgetfulness, and delusions and hallucinations. Such patients may show no other specific neurologic deficits and thus may be mistaken for psychiatric patients (Toglia, 1961).

Visual System

The visual pathways often provide significant keys in the localization of neurological disorders. As can be seen in Figure 2-5, the information from each eye may be divided into a right

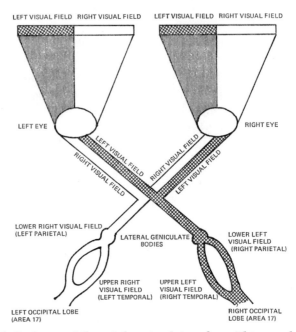

Figure 2-5. Pathways followed by visual impulses. This can be used to hypothesize the effects of given lesions to different areas of the visual system.

and a left visual field. The information from each eye travels via the optic nerve to the optic chiasm. The optic chiasm is located below the base of the third ventricle. At the chiasm, the two right visual fields integrate and travel to the left lateral geniculate body, a small knob over the posterior surface of the left thalamus. The two left visual fields also integrate and travel to the right lateral geniculate body.

From the lateral geniculate bodies, the information travels to the occipital lobe within the same hemisphere. The information from the upper half of each visual field travels through a pathway within the temporal lobe: The information from the lower half of each visual field travels via a pathway within the parietal lobe.

Lesions in different parts of the visual system cause different disorders of vision. For example, interruption of the optic nerve

| LEFT EYE | RIGHT EYE | NAME AND POSSIBLE DISORDER |

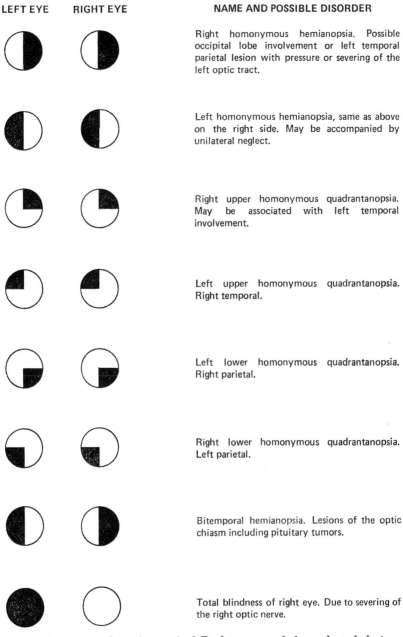

Right homonymous hemianopsia. Possible occipital lobe involvement or left temporal parietal lesion with pressure or severing of the left optic tract.

Left homonymous hemianopsia, same as above on the right side. May be accompanied by unilateral neglect.

Right upper homonymous quadrantanopsia. May be associated with left temporal involvement.

Left upper homonymous quadrantanopsia. Right temporal.

Left lower homonymous quadrantanopsia. Right parietal.

Right lower homonymous quadrantanopsia. Left parietal.

Bitemporal hemianopsia. Lesions of the optic chiasm including pituitary tumors.

Total blindness of right eye. Due to severing of the right optic nerve.

Figure 2-6. Examples of visual difficulties caused by selected lesions. These disorders may be caused by lesions other than those described here.

just after it leaves the left eye causes left eye blindness but does not affect the right eye at all. A lesion of the left occipital lobe could cause blindness in the right half of both eyes. Figure 2-6 presents some common disorders of vision and suggests areas where the lesion might be located.

THE CEREBRAL HEMISPHERES

Since the cerebral hemispheres are responsible for "higher mental functions" in humans, it is not surprising that these structures have been of most interest to the clinical neuropsychologist. Within this section the functions of the cerebral hemispheres as a whole will be discussed first, then differences in hemispheric functioning, and last, the functional significance of each major area within each hemisphere.

Tasks Dependent on General Cerebral Integrity

As indicated in the last chapter, all behavioral processes are mediated by functional systems involving many different areas of the brain. As a behavior becomes more complex, it becomes more dependent on many areas within the cerebral hemispheres. Consequently, any task which is complex enough or demands sustained and continuing attention is likely to be severely impaired by damage to any part of the cerebral hemispheres (Belmont, Handler, and Karp, 1972; Borkowski, Benton, and Spreen, 1967; Chedru, Leblanc, and Lhermitte, 1973; Coheen, 1950; Dee and Van Allen, 1971; DeRenzi, Faglioni, and Scotti, 1970; Kahn, Pollack, and Fink, 1960; McDonald, 1964; McDonald and Burns, 1964; Olbrich, 1972; Reitan, 1959c).

Cerebral Asymmetry

Although the two hemispheres are similar, they are not identical. Connolly (1950) established that the lateral fissure was longer in the left hemisphere than in the right hemisphere. This was subsequently confirmed in a number of reports (Geschwind, 1974). Wada, Clark, and Hamm (1975) found that the cerebral asymmetry was obvious as early as the twenty-ninth week of gestation, with those areas thought to mediate speech in the left hemisphere significantly larger.

From a clinical viewpoint, J. Hughlings Jackson in the 1870s first suggested that the left hemisphere was dominant in control of speech and the right hemisphere was dominant in control of nonverbal functions. Weisenburg and McBride (1935) confirmed the speculations of J. Hughlings Jackson. Others, such as Reitan (1966), also endorsed this view on the basis of clinical evidence. However, it was the research on the "split brain" individual, without a functional corpus callosum, that established the principle of differential hemispheric function.

The difference in functioning between the two hemispheres has generated a great deal of speculation attempting to explain the underlying processes in each hemisphere. Levy and Sperry (1968) suggest that the left brain is analytic while the right brain deals with data as a *gestalt* or whole. Others have suggested that the difference is related to serial versus parallel data analysis. It is also possible that the differences are not due to any inherent processing differences, but strategies designed to accommodate the tasks demanded of each hemisphere.

Not all individuals are left dominant for speech and right dominant for other functions. Although there is disagreement over the exact percentages, at least a small portion of the population is clearly right brain dominant for speech. In the present chapter, as a matter of convenience, the data will be treated as if all individuals were left hemisphere dominant for speech.

Right Hemisphere Functions

Over the past thirty years, the right hemisphere has been associated with many important functions. These include the ability to orient oneself in space, work with spatial coordinates, draw, remember nonverbal material, discriminate between colors, work with musical material, attend symmetrically to objects in space, perform automatic functions, control the left side of the body, and see in the left visual fields (Ettlinger, Warrington, and Zangwill, 1957; Hecaen, Penfield, Bertrand, and Malmo, 1956; Joynt and Goldstein, 1975; Levy, 1974; McFie, Piercy, and Zangwill, 1950).

An extensive body of research has confirmed the role of the right hemisphere in spatial orientation and awareness (Benton,

1967; DeRenzi et al., 1970; Kohn and Dennis, 1974a; McFie, Piercy, and Zangwill, 1960). This includes determining the slope and direction of a line (Benton, Hannay, and Varney, 1975; DeRenzi et al., 1970; 1971; Durnford, 1971; Fontenot and Benton, 1972; Hecaen, Wyke, and DeRenzi, 1972), as well as its location in space (Kimura, 1969; Taylor and Warrington, 1973).

The right hemisphere is important for general depth perception, stereoscopic vision, and general competency in dealing with space in three dimensions (Benton and Fogel, 1962; Benton and Hecaen, 1970; Carmon and Bechtoldt, 1969; Durnford and Kimura, 1971), as well as in two dimensions (McFie, 1970). The right hemisphere also plays a role in spatial reasoning (Archibald, Wepman, and Jones, 1967; Zaidel and Sperry, 1973), including the solution of mazes (Ratcliffe and Newcombe, 1973).

The right hemisphere is also important for activities such as assembling and drawing in which the spatial relationship of the parts of an object is important. Disorders of the right hemisphere cause disruption of these drawing and assembling processes. This symptom, commonly called *construction dyspraxia*, is one of the most common disorders of individuals whose right brains have been impaired (Heimburger and Reitan, 1961).

The ability to recognize faces has also been associated with right hemispheric function (Benton and Van Allen, 1972; Benton, Levin, and Van Allen, 1974; Bodamer, 1947; Bornstein and Kidron, 1959; DeRenzi and Spinnler, 1966a; Weinstein, Cole, Mitchell, and Lyerly, 1964). Patients with a disorder in this ability may be unable to remember nurses and doctors from one day to the next. The right hemisphere processes musical sounds, including pitch and rhythm (McFie, 1970). A patient with a right hemisphere injury may have no musical skills at all, even if s/he were formerly proficient at such tasks (Milner, 1958). Patients with disorders of the right hemisphere may also display a condition known as *impersistence,* in which they cannot do such simple, automatic tasks as keep their eyes closed for even a modest length of time (Fisher, 1956; Simernitskaya, 1974).

The right hemisphere contributes significantly to a number of visual functions. As seen earlier, it is important for the perception of the left visual field. It is also necessary for the memorization of visual nonverbal material (Kimura, 1961b, 1963; Milner and Taylor, 1972). The right hemisphere plays a role in the symmetrical appreciation of space. Patients with right hemisphere disorders may be unable to take into account the left sides of objects. This phenomenon has been variously labeled as *inattention* or *unilateral neglect* (Chedru et al., 1973; DeRenzi et al., 1970; Frantz, 1950; Gainotti, 1972b, Gainotti and Tiacci, 1971). Inattention may be accompanied by loss of vision in the left visual field, but this is not always the case.

Inattention may involve the neglect of the left side of a person's body and of all objects or parts of objects within the left visual field. Such patients may only copy the right side of a figure or read the right half of a sentence. They may deny the left side of their body, saying it belongs to someone else, or express hatred for an impaired left limb. The patient may have trouble dressing, because the left side of the body is not taken into account. There may be denial of any injury; the patient states that there is no reason to be hospitalized or helped.

The right hemisphere is also important for the discrimination of colors according to hue (Albert, Reches, and Silverberg, 1975; DeRenzi and Spinnler, 1967; Scotti and Spinnler, 1970). This should not be confused with the ability to name a given color, which is a left hemisphere task.

Right hemisphere functioning is also necessary for such basic abilities as time sense (Carmon, 1972), although patients with right hemisphere injuries are able to estimate short, elapsed times. The right hemisphere is also important in basic reaction time to environmental stimuli (Blackburn and Benton, 1955; Dee and Van Allen, 1971).

The right hemisphere also possesses some basic verbal abilities primarily receptive rather than expressive (Gazzangia and Hillyard, 1971; Gazzaniga and Sperry, 1967; Gott, 1973; Levy, Nebes, and Sperry, 1971). The right hemisphere can understand some speech, but cannot respond in a verbal mode.

The right hemisphere controls motor impulses to the left side of the body and receives the primary impulses from the left visual field, left ear, and left somatosensory receptors. The somatosensory receptors transmit such sensations as touch, temperature, pain, pressure, and information on bodily position. A right hemisphere injured patient may be unable to control the left side of the body, unable to appreciate somatosensory sensations on the left side, unable to see in the left visual field, and unable to hear well in the left ear.

Left Hemisphere

The primary and most obvious functions of the left hemisphere are verbal (Boller, 1968; McKeever and Huling, 1971; Weisenburg and McBride, 1935). These include the abilities to speak, write, read, and understand verbal material presented in any modality. Traditionally, these skills have been classified into two groups: expressive and receptive. Research, however, has shown that this oversimplification ignores interactions among all language skills.

Patients with dysfunctions of the left hemisphere may be unable to understand or articulate speech due to an impaired ability to break words into their basic phonemes (Luria, 1966; Yamadori, 1975). The same deficit may also disturb reading and writing (Luria, 1966). Patients may not be able to name objects or their attributes or describe what is going on in a picture or the real world (DeRenzi and Spinnler, 1967). There may also be an inability to demonstrate the use of an object (DeRenzi et al., 1968), to use correct grammar (Caplan, Kellar, and Locke, 1972), to produce understandable sentences (Gordon and Bogen, 1974), to recognize letters (Luria, 1966), to do arithmetic and recognize arithmetic symbols (Luria, 1966; Wheeler, 1963), to spell (Heimburger and Reitan, 1961), and to remember verbal material (Bisiache and Faglioni, 1974; Flowers, 1975; Hines and Satz, 1971; Newcombe and Marshall, 1967). There has been some controversy over whether these deficits can appear independently or whether they reflect an overall lowering of skills (Casey and Ettlinger, 1960; Luria, 1966, 1973). The left hemisphere injured patient is more likely to develop serious emotional disorders, including psychotic behavior (Black, 1975; Dikmen and Reitan,

1974; Gainotti, 1972). This may be due to the importance of verbal abilities in communicating and in understanding other people.

The left hemisphere is also involved in spatial behavior, but not to the same extent as the right hemisphere (Benton, 1961; Hecaen, Ajuriaguerra and Massonet, 1951; Luria, 1964, 1966, 1973). The right hemisphere is concerned with such basic spatial dimensions as slope or direction (DeRenzi in Hecaen et al., 1972). The left hemisphere contributes to the ability to cope with complex figures and spatial relationships, especially where some verbal coding is required by a task (Benton et al., 1974; Bortner and Birch, 1960; Brewer, 1969).

Luria (1966) has described a verbal type of spatial ability dependent on the left hemisphere. The left hemisphere is necessary in understanding the meaning of such spatial words as *below* or *above*. With certain left hemisphere injuries the patient may be able to understand all words except these spatial prepositions. The patient may also have trouble understanding such concepts as *bigger* or *less*.

The left hemisphere is responsible for motor control of the right side of the body and reception of somatosensory information from the right side of the body. It also receives projections from the right visual field and the right ear. The left hemisphere has control of coordinated motor activities involving both the left and right sides of the body (Wyke, 1971). The left hemisphere injured patient is less likely to recover from motor-sensory problems than the right hemisphere injured patient.

FUNCTIONAL UNITS WITHIN THE HEMISPHERES

Each hemisphere does not act as a unitary organ, but as a collection of separate areas contributing in a distinct way to the actions of the hemisphere and the brain as a whole. Consequently, the function of each division within the hemispheres and its contribution to the functioning of the entire brain can be examined.

On the basis of function, Luria (1966) has subdivided the cortex into *primary, secondary,* and *tertiary* areas. Each primary area is either a *sensory input* or *motor output* area. The primary sensory areas receive, via the receptors, information from either the outside world or the internal environment of the body. The major functions of these areas are to obtain and initially organize this information. The primary motor areas send information to the muscles of the body so that movement may occur. The destruction of the primary areas does not interfere with cognitive processes, but does cut the person off from some forms of sensory information or prevents some voluntary activities.

Secondary areas are adjacent to the primary areas and organize the information received by the primary areas into meaningful units. For example, the left temporal secondary areas change sounds received by the primary area into *phonemes* (speech sound units) so that spoken speech may be understood. Secondary areas have few connections to the outside world and must depend on primary areas for their information.

Tertiary areas receive information from the secondary areas. They act to integrate information received from different senses, as in the combining of visual and auditory data. These areas are responsible for higher cognitive functions, such as reading.

Temporal Lobes

The primary area of both temporal lobes is located in Brodmann areas 41, 42, and part of 22 (*see* Fig. 2-2) (Luria, 1966). These areas receive information from the auditory system. Each ear sends information to both temporal lobes. The majority of information received by each ear goes to the temporal lobe in the opposite side of the brain (Kimura, 1961). With an injury in either primary area, there is a partial loss of hearing acuity associated with the opposite ear. Complete loss of hearing, known as *central deafness*, may arise from the destruction of both primary temporal areas or the connections that lead to those areas (Jerger, Lovering, and Wertz, 1972).

The anterior-medial area of each temporal lobe is closely associated with the limbic system. Stimulation to these areas may cause visual or auditory hallucinations (Mullan and Penfield, 1959). Destruction may cause psychiatric problems characteristic of limbic disorders (Luria, 1966). Temporal lobe epilepsy in this area may be seen as fear or depression and may be accompanied by olfactory hallucinations (Weil, 1959). Epilepsy here may also lead to dreamy states or distortion of time and space parameters in the patient (Williams, 1968). Loss of these areas may cause the loss of new long-term memory, as is seen in hippocampal disorders (Meyer and Yates, 1955), but does not result in a loss of general intelligence (Blakemore and Falconer, 1967; Meyer, 1959; Milner, 1958, 1971, 1972; Milner and Teuber 1968). Unilateral or limited loss of the anterior temporal lobe may cause no discernible symptoms.

Damage to either temporal lobe posterior to (behind of) area 21 may cause a loss of the upper half of the opposite visual field. Thus, a left temporal lobe injury may cause a loss of the upper half of the right visual field in both eyes (Fox and German, 1935; Spalding, 1952) (*see* Fig. 2-6). This condition is termed *upper quadrantanopsia*.

Left Temporal Lobe

The left temporal lobe is involved in the decoding of speech (Kimura, 1961a; Lansdell, 1970; Neff and Goldberg, 1960; Rubino, 1970; Zurif and Ramier, 1972). Injury to the primary area may result in *word deafness*, in which the subject cannot understand speech (Gazzaniga, Glass, Sarno, and Posner, 1973). However, there is no accompanying deficit in writing, reading, or other cognitive processes (Jerger et al., 1972; Yamadori and Albert, 1973). Lesions of the primary areas may also interfere with an individual's perception of acoustic intensity (Swisher, 1967).

The secondary area (Brodmann areas 21 and 22) (*see* Fig. 2-2) is responsible for the analysis and integration of speech and the decoding of language phonemes (Luria, 1966, 1973; Zurif and Ramier, 1972). Lesions of this area cause an inability to understand or decode spoken speech. The secondary area also plays a role in the phonemic analysis necessary for reading, writing, and speaking. Consequently, lesions may lead to deficits in these skills as well. The patient's speech will also disintegrate because of an inability to monitor his or her own speech (Luria, 1966; Rochford and Williams, 1962). Often this speech will contain no substantives but only automatic phrases like "you know" (Luria, 1966). Patients may also show problems in analyzing rhythmic patterns (Lackner and Teuber, 1973; Luria, 1966). The left secondary area is also involved in verbal memory and recall (Meyer, 1959; Meyer and Yates, 1955; Milner, 1958; Stepien and Sherpinski, 1964), although in disorders of this area, there is no loss in intelligence (Neff and Goldberg, 1960). In milder forms of left temporal secondary disorders, the patient retains the ability to understand most speech, to read and write, but shows a tendency to confuse words with similar sounds, such as *bit* and *pit*. In all disorders limited to the secondary area, there is no change in hearing acuity.

The tertiary temporo-occipital area (just posterior to the secondary left temporal area) is partially responsible for the integration of auditory and visual information (Luria, 1966, 1973). Damage limited to this area does not affect speaking. However, the patient is unable to recognize or read letters or words, a condition known as *dyslexia* (Denckla and Bowen, 1973). In injuries confined to the left hemisphere, the patient will still be able to understand and appreciate complex visual stimuli (Luria, 1966).

Right Temporal Lobe

The right temporal lobe is not involved in the understanding of speech, but is responsible for the ability to decode complex, nonverbal patterns. Losses in the secondary area may disturb both visual and auditory pattern analysis (Kimura, 1963; Meier and French, 1965). The right temporal is especially important for rhythmic patterns that cannot be translated into a verbal code (Kimura, 1963; Luria, 1973; Milner, 1971; Shankweiler, 1966; Warrington and James, 1967). This function includes such musical abilities as pitch and rhythm (Milner, 1958).

The secondary areas are responsible for visual decoding (Hebb, 1959). Subjects with deficits have trouble completing a partially finished picture (Lansdell, 1970) and a great deal of trouble interpreting and remembering complex visual stimuli (Luria, 1966; Meier and French, 1965; Rubino, 1970). Kimura (1963) has suggested that the role of the right temporal secondary area is confined only to unfamiliar material. As the lesion involves more of the tertiary temporo-occipital area, more visual impairment is seen along with impairment of spatial ability.

Parietal Lobe

The parietal lobe is responsible for processing somatosensory input from the body. The primary area (Brodmann area 3) (*see* Fig. 2-2) is located within and posterior to the central sulcus. Each parietal lobe receives impulses from the opposite side of the body. The somatosensory input is arranged in such a way so that the reception areas for feet, legs, trunk, arms, hands, and face lie sequentially. The size of the reception area depends on its importance to the somatosensory modalities. Thus the hands, where senses of touch, pain, and location are very important, get a larger reception area than the torso.

Lesions in the middle of the primary reception area cause deficits in sensations from the hands and an inability to recognize objects by touch alone. This form of *astereognosis* due to a lack of tactile sensitivity must be differentiated from astereognosis that is due to a failure to integrate tactile input and information from the muscles and joints as described below (Neff and Goldberg, 1960; Roland, 1976; Roland and Larsen, 1976). Large lesions in the primary areas of either parietal lobe may cause some bilateral rather than only contralateral sensory disorders (Corkin, Milner, and Taylor, 1973).

The primary parietal areas are not responsible solely for somatosensory input. About one fifth of their cells direct motor output (Luria, 1973). In addition, the primary areas are constantly interacting with the areas of the frontal lobe responsible for major motor activity. This situation emphasizes the importance of sensory input for adequate motor output.

The secondary areas of each parietal lobe are located in Brodmann areas 5, 7, and 40 (*see* Fig. 2-2). This region deals with the more complex forms of sensations, those requiring integration of various somatosensory inputs. Lesions of this area will lead to astereognosis because of an inability to synthesize the primary sensations. For example, given a solid triangle while blindfolded, such a patient would be able to identify that the object had flat sides but would not be able to deduce the relationship of the sides to each other. This type of patient can only consider one attribute at a time rather than integrate all features into a spatial whole (Luria, 1966).

A patient with disorders of the secondary area will have difficulty integrating those impulses from the opposite limbs which aid an individual in locating the limb in space. Blindfolded, such a patient would not be able to imitate guided movements of the opposite hand since s/he would be unable to appreciate the location and movements of the limb. This deficit also forms the basis for the apraxic disorders reflecting an inability to perform a motor act despite intact motor strength and control. The disruption is the result of inadequately appreciated feedback that tells the brain where the limbs and body are at any given moment. *Apraxia* primarily affects the movements of the limbs opposite the injured parietal lobe. When a lesion is in the left hemisphere, there may also be oral apraxia interfering with spoken words. Fine, skilled movements are more affected in these disorders than are gross movements.

Another disorder of the secondary areas is *finger agnosia,* an inability to recognize which finger is touched by tactile stimuli alone (Goldstein, 1974; Heimburger and Reitan, 1961). In general, this occurs only in the opposite hand. A special form of finger agnosia, found after damage to the left parietal lobe, is discussed below.

Injuries to the parietal lobe, if deep enough, may interfere with the visual tracts from the thalamus to the occipital lobe. This results in blindness in the lower half of the opposite visual field in both eyes (*see* Fig. 2-6). This condition is called *lower quadrantanopsia.*

Left Parietal Lobe

The primary and secondary areas of the left parietal lobe are closely involved with speech and writing (Luria, 1966). Lesions of these areas may affect smoothness of speaking and cause difficulties when the patient must shift between sounds made by similar movements of the speech musculature. Disorders of writing arise when letters formed by similar muscular movements, such as *h* and *k*, are made. These deficits arise because precise sensory information is not available to the motor areas involved with speaking and writing.

There are two major subdivisions of the tertiary areas of the parietal lobe, the parietotemporo-occipital area (Brodmann's area 40) and the parieto-occipital area (Brodmann's area 39) (*see* Fig. 2-2). The parieto-occipital area is responsible for the integration of visual and somatosensory information. Since a combination of these inputs is normally used to locate one's body in space, disorders of this area can cause a disturbance of body schema (Butters and Brody, 1969; Sauguet, Benton, and Hecaen, 1971). The patient is unaware of the location of his body and the relationship of one body part to another. One of the major indications of this disorder is *bilateral finger agnosia;* the subject is unable to locate the fingers on either hand. If two fingers are touched, the subject is unable to say how many fingers are between them because s/he cannot appreciate the spatial location of the fingers (Gainotti, Cianchetti, and Tiacci, 1972; Kinsbourne and Warrington, 1962b).

Kinsbourne and Warrington (1964) have related finger agnosia to the role of the parieto-occipital area in spatial tasks. They have observed that lesions in this area produce deficits, such as an inability to spell, because letters were placed in the wrong order. For example, the word *cat* might be spelled *cta*. Others have also assigned a general spatial deficit to this area (Brain, 1941; Luria and Tsvetkova, 1964). This area is responsible for the construction dyspraxia characteristic of the left hemisphere and discussed earlier. It is necessary to differentiate this spatial disorder from the poor drawing caused by a lack of fine motor skills due to deficits in the primary or secondary parietal areas or the motor areas.

Lesions of this area may also interfere with an individual's ability to demonstrate the use of an object such as a key, although the person knows how to use the object (DeRenzi et al., 1968). The parieto-occipital area is also involved in the ability to understand and manipulate arithmetic symbols and processes (Benson and Weir, 1972). However, deficits in this area do not interfere with the ability to do well-practiced arithmetic problems requiring only memory and not arithmetic ability (Benson and Weir, 1972; Luria, 1966, 1973). For example, while the subject may be able to say that two and two is four, four minus two may be too difficult a problem. This area is also responsible for the understanding of words which denote spatial relationships, such as *above* (Luria, 1966). The inability to relate spatial and verbal concepts when this area is injured may also make it difficult for the patient to tell the time on a dial clock simply by the spatial positions of the hands (Luria, 1966, 1973).

The parieto-occipitotemporal area in the region of the angular gyrus plays an important role in many speech processes. This area is responsible for integrating information from all sensory modalities. Disorders of this area may lead to a loss of reading and writing skills and the ability to associate names to objects, a disorder known as *dysnomia* (Butters and Brody, 1969). The subject can do this, however, if the beginning of the word is presented (Luria, 1966; Oxbury, Oxbury, and Humphrey, 1969). For example, the patient may not be able to name a triangle but may get it after the examiner prompts with the first syllable, *tri*. A sufficiently large lesion may result in global aphasia with the loss of all language skills.

Lesions in the parieto-occipitotemporal area interfere with verbal memory (Warrington et al., 1971). Luria (1966, 1973) has suggested that this is due to a disturbance in categorizing verbal material correctly, a process essential to efficient recall. These patients may also show disorders of linguistic organization, making a variety of grammatic and semantic errors.

Disorders of the tertiary left parietal may cause an inability to name colors, although such subjects are able to separate or match objects by color (Netley, 1974; Wyke and Holdgate, 1973). Such patients will be unable to color objects correctly because of an inability to match color hues to the appropriate verbal labels directing what color an object should be.

Right Parietal

Deficits of the right primary and secondary areas are similar to those of the left brain. These effects will be generally less severe, because the nondominant left hand is not as important for skilled tasks and because of a lack of speech impairment in right parietal injuries.

The tertiary areas are responsible for awareness of the left side of the person's body or environment (Brain, 1941; McFie and Zangwill, 1960). Patients with disorders of the tertiary area may show many of the symptoms of inattention described earlier. The right parietal is also responsible for the recognition of faces and the sense of familiarity of objects (Hecaen and Angelergues, 1962; Luria, 1973). Warrington and Taylor (1973) ascribe both abilities to a general role for these areas in classifying nonverbal material.

The tertiary right parietal area plays a major role in such basic spatial abilities as determining slope and directionality of lines and assembling or drawing objects (DeRenzi and Faglioni, 1967; Piercy and Smyth, 1962; Warrington and James, 1967). It also is involved in arithmetic done "in the head," in which numbers must be spatially aligned (Cohn, 1961). Multiplication problems are particularly susceptible to disorders of this area. However, such patients do not lose the ability to perform arithmetic operations, as they would with left parietal injury.

Occipital Lobe

The primary sensory projection area of both occipital lobes is located in Brodmann's area 17 (*see* Fig. 2-2). Each primary area receives visual input from the opposite half of each eye. A complete loss of vision in either the right or left half of both eyes, a condition known as *homonymous hemianopsia*, may occur in total lesions of the primary area, although other lesions may also cause this condition (*see* Figs. 2-5 and 2-6). Partial lesions of the primary occipital areas will cause partial losses of vision (*scotomata*) in the opposite visual field in both eyes.

The secondary areas of both occipital lobes (Brodmann's areas 18 and 19) are responsible for the coding, integration, and synthesis of the point-by-point visual information received by the primary areas. Disorders of the secondary areas lead to errors in the schema by which visual data are integrated (Albert et al., 1975; Macrae and Trolle, 1956). Disorders of the secondary areas do not result in a loss of vision (Ettlinger, 1956).

Left Occipital Lobe

Luria (1966, 1973) has classified the major disorders of the left secondary areas as an inability to combine input into patterns *(visual agnosia)* and an inability to perceive two objects or two sensory attributes of a single object at the same time, *simultaneous agnosia.* This can make it difficult for an individual to recognize an object, because it cannot be seen as a whole but only as parts. In a less-severe form, an individual may not be able to appreciate a complex figure or picture because only one part can be seen. Disorders of the secondary area may also lead to disorders of the motor movements of the eye, causing the patient trouble in scanning the visual field or directing attention to important details (Bender, Postel, and Krieger, 1957; Cumming, Hurwitz, and Perl, 1970).

Disorders of the left secondary area cause an inability to read or recognize letters or numbers (Ajax, 1964; Benson, Segarra, and Albert, 1974; Greenblatt, 1973; Lhermitte and Beauvois, 1973; Rubens and Benson, 1971), and an inability to remember verbal material presented visually (Benson et al., 1974). As the lesion moves into the left tertiary temporal-occipital area, the patient is better able to appreciate visual forms but is still unable to read because of an inability to match visual and phonemic information. Lesions of the tertiary parieto-occipital and parieto-occipitotemporal areas have already been discussed.

Right Occipital

Lesions of the right occipital secondary areas are more likely to cause disorders of spatial relationships. Since objects can only be appreciated singly, the spatial relationship is lost. Deficits in this area may also lead to inattention, to an inability to recognize faces, and to an inability to appreciate complex, unfamiliar visual patterns. No deficits in verbal skills arise, except the neglect of the left side of a page in reading or writing. These patients also show deficits in recognizing color hues (Scotti and Spinnler, 1970).

Frontal Lobe

The frontal lobes are responsible for the planning, performance, and evaluation of all voluntary behavior. As such, they play a major role in all observable behavior.

The primary area of each frontal lobe is the motor strip located just anterior to the central sulcus (Brodmann's area 4) (*see* Fig. 2-2). Each motor area controls the action of the opposite side of the body, although each motor strip can take over control of the same side of the body as well. In general, the left motor strip can control the actions of the left side of the body more effectively than the right motor strip can control the right side of the body.

About 20 percent of the cells in the motor strip are sensory cells (Neff and Goldberg, 1960). This again emphasizes the importance of sensorimotor coordination in most voluntary behavior. The motor strip is aligned on the surface of the precentral gyrus, so that the motor area for a given part of the body is in general opposite the sensory area for the same part of the body in the postcentral gyrus. Each area of the body is represented on the motor strip proportional to the fineness of movement required of that part of the body. Those parts, such as the hand and face, involving the participation of many small muscles, are represented by relatively extensive areas of motor cortex.

The secondary areas of the frontal lobes lie just anterior to the precentral motor cortex. Brodmann's area 8, the frontal eye field, controls oculomotor activity. Brodmann's area 6 is concerned with the organization of general motor activities. In the left hemisphere, Brodmann's area 44 is responsible for the control of motor speech: This is often called Broca's area (*see* Fig. 2-2).

The secondary frontal areas are responsible for the continuous *chain of interchanging impulses* responsible for most motor activities (Luria, 1973). In essence, these areas organize behavior in detail. The motor area then sends the executive "orders" to the body. Tasks continually demand ever-changing reactions to adjust for the past movements and environmental demands. The secondary areas, using the feedback they receive from the sensory areas of the cerebral hemispheres, provide these adjustments. Consequently, they are extremely important for smooth, skilled behavior for the opposite side of the body. Lesions of the secondary areas result in jerky, disturbed movement in the opposite limb (Luria, 1966). More severe disorders of the secondary areas may lead to perseveration; the patient is unable to inhibit a movement and repeats it over and over.

The prefrontal cortex, the tertiary areas of the frontal lobes, consists primarily of Brodmann's areas 9, 10, 11, and 46 (see Fig. 2-2). The lesions of these areas, when severe, can be particularly striking, although small lesions may have no apparent effect (Hebb, 1945). This tertiary area is responsible for planning, structuring, and evaluating voluntary behavior. Severe destruction or impairment will result in the disintegration of behavior (Elithorn, Piercy, and Crosskey, 1952). The patient may be echolalic, perseverative, inflexible, mute, and nonreacting to environmental cues or instructions obtained from the self or from others (Luria, 1966; Luria and Tsvetkova, 1964). In general, the deficits are worse with bilateral rather than unilateral involvement of the prefrontal areas. In less-severe lesions, simple movements are preserved, but the patient is unable to perform complex activities or activities requiring successive changes.

Patients with tertiary frontal problems may have difficulty paying attention. They are often distracted by small noises or events that others are easily able to ignore (Luria, 1966). As a result, the patient's performance may actually be much worse than it would be without the distractibility. These patients are also very inflexible, finding it difficult to change activities or do things in an alternate manner (Drewe, 1974; Malmo, 1974; Milner, 1963).

The above disorders are associated with destruction of the lateral surface of the prefrontal area. Generally, lesions of the medial and orbital surfaces of the frontal lobe do not produce similar results. The function of these areas is intimately associated with the limbic and the reticular activating systems. With injuries to these areas, there may be changes in cortical tone, with the patient becoming apathetic or hyperactive (Luria, 1973). Emotional changes may be seen as well (Sanides, 1964). The patient may show a lack of inhibition by cursing and using obscene language (Kramer, 1955), by confabulation (Luria, 1966), or by emotional flatness. Some patients with behavioral problems have been treated by removing parts of these areas from the brain or cutting their connections to the rest of the brain. In some cases, this has resulted in an elimination of the behavioral problem (Paul, Fitzgerald, and Greenblatt, 1956). However, the patient may lose spontaneity or become apathetic as a result of such an operation. Disorders of the medial and orbital areas are more pronounced with bilateral lesions. As yet, no reliable right-left differences have been found for these areas.

Left Frontal Lobe

Lesions of the primary area of the left frontal lobe may lead to an inability to control the speech apparatus, causing speech to be garbled and slow or preventing speech altogether. Lesions of Broca's area result in motor aphasia. The person is able to utter individual sounds but cannot switch from one sound to another. If the lesion is severe enough, the patient will lose all expressive speech. Luria (1966) has also suggested that such injuries may lead to thinking disorders, because of an interference with the execution of internal speech, which he feels is the basis for thought.

Lesions of the left tertiary area may result in a complete loss of voluntary speech (Luria, 1958; Zangwill, 1966). Such patients may do poorly at tasks involving word fluency. For example, the patient may be unable to produce more than a few words beginning with a given letter (Benton, 1968; Milner, 1964; Ramier and Hecaen, 1970). The regulating role of speech may be lost. The patient will propose to do one thing but will actually do something else. The patient may not be able to change verbal instructions into acts, especially when the instructions are complex or symbolic (Luria, Pribram, and Homoskaya, 1964). The patient may also fail to scan the environment to become aware of what is occurring. As a result, the patient may reach decisions without gathering sufficient data (Luria, 1973). The patient may also show extreme memory deficits, especially for verbal material (Luria, 1966).

Right Frontal Lobe

Disorders of the primary and secondary areas of the right frontal lobe result in similar disorders as described with the left frontal lobe. However, no speech deficits generally arise from lesions of the right frontal lobe. Right frontal patients may lose the ability to sing, however, as a result of lesions to the secondary frontal areas (Botez and Wertheim, 1959). Motor disorders are not as serious to the patient in right frontal lesions since the nondominant left hand is less important in activities, and because the left hemisphere can provide some compensation for the loss.

Patients with disorders of the tertiary right frontal areas are impaired on spatial tasks, especially those which are complex. Deficits in visual-spatial integration have been reported (Teuber, 1963), as well as problems in maze learning (Corkin, 1965) and nonverbal visual memory (Milner, 1971). The serious speech deficits seen in left prefrontal disorders are not seen in right prefrontal injuries. Large right tertiary frontal lesions may exist without any obvious symptoms.

HIGHER CORTICAL BEHAVIORS

Before completing this chapter, it is important to emphasize the constant interaction of the functional units within the brain. Although each part of the brain plays a unique role in each behavioral configuration, no part can operate effectively without the others. Even such a simple task as voluntarily looking at something involves widespread cortical tone, reticular system; a decision to look at something, tertiary frontal; the sending of motor signals to the eyes, primary frontal; feedback from the eyes as to location of the eyes, primary and secondary parietal; reception by the visual area, primary occipital; integration of what is seen, secondary occipital; location of what is seen, sensory, motor, and tertiary parietal areas; and evaluation of what is seen, tertiary frontal.

Chapter 3

ISSUES IN NEUROPSYCHOLOGICAL ASSESSMENT

PURPOSE OF THE NEUROPSYCHOLOGICAL EXAM

IT IS RECOGNIZED that the neuropsychological exam must evaluate the full range of basic abilities represented in the brain (Benton, 1975; Swiercinsky, 1976). Benton (1975) has summarized these abilities as general intelligence, reasoning, memory, orientation, perceptual functions, perceptual-motor functions, language, flexibility, speed of response, attention, and concentration.

Smith (1975) has indicated that the exam should be able to serve as an aid in neurological diagnosis, a baseline for abilities, a prognostic instrument, and an aid in planning rehabilitation. Luria (1966) has emphasized the importance of reducing the symptomology of the brain-injured patients to its basic processes. Benton (1974) has termed this process the elucidation of "relationships between the structure and function of the nervous system."

Role in Neurodiagnosis

The neuropsychological exam serves as an aid to the neurologist or other physician in the diagnosis of the neurologically impaired patient. Although the exam is not needed for diagnosis in cases in which the diagnosis is clear-cut, the exam does provide additional and valuable information in difficult or unclear cases. The exam is useful in those situations where the client has definite neurological symptoms but no diagnosis can be established, as well as those cases in which a diagnostic choice needs to be made between a neurological and a severe emotional disorder. As will be seen later in this book, the latter diagnoses are among the most difficult to make.

The exam can also be used by the physician who wishes additional evidence to confirm a tentative diagnosis. In these situations, it is necessary for the neuropsychologist to give a full in-

45

terpretation of the possible neurological conditions suggested by the psychological results. This interpretation is then used by the neurologist in making the diagnosis.

Baseline for Abilities

The neuropsychological exam can serve as a baseline for a patient's abilities. As a patient improves, repeated administrations of the test battery can be used to plot the improvement. The repeated tests are also useful in identifying areas where there are residual deficits. This information is useful in counseling with the patient. It also enables the physician and neuropsychologist to evaluate any ongoing treatment plans for the patient.

Pre- and post-testing can also be used to evaluate the effects of surgery for a neurological condition. The effects of a given drug regimen can also be determined. This is especially important in the cases of young children receiving drugs for the conditions known as *minimal brain dysfunction.* Drugs to control such problems as hyperactivity can seriously affect a child's ability to learn under some conditions. It is important in these cases to have accurate measurements of the drug's effects. These enable the physician to balance the positive effects of the drug against any negative neuropsychological consequences. The baseline and subsequent testing can also be used for counseling the patient and his/her family. The patient and family can benefit by being aware of circumstances in which adjustments will be necessary. For example, the exam may indicate the patient will have difficulty in performing what are usually simple, everyday tasks.

Prognosis

A thorough analysis of the subject's condition can yield valuable information as to the patient's prognosis. As can be seen from the first chapters, spontaneous recovery of a behavior depends on the ability of a functional system to replace the injured areas of the brain. This can happen only if there are appropriate intact areas of the brain which can help reformulate the functional system. This process will be discussed in more detail in Chapter 9.

As the discussion above indicates, prognosis is based on the knowledge of which functional areas in the brain are damaged and which are intact. Consequently, precise diagnostic information on the functional areas involved is necessary for a fully adequate prognosis. This information is not typically found in a neurological diagnosis; such a diagnosis does not usually provide the information needed on the functional systems involved in a lesion. This can best be derived from a thorough, complete neuropsychological exam.

Rehabilitation

Rehabilitation programs require the same detailed functional diagnosis as does an accurate prognosis. The purpose of neuropsychological rehabilitation is to aid in the reformulation of disrupted functional systems by providing the alternate abilities to replace the function of the injured areas. This is done through using the intact areas of the brain and through repeated practice and feedback. The rehabilitation program helps provide functional reformulation that has not occurred spontaneously. The procedure is discussed in more detail in Chapter 9.

STRUCTURE OF THE EXAM

Clinicians have differed significantly in their approaches to structuring the neuropsychological exam. One approach attempts to adapt each examination to the needs and apparent deficits of each patient. The second approach has emphasized the use of a standard battery of tests for all patients.

Flexible Approach

The flexible approach to neuropsychological testing is based on the idea that each exam should be adapted to the individual patient. Rather than use a standard battery of tests, clinicians choose the tests and procedures within an exam, based on their impressions of the patient and information available on the patient from other sources. As a result, each examination may vary considerably from patient to patient. The clinician may use standard tests, or tests may be altered and adapted as the clinician attempts to form an opinion on the nature of the deficits (Christensen, 1975a; Lezak, 1976; Luria, 1966). Many of the conclusions reached in the exam are based on the clinician's qualitative interpretations of the test results and the patient's behavior. The conclusions are also founded on the clinician's experience and knowledge of the experimental literature.

This approach has several advantages. First, it acknowledges the individuality of the patient's deficits and attempts to adapt the exam to this individuality. Under the proper condition, such a technique can yield more precise measurements of a subject's skill on a given ability, rather than just the patient's score on a given test. Secondly, the exam can concentrate on those areas seen as most important for the patient. It can ignore areas not important for the patient's prognosis. Since the time for any exam is limited, this enables the clinician to more thoroughly investigate the areas seen as significant.

This approach can adapt the exam to different needs of the patient or physician. Again, this is a time-saving situation that allows more efficient use of the neuropsychologist's time. Finally, the approach allows the clinician to concentrate on tasks related to rehabilitation of the most important deficits that the patient shows.

The approach also shows several disadvantages. Since the content of the exam emphasizes the areas the clinician feels are important, it is possible that the exam can become a selective confirmation of the clinician's opinion. Since areas which are seen as irrelevant may never be tested, it may never be realized that a deficit has been missed. Since the tests are chosen just for the patient and his or her expected problems, the data may be biased towards confirming the original hypothesis. The use of tests not standardized for a clinical population or those which have been adapted also presents potentially serious problems. The interpretation of a test that has not been adequately standardized is always questionable. One's impression of what a score should mean for a given patient may be quite wrong. A test which appears to measure one thing in one population may measure something else entirely in a brain-injured population. In each of these situations, the accuracy of the individual clinician's judgment becomes the accuracy of the test. At present there are no measures of such accuracy, but it is likely that it varies considerably among clinicians.

The use of different exams and procedures for each patient precludes the experimental validation of individual tests in applied clinical settings. It also precludes an evaluation of the process as a whole, since conclusions come not from test scores but from the clinician's interpretation. It is possible, in such a situation, to continue using an ineffective test because it *appears* to work.

The structuring of an exam on an individual basis may mean that only some of the basic functions mediated by the brain are assessed. Rehabilitation and prognosis are dependent on the state of the brain as a whole; the lack of information on the entire brain can impair a rehabilitation program or invalidate a prognosis. In practice, it is not unusual to see patients with secondary deficits seemingly unrelated to their primary referral problem and the impression received from the patient. For example, it is not unusual for a patient with a major stroke to have had smaller, secondary disorders of cerebral circulation. The deficits may have existed before the patient's current problem. Whatever the source of the deficits, it is necessary that they be identified and considered in making any recommendations for a client.

Standard Battery Approach

The alternate approach to the neuropsychological exam has been advanced by Halstead (1947) and Reitan (1966). They pioneered the use of a standard battery of tests for brain damage which attempted to incorporate evaluation of all the major skills that should be reflected in a neuropsychological exam. The purpose of the battery was to allow the development of various "principles for inference of psychological deficit . . . as they would apply to the results obtained on individual subjects" (Reitan, 1959). In this approach, the same tests are given to all patients, regardless of the impression of the patient or the referral question. Typically, the tests are given by a technician rather than a doctoral psychologist, since the tests are given according to definite rules of procedure, without variations. The use of technicians allows more testing to be accomplished for the same cost, since the more expensive time of a doctoral-level neuropsychologist is not required for administration of the battery.

This approach presents several advantages. First, it can insure that all subjects are evaluated for all basic neuropsychological abilities as indicated at the beginning of this chapter. This makes it unlikely that a condition of importance could be overlooked. Secondly, it allows for the accumulation of data. These data can be used to identify objective patterns of scores that can be used in the diagnosis of brain damage. As such relationships are found, they establish an objective rather than intuitive basis for neurodiagnosis.

The discovery of such relationships also allows one to diagnose beyond the actual data presented. For example, inferences can be made regarding areas of the brain not directly tested. This could be done by finding patterns in the test results that reflected disorders of that area. Patterns within the data could also be related to diagnosing the probability of certain causes of brain dysfunction. Knowledge of causes can be useful both in providing a physician with tentative diagnoses, as well as in predicting the course and rehabilitation of a disorder.

There are also drawbacks to these methods. The time involved in testing any patient can be considerable. Problems, such as fatigue or loss of motivation, may develop. The time involved forces the use of a testing technician in order to insure a reasonable cost and reasonable use of a neuropsychologist's time. As a result, the neuropsychologist has little contact with the patient and thus loses the opportunity to make a qualitative analysis of the patient's behavior. Often an understanding of *why* a patient failed a task is as valuable as the fact that the task was failed (Luria, 1966). Such information can be very useful in making rehabilitation and diagnostic decisions.

Standard batteries are heavily influenced by the original choice of tests to include in the battery. The choice is often biased by the theoretical beliefs of the person doing the choosing. A poorly chosen test battery, no matter how many times it is given, will continue to yield unsatisfactory results. In different situations, different test batteries may be more effective. However, since no other tests are given by the user of a standard battery, this would never be discovered.

This standard battery method also fails to recognize that altering a test procedure is sometimes valuable in determining a specific deficit. For example, the Seashore Rhythm Test measures a subject's ability to remember rhythmic patterns and the subject's ability to concentrate. If a subject earns a low score, one cannot always be sure whether this was due to an inability to concentrate or to remember rhythms. By altering the procedure of a test, a better understanding of the basic underlying deficit may be acquired.

A standard battery may also overlook a specific, but unusual, deficit related to the client's condition. The possibility of this happening depends upon the comprehensiveness of the test battery employed. In some cases, failure to recognize such a deficit may affect the interpretation and understanding of the test results to a serious degree.

A standard battery may not be appropriate for all patients, especially when there are peripheral deficits, such as injury to the limbs, a serious visual loss, or a spinal cord injury. In such patients, their inability to do a given test may be related to a peripheral motor or visual problem rather than to a brain dysfunction. Consequently, the data from such a patient on a standard battery may be useless for diagnostic or evaluative purposes.

Finally, it should be recognized that the interpretation of even a standard battery requires considerable skill, knowledge, and experience. The standard batteries are easier to interpret as standard rules develop. However, the accuracy of such interpretation is at present too low to be clinically acceptable.

Combination Method

Since each of the first two approaches have clear advantages, some neuropsychologists have attempted to use an approach combining the best aspects of both. This entails using a comprehensive, standard battery augmented by individualized evaluation as suggested by each case. This approach possesses all of the advantages of the standard battery method. In addition, it allows for individual flexibility and analysis when it is necessary. This combined approach, used properly, can potentially yield more information than either the flexible or standard battery approach alone.

The main drawback to this alternative is the amount of time invested in a single patient, as this can be a very time-consuming process. It is incumbent upon the user to judiciously select the tests used in order to minimize this problem.

At present, there is no general consensus as to which of these approaches is ideal in any given clinical situation. Generally, such considerations as professional staff size, time, theoretical orientation, availability of technicians, and the role of the neuropsychologist in an institution help determine an individual choice. In the hands of a well-trained neuropsychologist, all three methods can yield accurate and useful assessments.

VALIDATION OF NEUROPSYCHOLOGICAL TESTS

An important emphasis has been placed in neurospychology on the validation of neuropsychological tests. The goal of such validation is simple. Tests or test batteries should be highly accurate in classifying both brain-damaged and normal individuals. Although this is a simple idea, in practice it has proven to be difficult to establish.

Neurological Criteria

The first problem in validation is establishing a criteria of who is brain damaged. Typically, the assumption has been made that the diagnosis of a physician is an accurate way to do this. This method has been seen in numerous studies.

A review of the literature suggests that this criterion may not be as accurate as desired. Storms (1972) found that a neurologist's evaluation for brain damage correlated better with a patient's degree of psychiatric disorder than it did with objective neurological tests. Yates (1954) has emphasized the questionable nature of the psychiatric diagnosis of "organic brain syndrome."

Such diagnoses are often based on a psychiatrist's opinion, rather than definitive neurological findings.

Single neurological tests have also been found to be inaccurate (Filskov and Goldstein, 1974). One problem with most neurological tests is that they are usually accurate in identifying certain disorders, but not others. Thus, a result indicating brain damage is likely to be correct. A result indicating normality, however, is questionable. Which disorders a test can accurately diagnose varies considerably among the major neurological tests.

Neurological Tests

Computed axial tomography, also known as the *CAT* or *EMI scan*, is highly accurate in diagnosing space-occupying lesions, such as tumors (New and Scott, 1975). It can also diagnose conditions causing enlargement of the ventricles or atrophy of the brain. It has been reported the CAT scan is 92 percent accurate in diagnosing tumors (Gawler, Bull, DuBoulay, and Marshall, 1975). The CAT scan works by taking x rays of the brain from many different angles. A computer then analyzes the results, in order to produce pictures indicating the density of each subarea within the brain. Since the density of tumors differs from that of brain tissue, the tumor can be clearly seen on the CAT scan pictures. In a similar manner, other disorders which cause density changes can be seen in the pictures.

Angiography allows the physician to get a picture of the cerebrovascular system. The physician introduces a radiopaque dye into the blood supply. After the dye is given enough time to circulate through the brain, x rays are then taken, indicating the distribution of the dye. This allows the physician to observe the location and size of the cerebral blood vessels. Abnormalities of the cerebral vessels may then be seen. Conditions occupying space may also be inferred, if they push a major vessel away from where it would normally be. Unlike the CAT scan, angiography is a potentially dangerous test. It can cause death under certain circumstances. Filskov and Goldstein (1974) found that the procedure was 85 percent accurate when used to diagnose appropriate disorders, such as vascular disease or tumor.

Pneumoencephalography involves the introduction of air into the ventricular system. This allows x rays to be taken of the size and shape of the ventricles and subarachnoid space. Tumors can be seen because they distort the size, shape, or location of the ventricles. Degenerative diseases can also be seen, because they usually result in enlarged ventricles. This procedure is safer than angiography, but has the unpleasant side effect of causing an extremely painful headache which lasts about twenty-four to forty-eight hours (Mayo Clinic, 1976). The pneumoencephalogram is about 80 percent accurate when used to diagnose degenerative diseases and space-occupying disorders (Filskov and Goldstein, 1974).

Electroencephalography involves the measurement of the electrical activity of the brain. This activity is usually quite stable and predictable under testing conditions. Variations from what is normally expected can be used to diagnose epilepsy as well as most other neurological conditions. However, the EEG is only about 60 percent accurate overall (Filskov and Goldstein, 1974). In addition, about 15 to 20 percent of the normal population produces EEGs similar to those of neurological patients (Mayo, 1976).

The *physical neurological exam* involves the investigation of the patient's physical health, cranial nerves, reflexes, sensory modalities, motor skills, psychiatric status, and mental abilities. Since this exam takes a considerable amount of time, many physicians will only do parts of the exam as they think appropriate. The way in which each area is tested is not standard, but varies considerably among physicians. Consequently, the effectiveness of the exam depends on the experience, skill, and thoroughness of the physician administering the exam. The exam is sensitive to gross disorders, but may miss more subtle deficits that are primarily reflected as behavioral or intellectual problems.

It is important in any research project attempting to validate a neuropsychological test to have all patients examined by the proper techniques. The results of such tests need to be interpreted by a qualified neurologist. For most studies, the use of a single examination method for all patients is usually questionable. For example, many studies have based their diagnosis on the results of the EEG. Other studies have used psychiatric diagnosis which may be based on a partial physical neurological exam and sometimes an EEG. In each case, results from these studies must be evaluated cautiously.

Experimental Group Structure

In examining a validation study, it is important to look closely at the structure of the brain-damaged experimental group. It is necessary to know the type and locus of brain injuries represented. The type of lesion is important, because each neurological disorder produces different patterns of results (*see* Chapter 6). Degenerative diseases, for example, may cause deterioration of all behavior. Consequently, almost any test would be found to be effective in diagnosing brain damage in such a population.

The location of the brain damage is also significant. Injuries in different areas of the brain produce different deficits. Using groups biased towards left, right, or diffuse injuries can distort the actual diagnostic effectiveness of a test. Many institutional settings do have biased populations available. Speech rehabilitation settings generally work with left- or diffuse-injured patients. Psychiatric institutions are likely to have patients with chronic, diffuse brain disease.

It is also necessary to look at the severity of injuries represented. The more severe the injuries, the more global the deficits. A test validated only on severe injuries is of questionable value. The most difficult clinical problems involve borderline, less-obvious deficits. It is this population for whom the tests must be effective.

The ideal experimental group consists of clinic patients referred because of a diagnostic question. After final diagnostic conclusion has been reached, this could be compared to the test results. It would be important that the final decisions are based fully on medical evidence, without considering the psychological test evidence. Although such a group is useful for establishing clinical relevance, it has rarely been used in published studies.

Control Groups

The appropriateness of the control group must be assessed in each study. Minimally, the control group should be matched with the experimental group for age, initial intelligence, education, and general health. For example, it is not appropriate to use a hospital staff as a control group for patients. Age is a particularly important dimension to consider, as numerous studies have shown declines with aging in many neuropsychological measures (deS Hamsher and Benton, 1976; Reitan, 1955b).

Psychiatric control groups present a number of problems. Psychiatric patients may be on tranquilizing medication that affects performance. Patients who have been in psychiatric hospitals for a long period of time also show a number of deficits, including listlessness, apathy, and loss of motivation. The patient's emotional problems may preclude cooperation with the examiner. All of these factors can interfere seriously with testing.

Methodological and Statistical Problems

Many studies fail to report how well patients were diagnosed by a given test. In these cases, the authors only report that there was a "statistically significant difference" between the control and experimental groups. This information is useful for an experimental evaluation of brain damage. It is not useful for a clinical evaluation. The clinician needs to know the effectiveness of a test for a single individual. Consequently, the clinician is interested in *hit rates,* the percentage of patients accurately diagnosed.

It is not sufficient to present overall hit rates. An overall hit rate of 75 percent might conceal an accuracy of 100 percent for the control group and 50 percent for the experimental group. Results can even be more distorted when a study has control or experimental groups of unequal number. If 80 percent of the subjects are normal, calling all patients normal would result in an 80 percent accuracy rate. Conversely, if 80 percent of the patients are brain damaged, diagnosing everyone brain damaged will also result in an 80 percent accuracy rate (Hartlage, 1966).

Another serious methodological problem is the dependence of most studies on only one test. In almost all clinical work, patients are evaluated by a series of tests. Conclusions are based on the combined results. Studies using multiple tests are of more interest and value to the clinician.

Cross Validation

A final problem with many tests is the lack of cross validation. The effectiveness of any test needs to be demonstrated in several studies by independent investigators. Ideally, these studies should use different types of subject populations. The lack of cross validation can cast considerable doubt on the effectiveness of any clinical test. This problem must be carefully considered when a clinican plans to adopt a given test.

SUBJECT FACTORS AFFECTING NEUROPSYCHOLOGICAL TESTING

A number of subject factors can influence neuropsychological test results (Hartlage, 1966; Luria, 1966). These factors include motivation, dominance, aging, chronicity, and other physical disorders of the patient.

Motivational Variables

Interpretations of test data are based on the assumption that a patient has performed as well as possible. If this is not the case, the test data may be essentially uninterpretable.

An important component of motivation is arousal. If a patient is taking medication which lowers arousal levels, this can lead to low motivation and cooperation. Such factors as lack of sleep, fatigue from numerous activities, or poor general health can produce similar results. Brain-damaged individuals vary considerably in their susceptibility to fatigue. Some patients can test for a full day with no problems. Others have difficulty maintaining a high level of performance for even one hour.

In any testing situation, attempts need to be made to take these factors into account. Breaks in testing may be scheduled according to the needs of the patient. With this procedure, most patients can be tested on an extensive test battery in a single working day. In many cases, the patient actually enjoys the testing, since it is a break from the inactivity s/he experiences in the hospital or at home. Some patients are not able to work more than a few hours each day, even with breaks. For these patients, testing can be scheduled over a period of several days.

Fatigue in a patient can also be used as a diagnostic factor. Luria (1966) has observed that patients fatigue faster when working with material that reflects their deficits. If a patient shows more fatigue with particular tests, those tests may reflect his/her underlying disorder.

Motivation may be low if a subject is reluctant to do the tests. This may come from a subject who is "afraid" of psychological tests. Many patients immediately assume that someone is trying to see if they are crazy. Such patients will usually respond to an explanation of the tests and will become more cooperative as a positive rapport with the examiner is established. It is important that programs using testing technicians insure that the technicians have the training to do this with difficult patients.

Reluctance to take the tests may also come from the psychiatric patient. Such patients may not respond to the normal motivational contingencies of the testing situation. With severely disordered patients, it may be necessary to use extensive reinforcers to get the patient to attend to the tests. These reinforcers may be social or they may have to be more concrete. Cigarettes, candy, privileges, cola, or other similar items can be used as concrete motivators.

When the lack of motivation is due to medication, it is necessary to work with the patient's physician. The doctor can be asked to take the patient off all nonessential medications likely to interfere with test performance. The length of time a patient needs to be off interfering medications varies with the patient, the dosage, and the drug itself. Generally, one to three days is an adequate length of time to eliminate the acute effects. Although there may be some residual effects, the patient can usually be tested and interpretable results obtained. The effects of medication can be rather substantial in some patients. Klonoff, Fibiger, and Hutton (1970) found a high correlation between drug regimen and neuropsychological test performance.

It should be recognized that, in some cases, drugs actually improve the patient's performance. These patients may be untestable when without medication. In such situations, consultation with the patient's physician can establish medication levels that maximize performance.

Despite all of the precautions taken, situations will arise in which test results are questionable because of motivational factors. In such situations, it is usually advisable to retest the patient in a subsequent session. Such a testing session should take place after corrections for the problems that interfered with the original testing.

Dominance

Not all patients are left hemisphere dominant for speech. There have been a number of studies attempting to identify the actual percentage of clients who are right hemisphere dominant or show mixed dominance (Boller, 1973; Goodglass and Quadfasel, 1954; Luria, 1966; Warrington and Pratt, 1973). The figures presented by Milner (1975) are probably the most useful. She found that 96 percent of the right-handed population was left hemisphere dominant, while only 4 percent were right dominant. In left-handers, 70 percent were left dominant, 15 percent were mixed dominant, and 15 percent were right dominant.

These figures changed if the client sustained early childhood brain damage. Of this group, 81 percent of the right-handers were left dominant, while 13 percent were right dominant, and 6 percent were mixed dominant. In the left-handers, 30 percent were left dominant, 19 percent were mixed, and 51 percent were right dominant.

These figures indicate that a substantial majority of the population is left brain dominant. This includes both right- and left-handed individuals. The only exception to this rule is the case of the left-hander with a history of early brain trauma. In most cases, it appears most profitable to assume that a patient is left hemisphere dominant.

In cases of complete right hemisphere dominance, neuropsychological test results will localize opposite to the manner described in this book. Once right dominance is recognized, however, these individuals do not present a difficult diagnostic problem. This is not the case with mixed dominant individuals. In cases of mixed dominance, abilities may be partially represented in both hemispheres or represented in full in either hemisphere. Since the pattern of how the abilities will be represented cannot be predicted for these individuals, they can present a very difficult diagnostic problem. Often the conclusions reached from the data of such individuals can only be tentative at best.

Mixed dominance may also cause serious problems for the client. If verbal abilities are represented in both hemispheres, the person may have trouble learning complex verbal skills such as reading. If the left hemisphere is responsible for cognition, but the right for dominant motor output and sensory input, there can be problems in directing motor output or evaluating sensory input. The lack of a dominant hemisphere directing behavior can lead to confusion and the inability to perform sequenced, coordinated activity smoothly.

Methods exist for identifying the dominance of an individual. Some involve injections of drugs to incapacitate one hemisphere and are generally not available to most neurospychologists. However, dichotic listening tasks can provide similar information (Beaumont and Dimond, 1974). In a dichotic listening task, verbal stimuli are presented to one ear or the other through earphones. It is then determined how quickly the person can react to these verbal stimuli. Sounds to the ear opposite the verbal dominant hemisphere should cause a faster reaction than sounds to the ear of the nonverbal dominant hemisphere.

In some cases, dominance may be deduced from the neuropsychological testing. In these cases, a patient shows a focal cognitive and a focal sensorimotor deficit. However, the cognitive deficit and the sensorimotor deficit both suggest lateralization to a different hemisphere, if the person is assumed to be left hemisphere dominant. If assuming right hemisphere dominance makes the cognitive and motor sensory deficits point to the same localization, then it is likely that the patient is right hemisphere dominant.

Several exams also exist to determine the dominant eye, hand

and foot (Crovitz and Zener, 1962; Oldfield, 1971; Reitan, 1959d). When a patient is mixed dominant this will often be expressed as differences in dominance among the eye, hand, and foot. However, it should be recognized that these differences also exist in individuals who are not mixed dominant.

Aging

As patients grow older, they generally do less well on tests measuring adaptive abilities or motor skills (Reitan, 1955b; Teuber and Rudel, 1962). Many of the neuropsychological tests fall into these categories. As a result, older persons tend to do less well on neuropsychological tests. This causes more older patients to be classified as brain damaged than is usually warranted. Consequently, analysis of the scores of older persons simply by looking at the level of performance is somewhat questionable.

In working with older patients, it is important to look more closely at the relationship of test scores to one another. If some tests are considerably more depressed than others, this information can be used for diagnosis and evaluation. Reitan (1955b) found that the pattern of scores seen in brain-damaged patients is the same for both younger and older patients. DeS Hamsher and Benton (1976) have suggested the possibility that these patterns do differ in older individuals, but their results were so tentative that the conclusions of the Reitan study must be accepted at present.

If there is a desire to look at the level of performance, it is necessary to provide age related normative data. At present this is available for a few major tests (Leuthold, Bergs, Matthews, and Harley, 1975; Wechsler, 1955; University of Wisconsin, undated). As there is presently increasing interest in the study of aging, it is likely that more data on aging effects will soon be available.

Chronicity

The effects of a recent acute disorder are generally more severe than the effects of an old, chronic disorder. There are a number of reasons for this effect. First, a current disorder is more likely to disrupt the integrity of the brain as a whole. Neurological lesions may cause increased pressure within the ventricles, swelling of the brain tissue, *edema*, and disorders of metabolism and circulation. There may also be a "mirror" effect in which the opposite hemisphere may show a deficit in the same place as the affected hemisphere (Bannister, 1973; Luria, 1966, 1973; Monakow, 1914; Smith, 1975). All of these conditions work to extend the effect of a lesion beyond its nominal boundaries.

An acute lesion may also result in blurring or loss of vision, *papilloedema*. This is a result of a raised intracranial pressure. The loss of vision can interfere with psychological test performance. Raised intracranial pressure may also interfere with motor skills and cause distracting headaches. These symptoms can also interfere with test performance.

Finally, the acute lesion looks worse, because the subject has not had time to recover. Luria (1963) has observed that functional systems spontaneously reform after a lesion's disruptive effects are removed. This reorganization of functional systems will improve performance on neuropsychological tests. It is not unusual to see a patient recover after a lesion with little or no observable functional loss.

Chronic patients look less severely impaired overall. Global measures of brain functioning will generally improve, often quite considerably. Such a patient may show only minor deficits where previously severe deficits had existed. In most cases, the lesions of chronic patients will show less localization to the injury. Recognition of each of these factors can be useful in classifying a disorder as acute or chronic.

Not all chronic patients show such hopeful pictures. Such factors as age, general health, the extent of the lesion, emotional reactions, and family support will affect the amount of recovery. These factors will be discussed more fully in Chapter 9.

Other Physical Disorders

Physical disorders other than injury to the brain may also interfere with test procedures. Broken arms would obviously interfere with doing manipulative tests, especially when the dominant arm is involved. Injuries to the spine may cause loss of motor control or sensory feedback to one or both arms. This can produce distorted motor or sensory test performance, which can easily confuse diagnosis. A variety of injuries may cause severe pain or headaches which also interfere with the tests.

In many cases, tests can be added to a battery to adjust for these special handicaps. For example, many spatial tests require a motor response which a spinal or peripheral arm injury might make impossible. Such tests can be replaced by those spatial tests (such as the Raven Colored Matrices) that do not require a motor response. Similarly, a patient who cannot talk cannot take most verbal tests. Such a patient could be asked to write rather than speak the answers. They could also be given a test like the Peabody Picture Vocabulary Test, which does not require a verbal response.

In all cases where test substitutions or alterations are made, the results must be considered cautiously. It is easy to misinterpret test scores under such circumstances. For example, the Peabody Picture Vocabulary Test tends to overestimate the verbal skills of low-IQ subjects. When using the test, one could attribute more verbal skills to the patient than actually exist. This could cause serious errors of interpretation.

COMPARING NEUROPSYCHOLOGICAL TEST RESULTS

When administering a battery of tests, it is important to be able to compare performance on tests which measure widely different skills. As one gains enough experience with a set of tests, this often becomes an automatic skill. However, the easiest way to accomplish this task is the use of T-scores rather than raw scores. T-scores are determined by a mathematical formula that can convert all scores from all tests to a standard scale. The T-score is determined by first subtracting the mean score from a normative group for a test from the person's actual score. The result is divided by the standard deviation of the scores in the normative sample. This result is multiplied by ten, and fifty is added to this answer. The formula for T-scores looks like this:

$$T = 50.0 + \frac{(\text{Score obtained} - \text{Average normative score})}{\text{Standard deviation (normative sample)}} \times 10.0$$

The T-score approach has several advantages. First, all scores are roughly comparable. Second, adjustments can be made for such factors as age and education. This is done by determining normative means and standard deviations for different age or educational levels. The normative scores corresponding to a given person's age or education may then be included.

All T-scores have an average score of 50 and a standard deviation of 10. Normal performance is usually considered to be between T-scores of 30 and 70. This range includes 95 percent of the normal population. Less than 3 percent of the normal population is misclassified by this technique. In some cases, the normal range is defined as being between 40 and 60. This range includes about two thirds of the normal population. If this range is used, about 17 percent of the normal population will be misclassified. However, a greater number of the brain-injured population will be accurately identified.

Chapter 4

THE DIAGNOSIS OF BRAIN DAMAGE

A MAJORITY OF THE RESEARCH within clinical neuropsychology has been directed toward the differentiation of the brain-damaged patient from all other patients. This research has attempted to develop a single test or test battery that can make this distinction. These studies have developed several methods of analyzing test results, including the following approaches: the level of performance, the differential score, the pathognomic sign, the difference between the right and left side of the body, the difference between the right and left hemispheres, the pattern of scores, and the statistical analysis (Hughes, 1976; Reitan, 1974b; Swiercinsky and Hallenback, 1975).

Level of Performance

This method compares the patient's score on a test to an expected score, or *norm*. The expected test score is determined from the performance of a normative sample of patients and controls. Such norms may take into account such factors as age, sex, education, and intelligence. Generally, these tests have a *cutoff* score. A patient scoring worse than the cutoff score is labeled as brain damaged; a patient scoring better is labeled as normal.

The cutoff score is set so that as few errors as possible are made in classifying an individual case. The cutoff score may be chosen to minimize the error of classifying the brain-damaged individual as normal. Alternately, it can be chosen to minimize the error of misclassifying the normal individual as brain damaged. This is done by lowering or raising the cutoff score. The cutoff score may also be set at an intermediate point where the chances of misclassifying either a brain-damaged or a normal individual are about equal.

Differential Score Approach

This approach compares a patient's test score on two tests. One test is theoretically highly *sensitive* to brain damage; the second

65

is theoretically insensitive to brain dysfunction. The insensitive test is supposed to reflect the individual's ability before any brain injury occurred, while the sensitive test reflects the effects of brain damage. If the sensitive test score is significantly worse, it is assumed that the difference is due to a brain injury.

In general, the two test scores are combined to yield a single score measuring their difference. This may be done simply by subtracting or dividing one score by the other. This single score is then analyzed by treating it in the manner described under the level of performance section.

This approach has three potential sources of error. First, the sensitive test may fail to reflect the brain damage present. At present, a test does not exist that is sensitive to all forms of brain dysfunction. Second, the insensitive test score may be lowered by the brain injury. Since all abilities depend upon the brain, all abilities can be affected by brain damage. No test is fully insensitive to brain injury. Finally, there are the errors involved in setting any cutoff point.

The differential score method has the advantage of recognizing that each individual starts at a different level of performance. Thus, the error of misclassifying all persons with low ability as brain injured is avoided.

Pathognomic Signs

This method is commonly seen in clinical neurology. It involves the observation of the patient's performance for signs characteristic of the performance of brain-damaged individuals. Pathognomic signs occur rarely in normal individuals. In clinical neurology, this would include such signs as an eye which will not move from side to side. In neuropsychology, the rotation of a drawing or the failure to draw the left half of a figure would be examples of pathognomic signs.

The number of pathognomic signs within a given test may be counted to yield a summary number. This number is treated as a level-of-performance score. In other cases, the simple presence of a particular pathognomic sign will be taken as an indication of brain damage.

Right-Left Body Difference

The two cerebral hemispheres control the contralateral sides of the body for most sensory and motor acts. If one side of the body performs significantly worse than the other, injury to the opposite hemisphere may have occurred. This approach is similar to the differential score approach in that one side of the body serves as the control for the other. For motor tasks in which the dominant side is expected to perform better than the nondominant, raw scores must be adjusted.

Generally, the scores from the two sides of the body are subtracted to obtain a single difference score. This score is then treated as described in the level-of-performance approach. This approach may yield inaccurate conclusions when an injury involves both hemispheres or when an injury to the spinal cord is involved, because such injuries may also cause lateralized motor or sensory deficits or impair performance bilaterally.

Right-Left Hemisphere Difference

This method is based on the functional asymmetry of the two cerebral hemispheres: A right brain skill is compared to a left brain skill. Significant differences in performance are assumed to measure lateralized dysfunction in the affected hemisphere. These scores are analyzed as are right-left difference scores. This method possesses the same advantages and sources of error as the differential score approach.

Pattern Analysis

Pattern analysis examines the relationships among the scores in a test battery. It seeks to recognize patterns consistent with specific injuries and particular neurological processes and has value in identifying mild disorders that cause relatively little disturbance in level of performance. It is also valuable in differentiating poor performances caused by factors other than brain injury. The major drawback to this method is the amount of knowledge about neurological disorders and the functional organization of the brain required to utilize this method properly.

Statistical Approaches

Multivariate statistical techniques have been employed in an attempt to derive maximum information from sets of test data. These techniques include such procedures as multiple regression and discriminant and factor analysis. Each of these techniques attempts to find underlying relationships within test data that would be useful in diagnosis.

Factor analysis has been used to find combinations of scores which represent pure abilities. Raw test scores do not do this, since any test reflects more than one behavioral function. A pure ability score should theoretically be more effective in identifying dysfunction in a particular area of the brain. As yet, such techniques have not accomplished this goal.

Discriminant analysis and multiple regression attempt to develop formulas that can directly discriminate between different criterion groups, such as a formula which discriminates brain-damaged from normal individuals. Such formulas have been shown to be highly effective in specific populations (Wheeler et al., 1963). The drawback to these techniques is their dependence on the specific populations used to derive the formulas. When used with an alternate population, even one from another hospital, they can lose a considerable amount of effectiveness. Consequently, it is necessary to validate the formulas for the specific population to be tested.

CLINICAL DIAGNOSTIC STUDIES: SINGLE TESTS

Studies on the diagnosis of brain injury have differed in the number of tests employed in the diagnostic process. Since the majority of studies have investigated the effectiveness of a single test, these studies will be considered first.

Because of the great number of tests investigated during the last thirty years, it is necessary to limit their presentation within this volume. Two criteria have been employed in selecting the following tests. First, the literature must indicate that the test is being used clinically at the present time. Many tests, popular in the 1940s and 1950s, have virtually disappeared in recent years. Secondly, there must be a body of well-designed research indicating the test is potentially useful to the clinician. Tests that are part of a larger test battery will be discussed with the test battery in the next section.

Spatial Tests

Complex spatial tests have long been popular as single tests of brain injury. This is based on the representation of complex spatial skills in both hemispheres.

Bender-Gestalt

The Bender-Gestalt Test is the oldest and one of the most popular spatial tests. It requires the subject to copy nine figures on a blank sheet of paper. These drawings are then evaluated by one of several scoring systems that have been derived in the literature. Each of these systems has attempted to identify qualitative signs indicating brain injury. In some cases, a sign may reflect either a brain injury or an emotional disorder. The most popular of these scoring systems include those proposed by Bender (1938), Pascal and Suttell (1951), Hain (1964), and Hutt (1969).

Investigators using these scoring systems have reported up to 70 percent accuracy in identifying brain-injured patients and 90 percent accuracy in identifying normal subjects (Brilliant and Gynther, 1963; Bruhn and Reid, 1975; Goldberg, 1959, 1974; Hain, 1964; Levine and Feirstein, 1972; McGuire, 1960; Orme, 1962; Tymchuk, 1974).

However, a number of other studies using the Bender-Gestalt Test have reported essentially negative results, particularly in situations requiring the differentiation of brain-damaged and psychiatric patients (Johnson, Helkamp, and Lottman, 1971; Mosher and Smith, 1965; Rosecrans and Schaffer, 1969; Watson, 1968). Several major review studies have criticized the Bender for its unreliability and inability to discriminate in psychiatric populations. The studies on the Bender-Gestalt have been criticized for the lack of adequate controls (Billingslea, 1963; Canter, 1976; Tolor and Schulberg, 1963).

The results from these studies indicate that the use of the Bender-Gestalt Test alone allows too wide a margin of error for clinical work. A poor score on the Bender may indicate problems for a client, but does not specify the nature of the problems. A good score does rule out the possibility of brain damage.

Minnesota Percepto-Diagnostic Test

The Minnesota Percepto-Diagnostic Test is an attempt to quantify the amount of rotation seen in drawings of Bender-like figures. It is based on the assumption that all brain damage will be reflected in rotations. The test employs two Bender-Gestalt figures, each presented against three different backgrounds for a total of six items. The designs and backgrounds are those found by the authors to yield more rotations than other designs (Fuller and Laird, 1963). The designs are scored by using a protractor to measure the amount of rotation in degrees. Normative data can be found in Fuller and Laird (1963).

The first Fuller and Laird (1963) study reported a hit rate of 90 percent in an organic population and 81 percent in a population with personality disorders. Both of the groups were identified by psychiatric diagnosis. Hit rates of 62 percent in an organic population and 86 percent in a normal group have also been reported (Crookes and Coleman, 1973). Two studies have reported high hit rates when the test is used with adolescents (Fuller and Laird, 1963; Fuller and Friedrich, 1974). Several studies reported an inability to discriminate between primarily schizophrenic and brain-injured patients (George, 1973; Holland, Lowenfeld, and Wadsworth, 1975; Watson and Uecker, 1966).

Overall, the Minnesota Percepto-Diagnostic Test has much less independent research support of its effectiveness than does the Bender. The studies that support it are questionable because of a number of experimental problems. The test's only advantage is a more objective scoring system than is seen in the Bender-Gestalt Test.

Background Interference Procedure

This test arose out of Arthur Canter's observation that distractions on a Bender-Gestalt response sheet (a coffee stain) impaired the performance of a brain-injured group more than any other group. The test requires that the subject draw the nine Bender figures on a blank sheet of paper and then draw them again on a paper printed over with irregular wavy lines. The test assumes that the interference of the wavy lines will be most disruptive for brain-injured individuals. The scoring system employs a modification of Pascal and Suttell's (1951) Bender scoring system (Canter, 1976). The score on the normal presentation is subtracted from the interference score to yield a measure of the effect of the interference.

To date, the literature on this test indicates a high hit rate in brain-damaged and control patients of about 88 percent (Canter, 1976). Using an older scoring system for the test, Canter (1966) reported a 73 percent success rate in differentiating brain-damaged from psychotic patients. Subsequent replications, using the newer scoring system, have reported higher hit rates (Canter, 1968, 1971, 1976). High reliability for the scoring system on the order of 0.9 has also been reported (Adams, 1966; Canter, 1976; Song and Song, 1969).

Overall, these studies have reported more accuracy in identifying the brain-damaged patient than is seen with the standard Bender-Gestalt Test. As with any new test, more research is necessary to evaluate its full effectiveness; at present, this test would seem to be a more useful choice than the standard Bender-Gestalt.

Memory for Designs

This test is similar to the other drawing tests, except that the designs must be drawn from memory (Graham and Kendall, 1960). The scoring system penalizes rotations and other errors common to the Bender scoring systems more than it does losses in memory (Graham and Kendall, 1960; McIver, McLaren, and Phillip, 1973). Consequently, the test yields a score comparable to those on the Bender-Gestalt Test (Quattlebaum, 1968).

Ascough and his associates (1974) reported hit rates of 77 percent for a brain-damaged group and 68 percent for a schizophrenic control. In groups diagnosed by a psychiatrist, Brilliant and Gynther (1963) reported hit rates of 88 percent for psychiatric controls and 63 percent for the organic group. A number of other studies have also reported positive results in the same range of effectiveness as those reported for the Bender (Grundvig, Ajax, and Needham, 1970, 1973; McManis, 1974; Shearn and Fitzgibbons, 1974).

However, Black (1974c) reported that the Memory for Designs Test was ineffective in diagnosing patients with mild frontal injuries. Watson (1968) reported that the test was unable to differentiate chronic schizophrenics from brain-damaged patients.

In general, the Memory for Designs appears to be somewhat more effective than the Bender-Gestalt Test with psychiatric populations. However, the difference between the accuracy of the Bender and the Memory for Designs does not appear to be great.

Benton Visual Retention Test

The Benton consists of three alternate but equivalent versions which may be administered under different conditions, including simple copying and copying from memory after various delays (Benton, 1945, 1963). The test contains ten cards, each of which contains several figures. A shortened eight-figure version is available (Benton, 1972), as well as a multiple-choice version (Benton, 1950). Norms are available for children and adults, as well as norms which take the subject's IQ into account (Benton, 1963, 1974; Benton, Spreen, Fargman, and Can, 1967).

Benton (1962) reported an overall hit rate of about 70 percent. He also noted that the test was most effective in identifying right hemisphere and diffuse-injured patients. Numerous other studies have also reported positive results (Benton, 1955; Brilliant and Gynther, 1963; L'Abate, Friedman, Volger, and Chusid, 1963; Lacks, 1971; Sterne, 1969, 1973). The hit rates have been in the 80 to 90 percent range for the controls and 60 to 70 percent for the brain-injured group. Watson (1968) reported that, although the Benton showed difficulty discriminating brain-injured from chronic schizophrenics, it was more effective than either the Bender-Gestalt or Memory for Designs in the same population.

Overall, the Benton has been found to be effective in a number of different populations. The research suggests that the Benton is preferable to either the Bender or the Memory for Designs. It also possesses better normative data and yields more information than either of those tests. With the Benton, the user can obtain information on both memory and spatial abilities.

Perceptual Maze Test

The Perceptual Maze Test, developed by Elithorn (1955), involves finding a pathway through a series of dots distributed on a triangular grid. The number of routes possible is limited, because the route must pass through a specific number of dots and progress steadily toward the top of the grid along fixed diagonals. The Perceptual Maze Test has been found to be effective in discriminating organicity with a hit rate of 70 percent or more. This test has been reported to be sensitive to right hemisphere dysfunction (Benton, Elithorn, Fogel, and Kerr, 1963) and left hemisphere dysfunction (Archibald et al., 1967; Colonna and Faglioni, 1966). Although the test has not been widely used in clinical settings, these results suggest that it may be a useful addition to any test battery.

Block Design Tests

These tests require clients to reproduce a pattern, usually using multicolored blocks. The most frequently used block test is a part of the Wechsler Adult Intelligence Test (WAIS) and will be discussed later. The *Koh's Block Design Test* is very similar to the Wechsler test. Because of the popularity of the Wechsler Intelligence Tests, the Koh test is not often seen.

Another block test is the *Grassi Block Substitution Test*. This test involves reproducing a design twice. On the first trial, the design is copied exactly as it is drawn. On the second trial, the design is reproduced with different colors. While several early studies reported that the test was effective (Grassi, 1953; Hirt, 1958; Ptacek and Young, 1954), serious questions have been raised about the populations used in those studies. Thomas (1963) found that the test was not better than chance in differentiating organics from normals. As a consequence, interest in this test has declined considerably over the last decade.

Benton (1973) has developed a three-dimensional, block-design test. The test has been found to be sensitive to most right brain injuries. Although there has been inadequate clinical research on this test, it is a promising instrument deserving continued evaluation.

Raven's Matrices

This test was originally intended as a culture-free measure of intelligence (Raven, 1960). While the test has not succeeded in this goal (Hecaen et al., 1972), it does appear to offer a measure of nonverbal reasoning. The tests consist of patterns with a "piece" missing. The client chooses one of five possible alternatives to fill in the missing shape and complete the pattern.

Poor performance on the Raven's Matrices has been associated with right brain injuries (Basso, DeRenzi, Faglioni, Scotti, and Spinnler, 1973; Costa, 1976; Urmer, Morris, and Wendland, 1960) and left brain injuries with aphasia (Basso et al., 1973). Colonna and Faglioni (1966) found that poor performance was related to the severity of a patient's left visual field deficit, while Zimet and Fishman (1970) found performance to be related to the severity of a patient's brain injury. Several studies have reported that the Raven is not a good screening device for brain injury (Arrigoni and DeRenzi, 1964; Costa and Vaughan, 1962). The use of the Raven's is also limited by the poor normative data which is currently available.

Verbal Tests

Because speech is important in everyday interactions, tests of verbal ability have found a prominent place in neuropsychology. These tests have attempted to measure the full range of verbal skills.

Shipley Institute of Living Scale

The Shipley consists of two subtests: a vocabulary test and a test of verbal conceptual thinking. The conceptual test involves finishing symbolic series, for example, an easy series would be "A, B, C, D, —." In developing the scale, it was assumed that the conceptual test scores would decline with brain damage while the vocabulary test scores would not. Although the test remains in use, the little evidence supporting its basic hypothesis is of questionable value (Shipley, 1940, 1946). Most of the research indicates a general lack of usefulness (Aita, Rietan, and Ruth, 1947; Fleming, 1943; Garfield and Fey, 1948; Margaret and Simpson, 1948; Parker, 1957; Ross and McNaughton, 1944.

Another early test based on similar principles is the *Hunt-Minnesota*, measuring vocabulary against design and word tests "sensitive" to brain damage. Some studies have supported the test (Avakian, 1961), but most evidence has been overwhelmingly negative (Aita et al., 1947; Canter, 1951; Malamud, 1946; Meehl and Jeffery, 1946; Yates, 1954).

Aphasia Tests

Numerous tests of aphasia have been developed within both neuropsychology and speech pathology. In general, the items on these tests are similar, although the tests do differ in the extent to which they cover particular deficits. Consequently, only those tests devised specifically for clinical neuropsychology will be included.

The *Spreen-Benton Aphasia Test* is probably the most comprehensive aphasia test available within neuropsychology. The test includes sections covering such functions as visual naming, tactile naming, digit repetition, word fluency, sentence repetition, identification by name, and descriptions of object use (Spreen and Benton, 1969). A modification of the Token Test (discussed below) and tests of reading, writing, and speaking are also included. Normative data for adult aphasics and normals can be found in Spreen and Benton (1969).

The *Token Test* has been developed as a screening test for aphasia. Originally introduced by DeRenzi and Vignolo (1962), an alternate and considerably shorter form was presented by Spellacy and Spreen (1969). The test requires the patient to manipulate plastic tokens in geometric shapes according to increasingly complicated instructions. For example, a subject might be asked to "touch the large red circle" or "put the blue circle under the white rectangle." The test has been found to effectively differentiate aphasics from nonaphasics with a hit rate of about

90 percent (Boller, 1968; Hartje, Kerstechensteiner, Poeck, and Orgass, 1973; Orgass and Poeck, 1966).

Other Verbal Tests

A number of other verbal tests are available including tests of achievement. The major individual achievement tests available today are the *Wide Range Achievement Test* (Jastak and Jastak, 1965) and the *Peabody Individual Achievement Test* (Dunn and Markwardt, 1970). These tests provide an assessment of the educational level of a patient. This information is useful in determining the kind of test performance that should be expected of a patient. The Peabody test is especially useful for patients who have difficulty speaking or writing because of motor deficits. Except for the reading pronunciation subtest, all of the subtests require pointing to the correct answer. Most neuropsychologists include some kind of achievement test as part of an evaluation.

Another test which has been recently applied to neuropsychology is the *Stroop Color and Word Test* (Golden, 1976b; Lewinsohn, 1973; Perret, 1974; Stroop, 1935). The Stroop test involves three measures for reading color names, naming colors, and naming the color of ink a color word is printed in (naming the color of the word *RED* printed in green). The Stroop has been found to discriminate highly between brain-damaged and control groups, including psychiatric patients (Golden, 1976). It may also be used to identify frontal disorders (Perret, 1974). Since the test is easy to administer, short, and applicable to any patient with more than a second-grade reading level, it is a potentially very useful test.

Categorizing Tests

Several sorting and categorizing tests have been derived including some by psychologists who felt that categorizing was a form of abstract thinking mediated by the brain as a whole (Goldstein and Scheerer, 1941, 1953; Weigl, 1941). Research has established little difference between normals and organics on these tests (DeRenzi, Pieczuro, Savoiardo, and Vignolo, 1966; McFie and Piercy, 1952; Newcombe, 1969; Parker, 1957). However, other tests of categorization have been more successful.

Wisconsin Card Sorting Test

This test, devised by Berg (Berg, 1948; Grant and Berg, 1948), used cards which have symbols differing in shape, color, and number. The patient must sort these according to a principle. The experimenter tells the patient if an answer is right or wrong, but does not reveal the principle. After ten correct sorts, the principle changes without warning and the patient must adjust. Milner (1963, 1964) uses 128 cards or until the subject successfully gets 6 principles. Milner has found this test highly successful with frontal-injured patients.

Category Test

This test was developed by Halstead (1947) and is included in the Halstead-Reitan Neuropsychological Battery, where it will be discussed in greater detail.

MOTOR AND SENSORY TESTS

The use of sensory and motor tests has been adapted from clinical neurology, where they are a primary part of the neurological examination. However, the tests within clinical psychology differ by their emphasis on quantification of deficit. The use of normative data adds to the sensitivity of the tests. In addition, the neuropsychologist looks at more complex motor and sensory functions subject to disruption by milder lesions than are basic sensory and motor skills.

Purdue Pegboard

This test, published by Science Research Associates (SRA) (1948), is a useful neuropsychological tool. Subjects are required to place pegs in a series of holes as quickly as possible using the right, then the left, and finally both hands together. The total administration time is less than five minutes.

Costa, Vaughan, Levita, and Farber (1963) found a 90 percent hit rate for the test in an initial study. In a second study, Costa's group achieved a 95 percent accuracy identifying a brain-damaged group and 73 percent accuracy in a control group. With psychiatric controls, Fernald, Fernald, and Rines (1966) reported a 70 percent hit rate in a normal group and 73 percent in an organic group, but only a 34 percent hit rate in a psychiatric population.

Vega (1969) reported 84 percent accuracy in discrimination using the Purdue Pegboard along with the *Finger Tapping Test* (Halstead, 1947). The two tests together did better than either alone, suggesting that although they are both motor measures (finger tapping measures the number of times a person can tap a telegraph key in ten seconds), they measure somewhat different functions.

Motor Impersistence

This syndrome was first defined by Fisher (1956) and was used as a clinical test by Joynt, Benton, and Fogel (1962). The test involves identifying the presence of the symptoms in the syndrome, including the abilities to keep one's eyes closed, maintain a protruded tongue, fix one's gaze centrally, deviate the eyes persistently to the left, hold one's breath, keep one's mouth open, fixate on a clinician's nose during visual field testing, squeeze a dynamometer evenly, say *ah*, and keep one's head steady during sensory testing. Severe cases of this syndrome have been reported in 25 percent of a brain-injured population (Joynt et al., 1962) and hit rates of about 70 to 85 percent have been reported in several studies (Ben-Yishay, Diller, Gerstmann, and Haas, 1968; Garfield, 1964; Levin, 1973).

The results to date on this syndrome are highly encouraging, especially since most of the observations can be made fairly easily and quickly. As with some of the other tests, more clinical research is needed to fully evaluate the Motor Impersistence Test's potential. However, it appears to be a fruitful area of investigation.

Spiral Aftereffect

This test requires the client to fixate on a spinning disk to see if it leaves a normal aftereffect. It has been believed that brain-damaged individuals fail to see the aftereffect. However, the results have been highly contradictory (Blau and Schaffer, 1960; Day, 1960; Davids, Goldenberg, and Laufer, 1957; Garrett, Price, and Deabler, 1957). Morant and Efstathiou (1966) have accounted for these deviant results by showing that the loss of aftereffect in the organic group is due to a patient's inability to keep his/her eyes centrally fixed, as in motor impersistence above. The authors demonstrated that when this factor is controlled, all differences between organics and controls disappear.

Suppressions

Suppressions occur when a subject is touched at two body points simultaneously but can report only one of them. Generally, the touches are on the two hands, a hand and the opposite cheek, or on any two symmetrical points on the body. The technique may also be extended to vision by wiggling a finger in the opposite place in the left and right eye fields, or to audition by making identical sounds in each ear. Although suppressions are relatively rare (Watson, Thomas, Anderson, and Felling, 1968), they are important since a reliable suppression almost invariably indicates brain injury, usually of a very serious nature. A suppression can only be recognized where the perception of single stimuli remains intact. This technique is also referred to as double simultaneous stimulation.

Auditory Measures

Important auditory functions are the perception of speech sounds and of rhythms. Tests for both of these functions will be presented later.

Lezak (1976) has suggested the use of the *Rey Auditory-Verbal Learning Test* with brain-injured patients (Rey, 1964; Taylor, 1959). This test of auditory memory includes memory after interpolated activity, a task potentially useful in the hippocampal-injured patient. No data as yet relate the test to specific deficits, and more research is needed before its usefulness can be determined.

Tactile Functions

A variety of measures have been developed for evaluating tactile abilities. Simple tactile perception may be measured by the *Von Frey Hairs*® (Russell et al., 1970), a device providing tactile pressures of varying strength. By finding the lightest perceivable touch, a rating of tactile sensitivity may be established in a given area of the body. A significantly higher threshold on one side of the body as compared to the other may suggest a central dysfunction.

Finger agnosia is tested in several different ways. Kinsbourne and Warrington (1962b) have described a technique in which two of the patient's fingers are touched and the patient with eyes closed or blindfolded must tell how many fingers are between the two touched. Reitan (1959c) touches only one finger and asks the patient which finger is being touched.

Personality Tests

Although there has been a great deal of interest among psychologists in the relationship of personality variables to brain injury, the amount of objective, usable research is very low. Before discussing this research, it is appropriate to remark upon a major problem in this area: the organic-functional dichotomy. Basically, this dichotomy reflects a belief that the impaired patient is impaired either due to an emotional disorder, such as schizophrenia (functional), or an organic disorder. Clearly, this is not an either-or dichotomy: The organic patient may be schizophrenic, and the schizophrenic may be brain-damaged.

Despite this, many tests of organicity have simply looked at the presence or absence of psychotic behavior. The absence of psychotic behavior does not mean that the patient is brain injured, since numerous other hypotheses, e.g. mental retardation, improper learning, lack of motivation, and medication, may be advanced for given behavioral deficits. Organicity can be established only through behavior indicating brain damage, not by a lack of other diagnoses.

MMPI

Since its inception in the early 1940s, there has been interest in the performance of brain-injured patients on the *Minnesota*

Multiphasic Personality Inventory (MMPI). Andersen and Hanvik (1950) attempted to establish a scale for brain damage, as did Williams (1952). Though the value of these scales is questionable, they were early prototypes to form MMPI scales for brain damage and have been followed by numerous other studies.

Hovey (1964) introduced a five-item scale that he found had a 50 percent accuracy rate with organics and over an 80 percent accuracy rate with normal controls. Similar results were reported by Zimmerman (1965) and Upper and Seeman (1968). Upper and Seeman concluded that the high rate of misclassification in the organic group made the test impractical.

Shaw and Matthews (1965) developed a seventeen-item scale that differentiated significantly between neurological and pseudoneurological subjects (psychiatric patients with neurological signs). Overall, they found the scale to have a 78 percent accuracy rate. On a cross validation they achieved a 73 percent accuracy: 67 percent in the psychiatric group and 78 percent in the organic group.

Watson (1971) developed a scale by comparing organic patients without psychiatric symptoms to psychiatric patients without any neurological signs. An eighty-item test was formed in a weighted and unweighted version along with a shortened thirty-item version in which the items were weighted according to their ability to differentiate the groups studied. The authors reported 85 percent accuracy in their initial study and success rates ranging from 58 percent to 71 percent in cross-validation studies. The cross-validation studies indicated that the scale worked only with male patients.

Neuringer, Dombrowski, and Goldstein (1975) reported hit rates of up to 76 percent using a population identical to that of Watson. However, Ayers, Templer, and Ruff (1975) were able to report only a 57 percent hit rate for organics and a 75 percent hit rate for schizophrenics. Holland et al. (1975) found the scale would not differentiate when emotional distress was controlled. They concluded the Watson scale primarily reflected emotional stress.

Two approaches have been suggested, using decision rules to

separate schizophrenics and organics. In these systems, the clinician answers a series of yes-no questions about the patient's MMPI profile. The pattern of answers to the questions leads the clinician to a diagnosis. Russell (1975) reported 80 percent accuracy with his schizophrenic group, and 72 percent with the brain-damaged group. No cross validations have been reported to date. A similar system was adopted by Watson and Thomas (1968), who reported hit rates in several samples ranging from 59 to 79 percent. Black (1974e), however, found it ineffective with a group of trauma-injured armed services personnel.

Another research approach has examined the performance of brain-injured patients on the traditional scales of the MMPI. Reitan (1955a) compared neurological patients with a normal control group. He found significant elevations for the brain-injured patients on the F (validity) scale and on the paranoia, psychasthenia (anxiety), schizophrenia, and mania scales. In a similar study comparing brain-damaged and psychiatric patients, a difference was found on the hysteria scale (Matthews, Shaw, and Klove, 1966). Watson and Thomas (1968), comparing psychiatric and brain-damaged patients, reported differences on hypochondriasis, depression, masculinity-feminity, schizophrenia, and social introversion. Lair and Trapp (1962) noted elevations in both psychiatric and organic groups on the neurotic triad (hypochondriasis, depression, and hysteria). Motto (1958) reported organics higher on psychasthenia and schizophrenia.

Overall, there was considerable variation in the results of these studies. One reason may be the composition of the neurological and psychiatric groups. Changes in MMPI profiles are to be expected as the psychiatric composition changes. Several studies have suggested that the MMPI profile may be related to locus of injury. In Black (1975), left brain injured patients had high scores on the F and K (correction scale that adjusts for reporting bad or good) scales and on depression, paranoia, schizophrenia, and social introversion, while the right brain group was essentially normal. Similarly, Dikmen and Reitan (1974) found that aphasics showed more severe psychopathology than non-aphasics. Vogel (1962) was unable to find a left-right difference, but this may have been due to the use of an overall measure of MMPI performance, rather than individual scale scores.

Presently, there are several promising research areas in the use of the MMPI with a neurologically impaired population. One is the use of the pseudoneurological scale developed by Shaw and Matthews (1965). A second area is the relationship of MMPI patterns to certain types of brain damage. If successful, such research could establish the MMPI as a valuable tool in differential diagnosis. Lastly, the key approach to diagnostic use of the MMPI, developed by Russell (1975) looks promising.

Rorschach

The *Rorschach Inkblot Technique* was developed by Hermann Rorschach around 1920. The test consists of ten inkblots, basically symmetrical in nature, that a subject must describe in terms of what objects or people the inkblots suggest. The use of the Rorschach as a test of brain damage was advocated by Piotrowski in 1937. Advocates see the Rorschach as a relatively quick method of uncovering personality dynamics and at the same time inferring the presence or absence of an organic condition. Detractors have termed the Rorschach as unreliable, idiosyncratic, and at best a poor indicator of attributes better measured by other instruments.

In his 1937 article, Piotrowski indicated ten signs that suggested brain damage. These included less than fifteen responses; poor responses; coloring naming, saying the card is pink rather than telling what the pink represents; few popular responses; perseveration; and the lack-of-movement responses. Piotrowski indicated that at least five signs were necessary to characterize someone as brain damaged.

Results in studies using Piotrowski signs have ranged from purely chance levels to claims of over 90 percent accuracy. As a whole, the research itself is questionable, as many of the methodological errors discussed in Chapter 3 are repeated. Those studies with good methodology have not been encouraging. Although Aita and his associates (1948) reported some of the Piotrowski signs to be discriminating in terms of a *t* test, the average number of signs was well less than five per patient. There was a tendency to diagnose only those with severe brain damage, patients about whom there is little question. Eckardt (1961) reported that the Rorschach was sensitive to intellectual impairment from any source. Similarly, Gottlieb and Parsons (1960) found that the Rorschach could not discriminate between psychiatric and organic patients.

Some advocates note that the Rorschach interpretation is an art, the rules of which cannot be specified. This is an irrefutable statement, since any failures can be blamed on the lack of proper clinical ability. If the Rorschach is to be used, there is a clear need for more rigorous research indicating the methods by which it can be useful in the diagnosis of brain damage.

TEST BATTERIES

As clinical neuropsychology has developed, it has become clear that the single-test approach has limited value for neurodiagnosis. The number of errors made using any single test is far too extensive to make reliable, individual diagnoses. There are no symptoms common to all brain disorders.

Although there are in existence many different test batteries, few have been researched or reported in the literature. Many batteries exist in only a few laboratories. Of those that have been researched, a number have been represented only by single studies and will not be discussed here (Spreen and Benton, 1965). Two others, which have been researched and will be discussed, were not originally intended as neuropsychological test batteries. Only one battery, designed specifically for neuropsychological investigation, has been extensively researched on a variety of populations and by a number of individual investigators in the literature. However, procedures used with these batteries are applicable to any general test battery.

Wechsler Adult Intelligence Test

The Wechsler Adult Intelligence Test (WAIS) is the end result of several decades of intellectual assessment. Extensive neuropsychological research has been conducted on this test and its immediate predecessor, the *Wechsler-Bellevue*. Its primary advantages are extensive standardization across age-groups and wide coverage of a number of intellectual abilities. It does not meet the requirement for a complete test battery as set out above, but it has been an important part of a number of major test batteries. The WAIS consists of eleven subtests. First, these and their neuropsychological significance will be discussed.

Vocabulary

This test asks subjects to define words orally. It has a high correlation with overall intellectual ability in the range of 0.8. Vocabulary is a highly overlearned task, and consequently, it was believed that it was little affected by brain disorders. Although this does hold to some degree (Gonen, 1970; Morrow and Mark, 1955), it is not always true (Russell, 1972). Vocabulary is especially vulnerable in severe aphasic disorders; disorders of following instructions, as are most tests; and in general deterioration, Alzheimer's disease. In cases where the person is unable to speak but appears alert, the Vocabulary Test may be replaced by the *Peabody Picture Vocabulary Test,* a nonverbal vocabulary test. However, care has to be taken in such situations as the Peabody tends to inaccurately estimate the IQ of low-intelligence subjects (Shaw, Matthews, and Klove, 1966; Pool and Brown, 1970).

In neuropsychological research, the Vocabulary Subtest often serves to establish a basal level of functioning against which other tests can be compared. If other tests are significantly below vocabulary, then there is a possibility of brain dysfunction.

Information

This test measures the client's store of general knowledge such as important dates or facts. It reflects the client's education, and general information tends to remain as stable in brain injury as vocabulary (Morrow and Mark, 1955; Woo-Sam, Zimmerman, and Rogal, 1971). This test is most often used as a comparison against which other test performance may be measured.

Comprehension

This assesses the client's ability to understand everyday situations. For example, a client might be asked why we have government, or how to interpret a proverb. Several studies have found that it was among the most stable of all the Wechsler subtests in brain-injured patients (DeWolfe, 1971; Russell, 1972; Woo-Sam, 1971).

Similarities

The Similarities Subtest measures the client's ability to find a common category for two objects, e.g. a tomato and a squash. This is clearly a test of verbal ability, but it does not correlate highly with verbal IQ. It is sensitive to brain injury, especially in the left temporal and parietal areas (McFie, 1975). In some patients, it may be the highest verbal score and thus help establish a tentative preinjury level.

Arithmetic

This is a test of a client's ability to do arithmetic story problems without paper or pencil. It requires skills in translating a word problem into arithmetic operations, as well as memory and arithmetic skills. Consequently, errors may not reflect deficits in arithmetic skills, which are better measured by an achievement test. Arithmetic is often the lowest score in normal individuals, many of whom become quite anxious at the mention of arithmetic problems. Wechsler (1955) advises that the patient not be told they are going to be given arithmetic problems when this subtest begins, in order to limit anxiety.

Digit Span

This is a test to measure a subject's immediate auditory memory capacity. The subject must repeat series of numbers presented orally, then repeat a second set of numbers backwards. The Digit Span Subtest is among the most sensitive tests of brain injury (DeWolfe, 1971; Woo-Sam, 1971), being somewhat more sensitive to left brain injury than right (McFie, 1975).

Picture Completion

In this test, clients are shown drawings and asked to tell what is missing, e.g. a face may be shown without an ear. This test measures familiarity with common objects, as well as the ability to decipher drawings. It is generally regarded as resistant to brain damage (Woo-Sam, 1971).

Digit Symbol

This is the most sensitive WAIS test to presence of brain damage. The client is presented the numbers 1 to 9, each associated with a nonverbal symbol. The subject is then given several lines of numbers under which the correct symbol must be placed. The subtest measures a wide variety of factors including motor speed, visual-motor coordination, and visual associative memory. Scores are generally low in nearly all lesions, although for a different reason in each case. The test must be used cautiously, however, since it is also sensitive to anxiety and psychiatric disorders (Rapaport et al., 1968). Kaufman (1968) has observed that other substitution tests similar to the Digit Symbol Subtest are effective indexes of pathology. An alternative to the digit symbol is the Symbol-Digits Modality Test, which includes written and oral versions (Smith, 1968, 1975).

Block Design

Tests of block designs have been found to be among the most sensitive indicators of brain damage. The client must construct a visually presented pattern with blocks. The test is most sensitive to right hemisphere lesions (McFie, 1975) but may also be depressed in left hemisphere injuries, especially those with severe involvement of the parietal lobe (McFie, 1960). The test is over 80 percent effective with right hemisphere and diffuse injured patients (Golden, in press).

Picture Arrangement

This test involves sequencing several cartoon pictures so that they tell a story. The test involves sequencing, social sophistication, and visual recognition and decoding. This test may be impaired in both right and left brain lesions.

Object Assembly

This test consists of several "jigsaw puzzles" made from cutting up pictures of common objects into several pieces. The subject must put the pieces together within a given time limit. This test involves visual organization, as does the Block Design Subtest, but is less sensitive. This may be because recognition of the object allows one to use skills other than spatial to complete the test.

Scoring the WAIS

The scores from all WAIS subtests are adjusted by tables in the WAIS manual (Wechsler, 1955) so that each test has an average score of 10 and a standard deviation of 3. Consequently, 50 percent of the population will score at 10 or above, while 83 percent will score at 7 or above. The use of the same scale in scoring each subtest allows the user to compare the performance on different subtests without difficulty. Generally, a difference of at least three points between subtest scores must exist before it is likely that there is a real difference in the person's abilities.

The first six tests of the WAIS—Vocabulary, Comprehension, Information, Digit Span, Arithmetic, and Similarities—are combined together to yield a verbal weighted score. This score is transformed by tables in the WAIS manual to a verbal IQ. There are separate norms available for each age-group from sixteen to over seventy-five years of age. In a similar manner, the remaining subtests—Picture Completion, Picture Arrangement, Block Design, Object Assembly, and Digit Symbol—are added to yield a performance weighted score from which a performance IQ is derived. The verbal and performance weighted scores are summed to get a total weighted score. This is also converted into an IQ score. Each of the IQ scores had an average of 100 and a standard deviation of 15. The range for normal intelligence is between 90 and 100. The legal definition of mental retardation is an IQ below 70.

Diagnostic Approaches to the WAIS

A great deal of research has been generated on the WAIS and the Wechsler-Bellevue as tests of organicity. Although the Wechsler-Bellevue and WAIS do yield different IQs (Fitzhugh, L. and Fitzhugh, 1964), research has established that the results which hold for the Wechsler-Bellevue hold for the WAIS as well (McFie, 1975). Consequently, their research will be considered together.

Although studies have differed in their assessment of the diagnostic accuracy of each of the WAIS subtests, there has been general agreement as to their relative effectiveness (Golden, in press; Lezak, 1976; McFie, 1969, 1975; Wheeler, Burke and Reitan, 1963; Wheeler and Reitan, 1962). Block Design, Digit Span, and Digit Symbol are considered the most sensitive to brain injury, yielding hit rates in the 75-80% range. Arithmetic, Object Assembly, Picture Arrangement, and Similarities are less sensitive. Their hit rates are estimated in the 65-75% range or less. Vocabulary, Comprehension, Information, and Picture Completion are the least discriminating; they are often used to estimate the intellectual functioning of an individual before a brain injury occurred.

The majority of approaches involving the WAIS have used the differential score approach, comparing *insensitive* tests remaining stable against *sensitive* tests decreasing with brain damage. The earliest attempt in this direction was the establishment of *hold* (insensitive) and *don't hold* (sensitive) tests (Wechsler, 1944, 1958) combined into a deterioration index.

The original deterioration index used Information, Comprehension, Picture Completion, and Object Assembly subtests as hold tests and Digit Span, Digit Symbol, Arithmetic, and Block Design as don't hold tests. The index was later revised, with Vocabulary replacing the Comprehension subtest and Similarities replacing Arithmetic. Neither of these formulas has been shown to be useful (Crookes, 1961; Norman, 1966; Russell, 1972; Woo-Sam, 1971; Yates, 1954). Russell (1972) has reported that only Comprehension is a hold test, while such tests as Object

Assembly and Picture Completion are only hold tests, in the sense that they are less affected by brain damage than are other performance tests. Morrow and Mark (1955) reported that only Vocabulary, Comprehension, and Information are good hold tests.

On the basis of such data, other general deterioration indexes have been suggested (Allen, 1947; Hunt, 1949; Norman, 1966), but these have not been generally supported (Woo-Sam, 1971). Gonen (1970) suggested Vocabulary and Information as hold tests, with Digit Symbol and Block Designs as don't hold tests. DeWolfe (1971) reported a success rate of 75 percent when simply comparing Digit Span and Comprehension. Watson (1972) found that comparing Digit Span and Comprehension would work at one Veteran's Administration Hospital, but not at another. These results suggest that the efficiency of the Wechsler deterioration ratios, used singly, depends very much on the population studied. It is doubtful that any single ratio will be found that will work for all populations.

Recognizing this limitation, attempts have been made to develop sets of ratios, each of which can be used for specific populations. The best known of these attempts was made by Hewson (1949). McKeever and Gerstein (1958) found the ratios about 70 percent effective with subjects who had IQs above 100, but was less effective than chance when a client's IQ was below 100. Overall, they obtained a hit rate of only 54.9 percent, little better than chance. Negative results have been reported elsewhere as well (Fisher, 1962; Wheeler and Wilkins, 1951).

Smith (1962) reported 81 percent accuracy in a brain tumor population and 73 percent in a control population with psychiatric problems. However, Smith noted that the ratios were less accurate with other classes of patients. Wolff (1960) reported hit rates of 71 percent using age-corrected scores. Although it appears that the Hewson ratios are more effective than the deterioration quotients, they are still no more effective than the individual subtests themselves.

Pattern Analysis

A more fruitful approach to the WAIS appears to be pattern analysis (Matthews, Geurtin, and Reitan, 1962; McFie, 1975;

Reitan, undated; Reitan and Davison, 1974). This approach relates depression on certain combinations of WAIS scores to known loci of lesions and to lesions varying according to process or chronicity. The patterns of WAIS scores associated with specific disorders will be discussed in the following chapters.

Wechsler Memory Scale

The Wechsler Memory Scale was originally designed by Wechsler (1945) for the investigation of alcoholic patients. Since memory impairment is often a symptom of brain disorder, there has been considerable interest in this test.

The exam consists of six subtests. The *Information* Subtest determines whether the subject knows simple facts such as who the current President is. The *Orientation Test* assesses whether a subject knows the year, month, day, and where he or she is. The *Mental Control* Subtest evaluates knowledge of the alphabet, counting, and simple repetitive addition. *Logical Memory* tests how much of a paragraph a person can remember. The fifth subtest is an adaption of Digit Span. The sixth subtest is a short version of the Memory-for-Designs Test. The *Associative Learning* Subtest evaluates the subject's ability to form verbal associations.

The research on this test has been disappointing, as many have failed to find differences between organics and other groups on the subtests (Parker, 1957). Bachrach and Mintz (1974) suggested that the design subtest was an effective discriminator, while Kljajic (1975) found comparisons among Digit Span, Associate Learning, Information, and Orientation subtests to be most effective. Holland (1974) and Howard (1950) found the paired associate learning test to be most useful. Milner (1975) has suggested using some subtests in a pre-post situation with interpolated activity as a test of delayed learning.

Halstead-Reitan Neuropsychological Battery for Adults

The development of the Halstead-Reitan Battery came in several steps. The initial work was by Ward Halstead at the University of Chicago beginning in 1935. Halstead attempted to develop a test battery that would reflect *biological intelligence* and aid in the evaluation of frontal lobe patients. This work culminated in the publication of Halstead's (1947) book introducing several tests that are an integral part of the neuropsychological battery.

The development of the remaining parts of the battery was completed by Halstead's student, Ralph M. Reitan, who set up his own neuropsychological laboratory at the University of Indiana Medical School. Reitan added the *Trail Making Test* (Reitan, 1955d, 1958), an abbreviated form of the Halstead-Wepman Aphasia Exam, the Reitan-Klove Sensory Perceptual Exam, and the Wechsler-Bellevue (Reitan, 1959). Reitan also included the MMPI and Wide Range Achievement Test; both have been described.

Trail Making Test

The Trail Making Test consists of two parts. Part A consists of twenty-five circles distributed over an 8½ by 11-inch sheet of white paper and numbered 1 to 25. The subject must connect the circles starting at 1. Part B also consists of twenty-five circles; thirteen are numbered 1 to 13 and the remainder lettered A to L. The subject must connect the circles alternating between numbers and letters, e.g. 1-A-2-B-3-C, etc. The time in seconds to finish is the score on each part.

The Trail Making Test was first used as a test of brain damage by Armitage (1946). Reitan (1958) reported that Part B was 81 percent effective with a brain-damaged population, and 88 percent effective with normal controls. A number of studies with similar populations have reported equally good results (Sterne, 1973).

Criticism for the test has come from a number of studies that have concluded that the test fails to differentiate psychotics from brain-damaged patients (Brown, Casey, Fisch, and Neuringer, 1958; Donnelly, Dent, Murphy, and Mignone, 1972; Gordon, 1972; L'Abate et al., 1962; Orgel and McDonald, 1967; and Watson, et al., 1969). These studies have been criticized, because the performance of the psychiatric patients was irretrievably confounded with medication effects, length of hospitalization, and motivational disorders.

It has been demonstrated that there is a significant correlation between the overall IQ and Trail Making Test performance (Boll and Reitan, 1973; Smith, 1963). There is also a correlation with age (Goul and Brown, 1970). Both factors must be accounted for in evaluating the significance of a score that is borderline. The University of Wisconsin Neuropsychology Lab (undated) has developed norms for both younger and older adults for all the tests in the Halstead-Reitan.

Category Test

The Category Test consists of seven subtests. Each subtest is based on a rule that allows the subject to deduce a number suggested by each item. For example, the rule in one subtest is that the number is equal to the number of objects shown in an item. The test involves the ability of the subject to hypothesize potential rules for each subtest, to test the rules out and to alter his or her behavior on the basis of immediate feedback.

This test is the single most sensitive test of brain damage in the battery. The Category Test has been found to be up to 90 percent effective in discriminating brain-injured individuals from normals (Wheeler, Burke, and Reitan, 1963).

It is less effective, however, in differentiating schizophrenic groups, with some studies reporting hit rates as low as 30 percent (Beaumont, 1975). This study reported reduced hit rates compared to studies with normals, because of a much higher incidence of poor scores among the schizophrenic population. Raising the cutoff point from Halstead and Reitan's fifty errors to sixty-four errors can accommodate this problem, but lowers the efficiency of the test in discriminating milder cases of brain damage (Golden, in press).

The Category Test has significant correlations with IQ (Logue and Allen, 1971; Lin and Rennick, 1974). When IQ is normal or above, a poor Category score is especially significant. Although the Category Test measures many of the same things as the Wisconsin Card Sorting Test, there are not yet any studies which have examined them jointly.

The Category Test has also been criticized for its length,

which may cause it to take a significant amount of time (up to two hours). Several shorter versions have been attempted, including one which is in regular use at the University of Wisconsin (University of Wisconsin, undated).

Aphasia Examination

Heimburger and Reitan (1961) modified the Halstead-Wepman Aphasia Test (Halstead and Wepman, 1949) by omitting items which were rarely discriminative. The aphasia exam covers such areas as naming, spelling, drawing, reading, speaking, understanding, left-right confusion, and arithmetic. The inclusion of copying tests using several geometric shapes and a key allows the test to be sensitive to right as well as left brain injuries.

Reitan (1959d) reported that the probability of brain damage increased with the number of aphasic symptoms. When no symptoms were reported the probability was only 20 percent. With one, two, three, or four symptoms, the respective probabilities were 38, 86, 87, and 100 percent, respectively. Russell et al. (1970) have presented an attempt to quantify the aphasia test results by assigning a weighted value to each item. A patient's score is equal to the sum of the weights of the items missed.

Rhythm Test

This test was adapted by Halstead from the *Seashore Test of Musical Talent*. The test consists of thirty items, each consisting of two rhythms. The client must indicate whether the two rhythms are the same or different. The test is successful for two reasons: (1) rhythmic deficits are seen with certain brain injuries, and (2) it requires sustained attention. Consequently, performance may be impaired by either left or right hemisphere injuries.

Speech Perception Test

This test consists of sixty multiple-choice items. The subject listens to a word on tape and must indicate which of four alternative spellings represents the word. All words have the same internal vowel (ee) and differ only in beginning or ending consonant sound. Poor performance reflects either poor discriminative hearing or an inability to match visual and auditory information. If a subject has less than a fourth-grade education, the test may be invalid, and a simpler test of auditory discrimination is needed. The author's laboratory is currently evaluating the use of the Goldman-Woodstock-Fristoe (1974) Tests of Auditory Discrimination for this purpose.

Finger Oscillation Test

Also known as the *Finger Tapping Test*, it examines a subject's ability to rapidly depress a lever similar to a telegraph key with the left and right hands. The subject is allowed ten seconds per trial, and the score is the average of five trials. A relative deficit on one hand reflects a possible lesion in the contralateral hemisphere.

Tactual Performance Test

This test uses a modified Sequin-Goddard® form board, a board with cutouts in which wooden shapes may be placed. In order to make this a tactile task, the subject is blindfolded and must use somatosensory rather than visual cues to replace the blocks. The test also reflects motor skills to a lesser extent. The subject first places the blocks with the dominant hand alone, then the non-dominant hand alone, and finally with both hands. This procedure yields learning scores and allows an analysis of the performance of both sides of the body.

After the test is completed, the board is put away, and the subject is asked to draw from (incidental) memory a replica of the board which can be scored both for remembering the shapes (Memory score) and the location of the shapes (Location score). In all, the test yields five basic scores plus a Total Time score. The Location and Total Time scores have been found to be highly discriminating between brain-damaged and control groups (Wheeler et al., 1963). Location is also a good measure of incidental spatial learning.

This test has been criticized because of the length of time it takes. Russell and his associates (1970) suggested limiting each phase of the test to ten minutes.

Perceptual Examination

This test was developed by Reitan and Klove (Reitan, 1959c) and consists of a number of procedures for evaluating sensory function. The first part tests for suppressions, *double simultaneous stimulation*, in the tactile, auditory, and visual modalities. Tests for the perception of a single stimulation are included, since suppressions cannot be scored if the subject is unable to perceive unilateral stimulation. Golden (in press) reports suppressions are rare, but they are almost always indicative of brain injury.

The Perceptual Exam also consists of a set of tests of more complex tactile functions. *Finger Agnosia* identifies the subject's ability to recognize which finger is touched while blindfolded. Similarly, *Fingertip Number Writing* examines the blindfolded subject's ability to recognize numbers written on the fingertips. Two tests of astereognosis are included: a coin recognition task and a task involving the recognition of simple geometric shapes, *Tactile Form Recognition*. The coin task demands a verbal response, while the second task has the subject point to a duplicate figure. On all these tests, scores are obtained for both the right and left hands.

Impairment Index

The Impairment Index is made up of those tests which are most sensitive to brain damage. The index is computed by counting the number of sensitive tests whose performance is worse than the cutoff point for that test (Reitan, 1959; Halstead, 1947). The number of tests beyond the cutoff point is divided by the total number of tests included in the determination of the Impairment Index. For instance, if seven tests are used to determine the index and three are beyond their cutoff points, the index would be equal to 3 divided by 7 or 0.43. Indexes of 0.5 or greater are considered indicative of brain injury. The tests included within the Impairment Index vary among researchers. However, the Category Test, the Total Time, Memory, and Location scores from the Tactual Performance Test, the Finger Tapping score, the Rhythm score and the Speech Perception scores are included in most formulas. Wheeler, Burke, and Reitan (1963) found the Impairment Index to be 90 percent effective in discriminating brain-injured and normal clients. Kiernan and Matthews (1976) have reported an alternate method of determining the Impairment Index. The method involves averaging the T-score of the tests in the index. The study reported this method to be equivalent to the previous method when used with younger subjects, but more effective when used with older subjects. This is probably because age-adjusted norms were used for the older patients. This helps to eliminate the misclassification of older subjects as brain injured simply because of the decline in scores which accompanies the normal aging process. An average T-score of less than 40 indicates brain dysfunction.

Modification of Halstead-Reitan

Most researchers and clinicians using the Halstead-Reitan have recognized that there is a need for continual improvement of the battery. Consequently, many include other instruments in their assessment, evaluating whether they may add to the overall effectiveness of the battery. A major set of additional tests has been developed by C. Matthews and H. Klove at the University of Wisconsin (Norton and Matthews, 1972). They have developed tests to evaluate tremors associated with extrapyramidal lesions and other subcortical disorders. These additional tests include evaluations of static (resting) tremor, voluntary tremor, and coordinated motion. These additional tests considerably extend the battery's ability to evaluate subcortical disorders.

Research on the Halstead-Reitan Battery

Extensive research has been done on the ability of the full Halstead-Reitan to discriminate between brain-damaged and other groups on the basis of level of performance alone. Wheeler, Burke, and Reitan (1963), using discriminant analysis, found the battery to be 90 percent successful overall and 80 percent successful in a cross-validation study of the discriminant equations (Wheeler and Reitan, 1963; also, *see* Reitan, 1955c, 1966). Klove (1974) has presented a review of this research, citing international studies which have repeatedly verified these results with researchers reporting up to a 95 percent hit rate using discriminative analysis. Other studies have attempted to validate the clinical interpretation of the Halstead-Reitan. These studies have reported success rates in the 90 percent range when used with patients with verified neurological disorders (Filskov and Goldstein, 1974; Reitan, 1964; Schreiber, Goldman, Kleinman, Goldfader, and Snow, 1976).

The major controversy in the research has been the ability of the Halstead-Reitan to differentiate between psychiatric and brain-damaged patients. Each of the studies in this area has found results for the brain-damaged group consistent with the studies reported by Reitan. The issue has been whether or not psychiatric groups perform better than brain-damaged groups.

Several studies have reported no discrimination with a schizophrenic control group (Donnelly et al., 1972; Klonoff et al., 1971; Watson, 1974; Watson et al., 1968a and b). Klonoff and his associates remarked on several of the problems encountered when working with a hospitalized chronic population. They found a high degree of correlation between the Impairment Index and drug regime. The subjects used in the Watson studies have been criticized for their lack of comparability in the length of hospitalization, the nature of the neurological diagnostic tests used, the number of patients who had received electroconvulsive therapy (E.C.T.), the drug dosages being received, and the amount of cooperation with the examiners (Klove, 1974; Levine and Feirstein, 1972).

Studies using acute rather than chronic patients and controlling for the factors discussed above have generally obtained good results (Barnes and Lucas, 1974; DeWolfe, 1971; Goldstein and Shelley, 1972; Goldstein, Deysack, and Kleinknecht, 1973; Levine and Feirstein, 1972; Small, Small, Milstein, and Moore, 1972). One reason for the better results with acute rather than chronic patients has been advanced by Lilliston (1973). She reported that the degree of neuropsychological impairment in schizophrenics is related to their score on a test of process (chronic) versus reactive, *acute* schizophrenia. She suggested that the reason for this may be that the chronic, process schizophrenic is more likely to be brain damaged.

Overall, the research indicates that it is difficult to differentiate the chronic schizophrenic from the brain-injured patient by the level-of-performance criteria alone. Less chronic cases, especially when there have been proper controls for medication, length of hospitalization, and motivation, can be diagnosed without serious difficulty.

Although a level-of-performance approach has proved ineffective with the chronic schizophrenic, this does not mean that such patients cannot be accurately identified. Other methods of analysis, particularly pattern analysis, offer an alternate method of discriminating the process schizophrenic from the brain-injured patient (*see* Chapter 6).

Luria's Neuropsychological Battery

A. R. Luria has been a significant contributor to international neuropsychology for several decades. In his 1966 book, Luria presented an outline of the neuropsychological battery used in his laboratory to diagnose clinical patients. Until recently, none of the materials used by Luria were available. These materials, as well as an instructional manual, have recently been published by Christensen (1975a, b, and c). Luria (1966) reports that the test procedures he advocates are very effective, but he does not include any data to support his statement.

The examination consists of a series of tests designed to measure all the basic verbal and nonverbal skills. It includes simple measures of basic motor and sensory skills, as well as measures of complex cognitive abilities. The emphasis in the tests is on observing the qualitative nature of the patient's performance, rather than attempting a quantitative analysis. Consequently, there are no objective guidelines on what constitutes a good or bad performance: The decision is left to the judgment of the clinician.

Reitan (1976) has stated that the major drawback of the Luria battery is that the only measure of its effectiveness is Luria's judgment. Because the battery has been published, researchers now have the opportunity to provide the necessary evidence. Within the next several years, evaluations should appear, assessing the effectiveness of this test battery.

Diagnosis with Multiple Test Procedures

At the beginning of this chapter, methods of analyzing the results of individual test procedures were discussed. As can be seen from the ensuing material, the use of a single test alone in any diagnostic procedure is highly questionable. No single test is effective enough to produce a practical level of accuracy by itself. As a result, the neuropsychologist must use a test battery. The composition of that battery generally depends upon the purpose of the testing situation. Generally, one of two major purposes is involved. The first is to screen from a large group those patients who need further neurodiagnostic or neurological evaluation. The second purpose is to fully assess and evaluate a patient who is known to be or who is likely to be brain injured.

Screening Procedures

In some situations, the psychologist has the responsibility of assessing unselected cases to identify areas where further evaluation is necessary. This occurs in many psychiatric hospitals or mental health clinics where psychological screening is routine with each patient. In general, examiners in such situations do not choose to use a lengthy test battery because of the time and cost involved and the small returns if the rate of neurological dysfunction is low in the population being screened.

The purpose of a screening is simply to identify those clients who would most benefit from further evaluation. It is important not to see such an exam as an end in itself, for the conclusions that can be reached from a screening exam are strictly limited. One can only conclude that the patient has some neuropyschological deficits consistent with a diagnosis of brain dysfunction. A screening exam cannot identify the nature of the disorder, the primary deficits, or the importance of the deficits of the patient's functioning. Nor can such an exam provide a reliable aid for treatment and rehabilitation.

The neuropsychologist employing a screening exam can use one of two approaches. First, s/he may employ several tests highly sensitive to brain damage. All procedures in neuropsychology are more sensitive to one kind of brain damage than to another, so the tests used in screening must complement each other. Several tests examined in this chapter would appear to be appropriate for use as a screening test. The Canter Background Interference Procedure of the Bender-Gestalt *seems* to be the most effective spatial test available. Of the verbal tests, a short battery screening for major aphasic deficits using tests such as Reitan's modification of the Halstead-Wepman or the Token Test would appear to be most effective. Other tests which might be considered would be the Trail Making and Digit Symbol Tests. A combination of the tests described in this paragraph would probably make an efficient and accurate screening battery.

With such a battery, the psychologist would be looking at the severity of any brain injury suggested by any of the tests. Severely depressed performance on any one of the tests would probably indicate the need for further evaluation. Performances suggestive of brain damage on one half or more of the screening tests would also indicate the need for further evaluation. A mild dysfunction on only one test is generally not sufficient for such a referral unless it is accompanied by relevant findings in the subject's history or behavior. Certainly, the appearance of any pathognomic signs would also be a reason for further evaluation. These would include perseveration, neglect of the left side of drawings, rotations, and other behaviors rarely seen in normals.

The alternative to this method is the use of a small test battery that can be analyzed much as a larger test battery. The tests in the battery need to be chosen so that each is sensitive to a different type of dysfunction rather than the more global tests most appropriate for the first technique. An example of this type of battery was presented by Golden (1976a). He used a test battery composed of Stroop Color and Word Test, the Trail Making Test, the Speech Perception Test, Object Assembly, Block Design, Similarities, Digit Symbol, the Seashore Rhythm Test, and the Reitan Aphasia Exam. Golden reported that the exam took slightly over one hour and had over a 90 percent accuracy in discriminating brain-damaged, psychiatric, and normal patients. This, of course, is not the only possible battery for such a purpose.

Preselected Populations

Many neuropsychologists are employed in situations where the patients who are evaluated are preselected. Such cases may be referred for diagnosis, because they are puzzling or present unusual features. In other cases, they are presented for evaluation of deficits for rehabilitation planning or other purposes. In all of these cases, a screening evaluation that can only conclude the patient may be brain injured is inappropriate and redundant. In these situations, only a full-scale neuropsychological exam as described in Chapter 3 should be employed.

The neuropsychologist has the choice in these circumstances to choose a battery with utility and effectiveness already demonstrated or to design a battery either for regular use or for each patient. The advantages and disadvantages of each of these positions have already been described.

The analysis of a test battery consists of two major steps. First, the level of performance by the patient must be inspected to see if the results as a whole suggest brain impairment. Second, the relative scores on the tests must be examined for indications of a localized disorder. In some cases, the results must also be examined to determine the cause of the disorder. This is especially valuable in trying to discriminate poor performance due to a disorder like schizophrenia from that due to a neuropathological process. Information on possible causes is useful to the physician in a case that has not been given a definite diagnosis. Ideally, any symptoms seen on the exam should be accounted for by any conclusions which are reached.

The first step in diagnosis involves assessing the level of performance on the test battery. This is accomplished by first examining the performance on the tests most sensitive to brain injury. Which tests these are will naturally vary considerably, depending on the test battery used. In the Halstead-Reitan, these tests would be the Impairment Index, the Category Test, the Trail Making Test (Part B), and Total Time and Location scores of the Tactual Performance Test. On the WAIS, the most sensitive tests are Digit Span, Digit Symbol, and Block Design. Other tests highly sensitive to brain dysfunction may be used as well. The larger the number of the general tests impaired, the higher the probability of brain damage.

In addition to the general tests, poor performance in specific areas can indicate a high probability of brain damage. On the Reitan Aphasia Test, four or more errors are associated with the presence of brain dysfunction (Reitan, 1959d). Motor or sensory deficits on one side of the body may indicate brain injury. Similarly, any severe deficit in a specific skill relative to all other skills may also indicate a neurological disorder.

However, it is not sufficient simply to look at the level-of-performance parameters. A patient who shows a low level of performance may have no neurological disorder; the patient could have scored low because of a psychiatric condition, fatigue, or because s/he has always had a low performance level. Alternatively, a patient with a good performance could have a mild disorder or a disorder in an area of the brain that produces few cognitive deficits. Consequently, a closer look must be made for any patterns suggesting a specific localization or a specific neurological disorder. These questions are considered in the next three chapters.

Chapter 5

LOCALIZATION

L OCALIZATION OF A BRAIN INJURY through psychological testing is a difficult process, because of the variability of the effects seen in brain injuries. The expression of a lesion in a specific area of the brain differs considerably, depending upon the severity of the lesion and its rate of growth, cause, and extent. The expression of a lesion will be altered by any secondary deficits, such as confusion, visual loss, or headaches. Patients' existing deficits can also complicate the results. Consequently, localization is not a process of simply finding deficits but of analyzing the patterns of the deficits and relating these patterns to specific locations and neurological processes. The conclusions reached should be able to account for the majority of deficits shown by a patient.

The major area of interest in neuropsychology has been the localization of disorders within the cerebral hemispheres. However, knowledge of deficits which arise from lesions of the spinal cord, brain stem, cerebellum, thalamus, and basal nuclei also need to be recognized by the neuropsychologist in order to avoid misdiagnosis of these conditions. While some disorders such as spinal cord injuries may normally rarely be seen by the neuropsychologist, they are sometimes present as complicating conditions along with a brain injury. For example, this can be relatively frequent in a population with a high percentage of traumatic injuries.

Spinal Cord Injuries

Spinal cord injuries never cause deficits in cognitive skills. Deficits may include weakness, pain, and somatosensory loss in the trunk or limbs of the body. The deficits may be bilateral or unilateral. All psychological tests with significant motor or somatosensory components can be affected, including many cognitive tests that have somatosensory or motor components. This includes a high percentage of the spatial tests available, as well as

104

such tests as the *Tactual Performance Test,* which demands both motor and somatosensory skills.

For patients who have a significant impairment as a result of a spinal cord injury, especially those involving the dominant hand, it is best to use tests that are not too dependent on motor skills. Tests like the WAIS verbal tests, Picture Completion, Picture Arrangement, the Category Test, Speech Perception, Rhythm, and the Raven's Matrices Tests, can be used to evaluate these patients.

Brain Stem and Cerebellar Disorders

These lesions do not usually result in cognitive deficits. The major deficits are motor and sensory. Performance on tests of complex cognitive functions, such as the Category Test, are generally within normal limits.

These deficits may be recognized because of the scattered symptoms on the tests involving motor and somatosensory components. Other tests measuring similar skills, but not as dependent on motor and somatosensory components, are usually intact. Deficits of the cranial nerves may also be seen (*see* Table 2-I). The patient may also show significant motor tremor. The tests developed by the University of Wisconsin for measuring static and voluntary tremor (described in Norton and Matthews, 1972) are especially useful in recognizing these disorders.

Severe brain stem disorders, especially those involving the Reticular Activating System, may cause gross disturbances in consciousness and arousal. These defects make it impossible to test the patient or may severely impair performance even though cognitive areas of the brain are intact. Such patients, if testable, will often show grossly impaired scores on all tests.

LATERALIZATION OF LESIONS OF THE CEREBRAL CORTEX

Laterality of lesions to the cerebral hemispheres is determined by identifying the evidence suggestive of a right or left hemisphere injury. The evidence comes from several primary sources: (1) performance suggestive of brain injury on tasks primarily reflecting the performance of one hemisphere; (2) impaired performance on one side of the body as compared to the other; (3) impairment on right or left brain hemisphere tasks, as compared to tasks mediated by the opposite hemisphere. All of the indications are then considered as a whole to investigate whether the pattern is suggestive of right, left, diffuse, or scattered impairment.

Tests Lateralizing to Left Hemisphere

The primary tests lateralizing to the left hemisphere are those involving verbal skills. These include tests relating to the understanding and expression of speech, as well as the use of speech symbols.

On any test of aphasia, signs indicating *dysnomia*, inability to name objects; *dyslexia*, reading impairment; *dysgraphia*, inability to write; or *visual-letter dysgnosia*, confusion between numbers and letters, are almost always indicative of left brain injury (Wheeler and Reitan, 1962). Impairments on tasks such as *dyscalculia*, inability to perform arithmetic operations; *central dysarthria*, slurring of speech or loss of motor speech; *spelling dyspraxia*, inability to spell simple words; and *right-left disorientation*, confusion between right and left, are generally indicative of left brain injury but do occur sometimes with lesions lateralized to the right hemisphere (Wheeler and Reitan, 1962).

Poor performance on tests of verbal recall is also indicative of left brain injury (Riseman et al., 1971). This includes tests of paired associate learning from the Wechsler Memory Scale (Black, 1973) and sentence learning (Ettlinger and Moffett, 1970). Tests of speech understanding (Speech Perception) are usually indicative of left brain impairment as well (Goldstein and Shelly, 1973; Reitan, 1964). Impairment on the Token Test is also highly correlated with left brain involvement (Swisher and Sarno, 1969). On the WAIS, left brain involvement may be seen by low scores on the Digit Span, Similarities, and Arithmetic Subtests. Of the three, the Digit Span is generally more sensitive.

Several other tests may be impaired in left brain injuries, but these may also be down in right brain injuries so are not of lateralizing significance. This includes impairment on most of the visual-spatial construction tasks, such as the Bender-Gestalt (although extremely poor performance may indicate a right brain injury), the Category Test, Digit Symbol, Arithmetic, Picture Completion, Tactual Performance Test (total score), and other tests sensitive to brain damage in general. Although these tests are not useful in lateralizing, there are specific instances in which they aid the localization process.

Tests Lateralizing to the Right Hemisphere

A number of the tests presented indicate a right hemisphere deficit. The inaccurate execution of the spatial character of simple drawings, like a Greek cross on the Halstead-Wepman Aphasia Test, are generally indicative of right brain injury, *construction dyspraxia* (Heimburger and Reitan, 1961; Klove and Reitan, 1958; Wheeler, 1963; Wheeler and Reitan, 1962).

Performance on tasks involving mazes may also indicate right brain dysfunction (Kershner and King, 1974). A major test using mazes is the *Elithorn Perceptual Maze* (Archibald et al., 1967; Benton et al., 1963). Impairment in facial recognition (DeRenzi and Spinnler, 1966b; Hilliard, 1973) and in other visual matching tasks (Kershner and King, 1974) is also indicative of right brain disorders.

Impairment on tests involving spatial or sequential skills also may be an indicator of right brain dysfunction. These tests include the Memory and Location scores from the Tactual Performance Test (Goldstein and Shelly, 1973), Raven's Matrices (Costa and Vaughan, 1962; Costa et al., 1969), and Block Design and Picture Arrangement (Klove, 1960; McFie, 1969, 1975).

When it occurs, unilateral spatial neglect is a significant sign of right brain dysfunction. The patient ignores the left side of presented material. Consequently, a patient may draw only the right half of a figure or read only the right half of a sentence. This phenomenon is often accompanied by a left visual field loss (Critchley, 1953; Oxbury, Campbell, and Oxbury, 1974).

Other single indications of right brain dysfunction may include temporal disorientation, as measured by the Wechsler Memory Scale (Wang, Kaplan, and Rogers, 1975), and a loss of stereoscopic vision (Benton and Hecaen, 1970). Rhythm deficits may indicate right hemisphere disorders, but it may also be impaired in left hemisphere problems. In general, a deficit on the Rhythm Test in the absence of speech deficits suggests a right hemisphere disorder.

Right-Left Comparisons

Comparisons involving the right and left body sides and tasks mediated by the right or left brains are common ways of diagnosing laterality. Such methods have the advantage of using a basal level for each patient, rather than a level-of-performance or sign approach alone. Generally, consistent differences in these scores indicating laterality are much more important than conclusions reached from level-of-performance or sign approaches.

Sensory Comparisons

It is generally assumed that the basic sensory performance of the right and left sides of the body are equal. Consequently, any impairment on one side relative to the other is seen as an indicator of damage to the hemisphere contralateral to the impaired side. This holds for tactile, auditory, and visual comparisons.

As noted earlier, one of the most serious sensory signs is a reliable suppression coming from double simultaneous stimulation. Not only does the presence of a suppression on one side imply involvement of the contralateral hemisphere, but it also implies the probable destruction of brain tissue as seen in malignant tumors or cerebrovascular bleeding. Because of the importance of suppressions when they do appear, it is incumbent upon testers to repeat the procedures to insure that the suppression is real, rather than as a result of the patient's confusion or errors in procedure (Goldstein, 1974).

A loss of vision in the entire left or right visual field generally implies the involvement of the contralateral hemisphere, as does the loss of one half of either visual field in both eyes. However, the complete loss of sight in one eye is rarely due to cerebral hemisphere involvement alone. The reader is referred to Figures 2-5 and 2-6 on visual pathways for the possible significance of each visual disorder. Impairment of hearing, higher threshold, may accompany damage to the contralateral hemisphere, especially after an acute injury involving the auditory areas.

Several tactile tasks may indicate right-left differences. Von Frey Hairs may be used to identify loss of tactile sensation (Russell et al., 1970). Finger agnosia, the inability to name a finger, is generally worse on the side opposite the injury. In addition, impaired performance bilaterally may also be indicative of left brain involvement (Gainotti et al., 1972; Gainotti and Tiacci, 1973; Reitan, 1959c; Russell et al., 1970). Differences between the two sides of two to three errors are generally significant using the Reitan (1959c) procedure of twenty trials for each hand.

Fingertip Number Writing (Reitan, 1959c) involves the writing of numbers on the client's fingertips which he must recognize. Generally, this task is sensitive to many types of brain involvement, as well as problems in attention. Results indicating three or more errors on one hand than on the other generally suggest lateralization to the opposite hemisphere.

Another common sensory task is astereognosis, the recognition of objects placed in one hand. Impairment in one hand compared to the other is generally seen as significant. Since the objects to be named are generally simple shapes which are never missed by normals, even one error may be useful in determining lateralization (Kohn and Dennis, 1974b; Reitan, 1959c). Reitan (1959c) has the patient point to the object's replica rather than name the object to avoid mistakes due to aphasia rather than tactile impairment.

Motor Impairment

Evaluating motor differences is somewhat more difficult than evaluating sensory differences, since the dominant hand is generally expected to do better than the nondominant hand. Consequently, the neuropsychologist must take into account this expected difference in analyzing results. If the dominant hand performs more poorly or equal to the nondominant hand on any motor task, this is possibly indicative of an injury to the contralateral hemisphere. However, impairment in the nondominant hand must be significantly larger than the expected difference before involvement of the nondominant hemisphere is hypothesized.

On the Halstead-Reitan, the major measure of motor skills is the Finger Tapping Test, which measures the speed of tapping by the index finger on both hands. In general, the left hand (nondominant) is expected to be about 10 percent slower than the right hand. Consequently, any situation in which the dominant hand is not 5 percent or more effective than the nondominant hand suggests the possibility of dominant hemisphere damage. If the dominant hand is slower than the nondominant, this is strongly indicative of dominant hemisphere dysfunction. To hypothesize lateralized nondominant hemisphere dysfunction, the performance of the left hand should be at least 20 percent below that of the right hand (Reitan, 1959d).

Grip strength may also be used as a measure of motor skills. The most useful instruments are those having adjustments for different hand sizes, since the handgrip can affect scores considerably. The same rules that apply to the analysis of finger tapping can be applied to gross motor strength.

The Purdue Pegboard provides comparisons of right and left hand performance on a task involving fine motor skills, as well as concentration (Costa et al., 1963). Norms for the test are presented by Costa and his associates. As with the other motor tests, more impairment on one hand as opposed to the other implies the involvement of the contralateral hemisphere.

The Tactual Performance Test is a complex task involving both motor and sensory components. As described earlier, the test is a form board into which the subject must place blocks while blindfolded. The client does this first with his dominant hand, then the nondominant, and finally with both hands. In general, the client is expected to improve by about one-third from trial to trial due to learning. For example, if it takes six minutes to do the test with the dominant hand, then it should take about four minutes with the nondominant hand and about two and one-half minutes with both hands.

Deviation from this expected performance is indicative of a brain lesion. If the time for the nondominant hand is not better than the time for the dominant hand, a lesion of the nondominant hemisphere is likely. If the time for the dominant hand is impaired, with significant improvement for the nondominant hand (about 40% or more), this is suggestive of dominant hemisphere dysfunction. An overall poor performance is suggestive of right or diffuse involvement.

Comparisons Involving WAIS Scores

One of the more controversial left-right indicators has been the difference between the performance and verbal IQ. It has been suggested that the verbal tests reflect left hemisphere function while the performance (nonverbal) tests reflect right hemisphere function. Thus, in right brain injury the left brain score (verbal) should be higher (Balthazar, 1963; Balthazar and Morrison, 1961; Black, 1974b; Dennerll, 1964b; Doehring, Reitan, and Klove, 1961; Fields and Whitmyre, 1969; Goldstein and Shelly, 1973; Kershner and King, 1974; Reitan and Klove, undated; Russell, 1972).

Despite the impressive number of studies supporting this score, several studies have reported the score to be useless, if not misleading (Heilbrun, 1959; Meyer and Jones, 1957; Pennington, Galliani, and Voegele, 1965; Reed, Reitan, and Klove, 1969; Smith, 1966). The Pennington and Reed cohorts dealt with children with serious lateralized damage at birth, a group where such results might be expected (*see* Chapter 7). However, the other studies (especially Smith, 1966) have dealt with populations where confirming results would normally have been expected.

The conclusion reached from the literature is that the performance-verbal IQ (PIQ-VIQ) difference is a useful score, but only in some cases. An examination of the conditions under which the score fails is useful, because the same reasoning processes can be applied to a number of different tests.

The major problem in comparing the PIQ-VIQ differences is that not all the performance tests are pure right brain tests, while not all the verbal tests are pure left brain tests. For example, all of the performance tests except Picture Completion require motor manipulation. In dominant hemisphere disorders, the motor skills of the dominant hand may be severely impaired, causing some hindrance in the performance test in relationship to the individual's dependence on the dominant hand and the severity of the impairment.

On the other hand, an individual with an injured right brain might be able to compensate for impaired spatial ability by using verbal skills to complete the performance items. Impairment in verbal skills, however, might lead to impairment in Picture Arrangement, which involves telling a story, or Picture Completion, where a missing detail must be identified. In all of the tests, an inability to remember and follow instructions might impair performance.

The verbal tests are less affected by right brain impairment. The major exceptions to this are the Arithmetic Test, which demands some spatial skills, and the Digit Span Test, where the backward repetition of numbers demands spatial-sequencing skills. The Vocabulary, Comprehension, and Information Tests are relatively insensitive to right or left brain injuries, except when motor aphasia or severe impairment in the ability to understand is present. Similarities tend to reflect left brain integrity, but can be depressed in right brain injuries as well.

Another factor is the chronicity of the injury. Acute, lateralized disorders will often create clear performance-verbal differences. As a subject recovers, there tends to be an improvement in the lowered scores. This often reduces or eliminates any significant difference in the scores.

Other score comparisons from the WAIS have also been proposed for lateralization. Simpson and Vega (1971) proposed six comparisons of scores that, when positive, indicate left brain involvement: Vocabulary greater than Comprehension, Vocabulary greater than Arithmetic, Vocabulary greater than Similarities, Picture Completion greater than Arithmetic, Picture Completion greater than Similarities, Picture Arrangement greater than Arithmetic. Five score comparisons indicate right brain involvement: Information greater than Picture Arrangement, Information greater than Object Assembly, Digit Span greater than Digit Symbol, Digit Span greater than Picture Arrangement, Picture Completion greater than Object Assembly. The user would have to use the weight of these eleven comparisons to make a decision as to whether or not they implied left or right injury. Parsons and his associates (1969) suggested that a comparison of Block Design and Vocabulary would help lateralize. If Block Design is the larger score, this suggests a left brain injury, while a larger Vocabulary score suggests a right brain injury.

As noted earlier, Digit Span may be used to lateralize brain injury. If both digits forward and digits backward are down (normal for an average adult is remembering six numbers in a row forward, five backward), this indicates a left hemisphere injury. If digits backward is impaired but digits forward normal, this implies a right hemisphere injury. Generally, digits forward must be at least three digits longer than digits backward to strongly indicate a right brain dysfunction (Klove, 1959; Kraus and Selecki, 1967; Rudel and Denckla, 1974; Weinberg, Diller, Gerstmann, and Schulman, 1972).

Comparisons Involving Other Tests

Reitan and Tarshes (1959) have proposed the use of the Trail Making Test as a lateralizing score. If the performance on Part A, connecting the circles by numbers, is impaired compared to Part B, connecting the circles by numbers and letters alternately, this is indicative of right hemisphere involvement. If Part B is significantly impaired compared to Part A, this indicates a left hemisphere injury.

Performance on drawing tests may also be interpreted as left or right hemisphere performance. As indicated in Chapter 2, deficits on very simple drawings, even in drawing a straight line, are indications of right hemisphere dysfunctions. However, more complex drawings may be done badly by both right and left hemisphere injured patients. In left hemisphere patients, the problems are reflected in simplified, reduced drawings, which usually retain the elements correctly oriented to one another. The left hemisphere injured patient may also show some problems with angles in the drawings.

The right hemisphere injured patients will include details,

but the spatial arrangement of the parts will be disrupted. The right hemisphere patient is much more likely to show unilateral spatial neglect. Finally, the right hemisphere impaired patient is more likely to include extra, unrequested drawings (Arrigoni and DeRenzi, 1964; Gainotti and Tiacci, 1970; Hecaen and Assal, 1970; Warrington et al., 1966).

Diffuse Brain Injury

In diffuse brain involvement, there will be deficits in functions mediated by both hemispheres. Sensory and motor deficits will be bilateral, and neither hemisphere will appear more severely impaired than the other. A number of disorders show a combination of a localized and a diffuse disorder. The scores in general are down. However, scores representing a localized area are severely impaired, compared to the level of the other scores. This pattern is important to recognize, since it is seen in cerebrovascular disorders and other neurological problems (*see* Chapter 6).

In all diffuse disorders, indicators of general brain integrity will be uniformly impaired. In contrast to the pattern of localized lesions, there will be few, if any, scores indicating normal performance. Measures involving comparisons of left and right hemisphere tests will not point in any consistent manner to either hemisphere.

Localization of Brain Dysfunction

One problem in localization is that disorders do not always localize along the lines assigned to a particular functional area. Often an area of the brain is only partially disrupted, so an ability is affected to a lesser degree than normal. Finally, we must deal with the secondary effects of an injury as discussed earlier. Each of these factors complicate a localization, but do not necessarily prevent it.

Two major methods are used in making a localization of the dysfunction. First, an identification is attempted, through pattern analysis of the test scores, of the basic deficits underlying a given set of test results. With that information, the experimental results may be applied as discussed in Chapter 2, assessing where the deficit would have to be in order to cause such results. Luria (1966) has termed this process *syndrome analysis*. The second method can be used when a regular set of tests is employed. Through research, patterns of results specific to these tests may be identified for different areas of brain localization. In short, this becomes a pragmatic rather than a theoretical approach to the problem of localization.

It is felt that both syndrome analysis and regular testing approaches are applicable to the work of the neuropsychologist. Each method can serve to verify the other. Both have strengths in different types of disorders and so can supplement one another in difficult cases. The theoretical function of the brain was reviewed in Chapter 2. Here, the test scores from conditions resulting in different, localized injuries will be examined. It should be remembered that this discussion can only offer general guidelines rather than strict, unchangeable rules.

The Frontal Lobes

Lesions of the orbital frontal areas are particularly difficult to diagnose, since they are generally reflected in emotional symptoms with minor deficits at best in the normal measures of frontal integrity. These lesions, especially when they involve the left or the bilateral frontal lobes, may be reflected in a lack of anxiety (Scherer, Winne, and Baker, 1955), a lack of inhibition in social situations (Crown, 1953), impulsiveness, mild euphoria, and apathy. Hebb and Penfield (1940) suggested such lesions have no effect on sorting or abstraction problems. Hamlin (1970) reported no long-term decline eight to fourteen years after orbital lesions.

Bilateral lesions of the lateral frontal lobes, on the other hand, can produce marked and obvious deterioration of behavior, including the loss of time-and-place orientation (Benton, 1968). This can cause loss of behavior across all complex abilities, depending on the seriousness of this disorder. These lesions do not interfere with basic sensory input processes, although this may be difficult to measure in light of the patient's generally deteriorated condition. The effects of these lesions depend greatly on the cause: Lesions associated with surgical procedures generally show fewer deficits than those associated with frontal degenerative diseases (*see* Chapter 6).

Left Frontal Lobe

Lesions of the left prefrontal area result in deficits on tests of categorizing and flexibility. This can be seen by deficits on the Halstead Category Test requiring the subject to deduce principles from a series of slides (Halstead, 1947; Reitan, 1959c, 1964). Left prefrontal patients also show severe deficits on the Wisconsin Card Sorting Test, another measure of categorizing (Milner, 1963, 1964). Prefrontal lesions may also result in impairment on Part B of the Trail Making Test, which requires alteration between letters and numbers (Reitan, undated), and on the color-word page of the Stroop Color and Word Test, which involves the suppression of a word-naming in favor of a color-naming response (Golden, 1976b; Perret, 1974).

On the Wechsler Intelligence Test, depressions may be seen on Digit Span (Mahan, 1976; Markwell, Wheeler, and Kitzinger, 1953; McFie, 1969, 1975) with only slight impairment in the IQ score (Smith, 1964, 1966). Deficits in word fluency and verbal associative learning may also be present (Benton, 1968; McFie, 1975).

In general, no other deficits are seen in lesions limited to the left prefrontal areas. Indeed, the presence of several of the above deficits without other impairment should lead to the hypothesis of a left prefrontal deficit. When these and other deficits are present, the lesion may be elsewhere in the brain. Caution must be particularly taken with tests, like the Trail Making and Category Tests, which are sensitive to brain injury in general.

Involvement of the secondary and primary areas produces significant signs. Injuries may cause complete loss of speech or difficulty with complex words reflected in slurring or mispronounciation, central dysarthria; slowness of speech (Schiller, 1947); loss of writing skills, dysgraphia; and perseveration.

Motor deficits are common to these lesions, reflected in low scores on the dominant hand on such tests as the Finger Tapping, Grip Strength, Purdue Pegboard, and the Tactual Performance Tests. Generally, there is no relative impairment on the nondominant hand, although there may be a decrease in level of performance on the nondominant hand. Lesions limited to the frontal lobe will not produce sensory suppressions and result at most in sensory deficits in complex sensory tasks, such as deciphering numbers written on one's hands.

Tasks reflecting right brain integrity will generally be intact, except when they require a verbal response or involve the dominant motor skills. The degree to which this will occur depends upon an individual's dependence on his or her dominant hand. If the motor impairment is severe enough and speech involvement slight, these patients may even show a larger drop in performance as compared to verbal IQ.

Right Frontal

Right frontal lesions are among the most difficult to recognize, because they can be largely asymptomatic. The right prefrontal patient does not show the severe deficits on the Wisconsin Card Sorting Test, Category Test, Trail Making Test or Stroop Color and Word Test as does the left frontal patient, although these deficits may be present in some cases.

McFie (1969, 1975) has associated deficits in Picture Arrangement and the Memory for Designs Test with right frontal deficits. Mahan (1976) has suggested that the major deficits are seen on Picture Arrangement and Digit Span. As with left frontal injuries, right frontal patients show little change in overall IQ (Smith, 1966).

Benton (1968) has suggested that right frontal injuries can be seen on complex spatial-construction tasks, especially those involving three-dimensional figures. There is also an impairment with right frontal patients in general spatial skills, which can be reflected in scores on many spatial tests, especially if the lesion is severe.

Lesions involving the posterior right frontal show deficits on the nondominant hand in the motor tests such as Finger Tapping, Purdue Pegboard, and the Tactual Performance Tests. In more severe injuries, the Tactual Performance Test as a whole may be disrupted due to spatial impairment. In frontal injuries, on both sides, the Finger Tapping Test will generally show more impairment than the Tactual Performance Test (Reitan, (1959d), except when the deficits are limited to the prefrontal areas alone.

Temporal Lobes

There are a number of important patterns of deficits common to the two temporal lobes. Lesions of the primary areas of either temporal lobe will result in a loss of hearing acuity in the contralateral ear. If the lesion involves actual tissue destruction, this is likely to result in auditory suppressions involving the opposite ear.

Lesions to either temporal lobe may result in a loss of the upper visual field of the opposite side of both eyes (Fig. 2-6). As a temporal lesion moves more posteriorly, this movement is shown in better Finger Tapping scores (reflecting an intact motor area in the posterior frontal lobe) and more sensory signs, especially in such complex tasks as the Tactual Performance or Fingertip Number Writing Tests. As with all other sensorimotor symptoms, these will occur primarily on the side of the body opposite the lesion.

Anterior-medial lesions in both temporal lobes are difficult to diagnose, because of the close association between these areas and the limbic system. To the degree that there is hippocampal involvement in the lesions, there will be memory deficits, although the character differs, depending on the side of the lesion. Bilateral involvement may lead to the complete loss of new, long-term memory characteristic of bilateral hippocampal disorders. Otherwise, effects may be rather minor or nonexistent (Meier and French, 1966; Paolino and Friedman, 1959). Visual, auditory, or olfactory hallucinations may accompany epileptic foci in the anterior temporal lobes (Bennett, 1965), as symptoms of emotional disorders may also (Meier and French, 1965). No clear and reliable method has been found, as yet, for discriminating such emotional disorders differentially from other emotional problems.

Left Temporal Lobe

The major deficits in left temporal lobe disorders are speech problems. Disorders of the secondary areas of the left temporal lobe result in an inability to discriminate phonemes. This is reflected in a low score on Speech Perception, and often a low score on the Seashore Rhythm Test as well, although this is not necessary to establish the diagnosis. In more severe disorders, the patient completely loses the ability to decode phonemic speech; in less-severe injuries, this is reflected as a problem in deciphering similar phonemes. This disorder also interferes with the person's ability to speak, read, and write as a secondary result of the phonemic disorder (Luria, 1966). Numerous signs are seen on tests of aphasia with secondary temporal lesions. Deficits are usually seen in measures of verbal learning, such as the Digit Span or Sentence Learning Tests (Fedio and Mirsky, 1969; Glowinski, 1973; McFie, 1969, 1975). McFie (1969, 1975) has also associated deficits on the Similarities Test with left temporal lobe function.

As a deficit moves towards the more posterior temporal lobe, there are selective auditory-visual problems, such as dyslexia, and less impairment in Speech Perception. Lesions in the parieto-temporo-occipital area will cause an inability to name objects, as will temporal injuries themselves; but the more parietal-lesioned patient will be able to get the word if given the initial phoneme(s). These patients also show more deficits on somatosensory measures.

Right Temporal Lobe

Lesions to the right temporal lobe involve disorders in both visual and auditory measures. There is often a loss in pitch perception or Rhythm scores (Fedio and Mirsky, 1968; Reitan, undated), without a similar loss in speech perception. The patient may suffer from a complete loss of musical skills, *amusia*.

Visual deficits may be seen on the *McGill Picture Anomaly Test;* the patient must indicate what is wrong with a picture (Milner, 1962; Shalman, 1961), but only in those cases where there is a relatively rare, severe deficit (Milner, 1975). Others have associated the right temporal lobe lesions with deficits on Picture Arrangement (McFie, 1975; Meier and French, 1966), Object Assembly (Meier and French, 1966), Memory for Designs (McFie, 1975), and the Rey Figure, a highly complex, unusual drawing (Milner, 1975). Kimura (1963) has concluded that the major deficit in the right temporal lobe is an inability to work with unfamiliar material, so that the tests successful with any given person or group may vary. As the deficit moves towards the temporo-occipital and temporo-parieto-occipital areas, the deficits are more spatial in nature. As in the left temporal lobe, the closer the lesion to the parietal lobe, the greater the degree of sensory loss.

Parietal Lobes

Deficits in the primary area of the parietal lobe cause losses in the reception of somatosensory impulses from the opposite half of the body. Such losses on a tactile level may be measured by the Von Frey Hairs (Russell et al., 1970). A significantly lower sensitivity for one side of the body implies involvement of the parietal lobe opposite the affected side. Destruction of tissue in the primary area leads to the presence of tactile suppressions. Loss of discrimination in the hands will also lead to such symptoms as finger agnosia, astereognosis, and deficits in fingertip writing.

Deficits in the secondary areas will lead to an inability to integrate the stimuli received by the parietal lobe, again leading to deficits in finger agnosia, astereognosis, and fingertip writing, but not to deficits of primary tactile sensitivity. Deficits in the tertiary areas lead to different symptoms, depending on the laterality.

Deficits in any of the parietal areas will generally cause a greater deficit on the Tactual Performance Test than on measures of motor control, like the Finger Tapping Test. However, motor deficits will be seen on the hand opposite the injury, if the motor strip no longer receives effective sensory feedback. This will be seen most clearly in tasks involving fine motor control, such as the Purdue Pegboard. Parietal deficits may also be seen in lower visual field losses in the opposite visual field (Fig. 2-6).

Left Parietal Lobe

Disorders of the left parietal show major sensory problems in the right body. On the Tactual Performance Test, this will usually be expressed as a specific deficit of the right hand, as compared to the left hand or both hands. It will also be expressed in unilateral right-handed finger agnosia, astereognosis, and fingertip writing, depending on the location of the deficit. Bilateral finger agnosia may be present if there is tertiary parieto-occipital involvement.

Disorders of the tertiary areas result in a number of basically verbal and spatial disorders. The subject may be unable to accurately recognize or name body parts or appreciate their spatial position, finger agnosia, and may be unable to locate himself in space, causing him/her to show disorientation in left-right directions.

These lesions will cause losses on several WAIS subtests, including Arithmetic, Digit Span, and Block Design (McFie, 1969, 1975), and sometimes, Similarities (Mahan, 1976). Although a subject will still be able to speak, he or she is unable to name objects, dysnomia; and has deficits in reading, dyslexia; and writing, dysgraphia. Spelling disturbances are commonly seen, spelling dyspraxia, as well as confusion in recognizing and separating numbers and letters. The patient may have problems in demonstrating the use of objects, even though the patient knows the use. Disorders of grammar may also become evident.

The tertiary parietal areas will also show disorders of the understanding of relational words, as well as arithmetic relations and operations, dyscalculia. Deficits in verbal learning will be present (McFie, 1969). Lesions of the parieto-occipito-temporal area may result in more severe symptoms, including the complete loss of verbal skills, or *global aphasia.*

A syndrome indicating parietal deficits is made up of four of the disorders described above. First described by Gerstmann, *Gerstmann's syndrome* consists of finger agnosia, agraphia, acalculia, and right-left confusion (Gerstmann, 1971; Wilkins and Brody, 1971). As a sign of left parietal involvement, this group of symptoms has been very controversial, with some seeing it as an invariable result of parietal disorders and others seeing it as a syndrome arising from many disorders (Benton, 1961; Strub and Geschwind, 1974). An excellent study by Heimburger and his associates (1964) established that in 57 percent of the cases with these four symptoms, the disorder was located in the parietal lobe, usually in the tertiary areas; in 13 percent, the disorder was not in the parietal lobe; and in 30 percent it could not be determined if the parietal lobe was responsible. Thus of the identifiable cases, over 80 percent of the patients with this syndrome had lesions in the left parietal lobe.

Right Parietal Lobe

Here, the sensory deficits involve the left side of the body. On the Tactual Performance Test, there is a general lowering of scores due to the role of the right parietal in spatial synthesis, as well as a specific loss on the left hand. Right parietal lesions are also seen in the deficits on such tests as Block Design, Picture Arrangement, drawing a Greek cross, the Trail Making Test (especially Part A), Bender-Gestalt and most other construction tests, and in arithmetic, especially problems involving the spatial relationships of numbers (Mahan, 1976; McFie, 1969, 1975; Reitan and Klove, undated). Deficits are also present in visual memory and tactile memory tests, including the Memory and Location scores of the Tactual Performance Test, the Memory for Designs and the Benton Visual Retention Test (McFie, 1969). In general, these deficits are more severe in lesions of the tertiary areas of the right parietal lobe than they are in other lesions. Reitan (Wheeler and Reitan, 1963; Wheeler, 1963) uses the drawing of the Greek cross as a major sign of right hemisphere and right parietal involvement.

A major pathognomic sign of right parietal deficits in particular and many right brain lesions to some extent, is unilateral spatial neglect, or inattention. On the tests normally given, this is usually expressed as an omission of the left half of a figure or reading only the left half of a line. Such subjects also have difficulty with dressing, a deficit which may be noted in a referral for a patient.

Occipital Lobes

The major characteristic of primary occipital lobe lesions is partial or complete loss of the opposite visual field in both eyes, *homonymous hemianopsia.* This does not cause any practical difficulties when the lesion is in the left occipital lobe, as the person will generally compensate for the deficit by eye and head movements. In the right occipital disorder, however, the inattention phenomenon described above may cause the patient to ignore the left visual field.

Less-extensive deficits of the primary area can cause specific, irregular deficits in the opposite visual field corresponding on a point-to-point basis to the deficit in the occipital lobe. Visual suppressions may also be seen.

Disorders of the secondary areas cause symptoms of visual agnosia, in which the subject cannot recognize objects by sight. Thus, bilateral lesions can disturb tests involving picture recognition, including many of the WAIS performance tests. Left lesions may show disturbances in recognizing numbers or letters. Right lesions will interfere with nonverbal and complex material, although the intact left side can compensate for some of this deficit.

The tertiary deficits of the occipitotemporal, occipitoparietal, and occipitotemporoparietal areas have already been described.

Diagnosis of Lateralization and Localization

The first step in determining the lateralization and localization of a neurological disorder is the organization of the data gathered from the patient. In order to do this, a process slightly modified from that suggested by R. M. Reitan is effective. Each test whose performance indicates a possible brain dysfunction can be listed on a sheet of paper. If the test suggests a left brain dysfunction, it is placed on the left side of the page. If the test suggests a right hemisphere dysfunction, it is placed on the right side of the page. Tests which suggest a diffuse disorder or are sensitive to brain damage in general are placed in the center of the page. Information, such as educational level and performance, is also placed in the center.

Tests that are especially well performed are also placed in the appropriate column but enclosed in parentheses on the data page. These tests are included since they often will help rule out a possible disorder. For instance, the absence of tactile deficits of any kind would strongly argue against a parietal lesion. An example of such a page in one case can be seen in Figure 5-1.

After the data are organized, initial decisions are made as to the

Verbal IQ < Performance IQ
(80 < 110)

Category (96 errors)
TPT Total Time
(19 minutes)

Block Design Scale–8

Aphasia: Dyslexia
      Dysarthria
      Dysnomia

Digit Symbol
Scale Score 6

Mild construction
dyspraxia

Speech Sounds Perception
(30 errors)

< Picture Arrangement
  Scale Score–10 >

Tactual Performance Test
(L–10 minutes)
(R–5)

< Picture Completion–10 >

< Object Assembly–11 >

Arithmetic (Scale Score–5)

< Tactual Performance Test
  Memory–8
  Localization–7 >

Digit Span (Scale Score–4)

Finger Tapping
R–44
L–44

Rhythm–10 errors

< Trails A–20 seconds >

Auditory Suppressions (1)

Tactile Suppressions (2)

Finger Agnosia
 R–8 errors
 L–2 errors

Finger Number Writing
R–12 errors
L– 4 errors

Tactile Form Recognition
R–2 errors
L–0 errors

< No visual suppressions >

Trails B (180 secs, 2 errors)

R= right hand
L= left hand

Figure 5-1. Example of how the neuropsychological data may be organized in the case discussed in the text.

likelihood of brain dysfunction, using the processes described in the last chapter. Then the data for each hemisphere are compared to see if there are indications that one hemisphere is more seriously involved than the other. For example, in Figure 5-1 there is a heavy preponderance of data indicating left brain dysfunction. Consequently, a focal lesion within the left hemisphere may be postulated.

The data for the left hemisphere can then be examined for indications of localization. In this case, the combination of tactile suppressions, a poor right-hand Tactual Performance Test score, aphasia symptoms, disturbances in Speech Sound Perception, auditory suppressions, the drop in verbal IQ, and the equal performance of the right and left hands on the Finger Tapping Test suggest a parietotemporal lesion. This is further supported by the severity of the deficit on the right hand of the Tactual Performance Test, as compared to the right hand deficit on the Finger Tapping Test.

After reaching a tentative localization, the other deficits that are reported must be examined to see if they can be accounted for by that hypothesis. In this case, there is reduced performance on the "right hemisphere tests" of Block Design and Rhythm and indications of mild construction dyspraxia. As noted earlier, each of these deficits may be associated with left temporoparietal dysfunction as well. Consequently, the hypothesis of left temporoparietal involvement can account for the results as a whole.

Alternatively, it may have been concluded that the right hemisphere was showing deficits that could not be accounted for by the left hemisphere lesion. These deficits may have indicated a second focal lesion in the right hemisphere or diffuse involvement of the right hemisphere. There may also be scattered deficits inconsistent with either a diffuse disorder or a focal lesion. Each of these alternatives indicates a possible neurological disorder when combined with the left hemisphere results. For example, a focal deficit in one hemisphere and a diffuse deficit in the other are seen in many cases of cerebrovascular lesions. The importance of each pattern is indicated in the next chapter.

If neither hemisphere appears more seriously involved, the data from each of the hemispheres must be examined to see if the deficits are localized, diffuse, or scattered. Some disorders will cause diffuse bilateral impairment, while others may cause lateralized focal lesions in both hemispheres.

It is important in this process to carefully consider the severity of the deficits in each hemisphere as well as the locus. Such information can be extremely valuable in assessing the probable underlying neurological disorder. In addition, the severity of any deficit on generalized tests must be taken into account as well. Some localized lesions will affect generalized tests to a much greater extent than others.

At this point, several decisions should be made by the diagnostician. First, the overall level of impairment as determined by the generalized tests should be ascertained. Second, the condition of each hemisphere should be determined. Generally, this would indicate either a focal involvement, a diffuse involvement, scattered impairment, or a normal, unimpaired performance.

At the same time, analysis may be made of the basic brain functions that have been impaired. In this case, there is a deficit in both primary and secondary functions of the temporal lobe, as well as primary, secondary, and tertiary functions of the parietal lobe.

A number of precautions need to be taken by the diagnostician in the diagnostic process. First, a test may not measure what it seems to measure. A deficit in Block Design, for example, may not be a loss in spatial ability but a loss in motor skills. A deficit in Picture Arrangement may reflect a spatial, sequential, or verbal dysfunction. Consequently, it is often necessary to closely analyze and consider each test before a decision is made on the localizing value of a test in a given case.

Secondly, there may be people tested whose poor performances are unrelated to brain injury. In some cases, these deficits were present before the brain injury, either because of the failure of a skill to adequately develop or through a previous disorder. Therefore, a hypothesis may not account for all the evidence. It must instead, be based on the weight of the evidence. However, these "extra" deficits should be noted as they are important in making a prognosis or planning a rehabilitation program.

In addition, the consequences of any hypothesized disorder should be examined. For instance, if right parietal disorder is hypothesized, this would suggest there should be a loss in left tactile functions. If these are not present, an alternate hypothesis must be considered or the lack of deficit explained. An alternate hypothesis to a right parietal disorder would be a right frontal disorder, which might cause some of the same losses in spatial skills but not result in tactile deficits.

Finally, it must be recognized that, even at this point, a diagnosis is not necessarily final. The neuropsychologist must ascertain whether the pattern of deficits is consistent with a neurological disorder. This is especially important in a case where schizophrenia must be ruled out, as shall be seen in the next chapter. This process is also important in those cases where the overall performance seems to be normal, but there are selective deficits suggestive of a lesion. This process may also aid in properly classifying cases with scattered dysfunctions, which may be a result of a disorder, such as multiple sclerosis, or may reflect only a poor normal performance.

Chapter 6

NEUROLOGICAL DISORDERS

NEUROPSYCHOLOGICAL TEST RESULTS are affected not only by the location of a brain lesion but its etiology as well. Diagnosis of the cause by neuropsychological tests is difficult, since each neurological disorder may produce a variety of test results. These are dependent on such factors as the stage, extent, and location of the disorder. In addition, different neurological conditions may produce similar test results.

Single neuropsychological test results cannot diagnose a neurological disorder. A diagnosis can only be inferred from an analysis of the relationship of all test results, a process which requires a knowledge of neuropathological processes and an awareness of the probable course of each disorder and the secondary problems that may arise. Often, only tentative alternatives may be advanced as a diagnosis.

Knowledge of neurological disorders can be valuable for the neuropsychologist; recognition of a specific pathological process may enable him/her to accurately classify a borderline case. In a psychiatric setting, some patients who have not been identified as victims of a pathological process may be revealed by testing and careful analysis. In other cases, the neuropsychologist may be asked whether a pattern of deficits is a likely result of a specific neurological disorder. This can be important in legal cases determining responsibility for a patient's disorder.

Knowledge of neuropathological processes can also be useful in deciding upon a prognosis, since the course of some disorders is much more benign than others. Similarly, the information may be used in assessing rehabilitation potential: Taking the neurological process into consideration can greatly enhance the accuracy of such evaluations.

In this chapter, the major neurological disorders are considered, and both neurological and neuropsychological aspects will be discussed. In addition, the differential diagnosis of schizophrenia will be considered. This is due to its importance in many settings using neuropsychological testing.

SCHIZOPHRENIA

The differential diagnosis of schizophrenia from brain damage continues to be a controversial issue in clinical neuropsychology (Heaton, 1976). Many individual tests have been shown to be ineffective in differentiating between these groups (*see* Chapter 4). Part of this problem is due to such factors as lack of motivation, drug regime, the length of hospitalization, and lack of response to normal reinforcers. In many studies in the literature, there seem to have been no attempts to consider the influence of these factors. Procedures which can help control these problems were discussed in Chapter 3.

When these procedures are undertaken in testing psychiatric patients, many acute and chronic schizophrenics show normal neuropsychological profiles (Levine and Feirstein, 1972). Since these subjects do not test as brain injured, there is no problem in diagnosis.

However, sizable numbers of schizophrenics perform at a level indicative of brain damage. To assess these patients accurately, a localization and process diagnosis must be made. If the profile shows a localized disorder, it is highly unlikely that this is the result of schizophrenia. Consequently, only profiles showing diffuse or scattered deficits must be considered for a diagnosis of schizophrenia.

For the patient with scattered signs, the condition must be analyzed to see if it reflects any known disorders. Primarily, these would include such processes as Parkinson's disease or multiple sclerosis. The possibility of incipient multiple tumors must also be considered.

The schizophrenic with diffuse deficits generally presents a much different picture from that seen in true neurological disorders. Tests measuring higher cognitive functions are seriously impaired; tests demanding sustained concentration and attention are also severely disrupted. Complex tests are done poorly. These test results suggest severe, diffuse brain impairment. In contrast, most basic motor and sensory skills are intact. Some scattered tests, which may seem randomly chosen, may be performed normally. It is this contradictory pattern which defines the schizophrenic profile. One set of results suggests a severely impaired brain bilaterally, whereas the other indicates normality in processes which should have been disrupted. This pattern is quite different from what we would see in diffuse cerebrovascular disorders or degenerative diseases, such as Alzheimer's.

The test results of the schizophrenic also tend to be quite inconsistent across sessions. In questionable cases, it is useful to do a retest; the brain-injured client will show primarily the same pattern, whereas the schizophrenic can give quite different results. The schizophrenic is also more likely to show intratest inconsistency. For example, easier items are missed while more difficult areas are done without error.

Before classifying a case as not brain damaged, it is important to consider all possible neurological diagnoses and rule them out. In addition, the basic inconsistency of the test results should be documented. When both these conditions are met, it is likely that the profile reflects emotional rather than organic problems.

TUMORS

Tumors come in a variety of forms. They may be divided into two categories: infiltrative tumors, which take over and destroy brain tissue, and noninfiltrative tumors, which cause deficits by compressing brain tissue until it cannot function normally.

Infiltrative Tumors

The most common infiltrative tumors are the *gliomas*. These arise from disorders of the *glia*, the supporting cells of the brain tissue. The most common and most destructive of the gliomas is *glioblastoma multiforme*. This tumor generally arises in middle age and is usually found in the cerebral hemispheres. Glioblastoma multiforme grows very rapidly, and symptoms may arise in several weeks. When surgical removal is incomplete, it will often grow again.

Neuropsychological signs of glioblastoma multiforme are rather clear cut. There is always a strong focal area where destruction is severe and nearly complete. If primary sensory areas are involved, there are suppressions. Due to the speed of growth of these tumors, there is a general decline in adaptive abilities, reflected in poor performance on almost all tests sensitive to brain dysfunction, such as the Category Test. Generally, there is a clear difference between the performance and verbal IQ, with the Impairment Index almost always near 1.0.

Astrocytomas are infiltrative tumors of *astrocytes,* a type of glia cell. They are generally slower growing than glioblastoma multiforme, although they may vary considerably from very slow to approaching the growth rate of glioblastoma multiforme. Generally, patients with an astrocytoma will have a longer history of increasing problems than the patient with glioblastoma multiforme.

As with glioblastoma, these tumors show definite local symptoms due to destruction of healthy brain tissue. Due to their slower growth, however, they may not show the widespread effects common to the faster-growing gliomas. As the astrocytomas growth rate increases the neuropsychological effects will closely duplicate those seen in glioblastoma.

A rare, slow-growing tumor found in young adults is *oligodendroglioma* (Bannister, 1973). The widespread effects in this tumor are few and small, because of its slow rate of growth. Its significance lies in the generally young age of the individuals in which it is found.

An alternative method of classifying the gliomas is by grade. The grade of a tumor is determined by its *malignancy,* the tendency of a tumor to grow at a fast rate, causing severe destruction of brain tissue and eventually, death. A slow-growing tumor accompanied by little impairment would be classified as a grade 1 tumor, while a fast-growing, destructive glioblastoma multiforme would be classified as grade 4. Grades 2 and 3 represent intermediate rates of growth and intermediate severity in neuropsychological deficits.

Noninfiltrative Tumors

The most common of these are *meningiomas,* representing about 15 percent of all brain tumors (Robbins, 1974). These arise in the arachnoid layer of the meninges, creating an irregular growth that presses upon the brain tissue. The neurospychological effects of the meningioma are generally less localized and less severe than glioma. They rarely give rise to suppressions or to severe deficits in behavior as is seen in the gliomas. The Impairment Index tends to be less severe (on the order of 0.4 to 0.8). A meningioma produces its behavioral effects by compression of the brain. This area of more severe deficits is often surrounded by areas of less-severe effects. There are few clear lines of demarcation.

Metastatic tumors arise secondarily to cancerous tumors, which start in such areas as the lungs, breasts, adrenals, and lymphatic system and are usually multiple. Metastatic tumors represent up to 40 percent of all the tumors seen in the elderly (Earle, 1955). They are generally fast-growing tumors, similar to glioblastoma (Bannister, 1973). They may grow within, *intrinsic*, or outside, *extrinsic*, of brain tissue, often times showing both forms (Robbins, 1974).

Metastatic tumors show test results indicating multiple focal areas of destruction. The foci can range considerably in size. Individual skills may be relatively intact in those areas not yet infiltrated by tumor. This will cause an alternate pattern of relatively good and bad areas. Sensitive tests are uniformly down. In later stages of the disorder, one may only be able to see diffuse loss of most neurospychological abilities.

Acoustic neuromas arise at the origin of the 8th cranial nerve (*see* Chapter 2). Their initial symptom is ringing in the ears, followed by partial deafness. The patient shows signs of intracranial pressure and may have difficulty in distinguishing speech sounds or rhythmic patterns, due to interference in the information reaching the temporal lobes. These tumors are not accompanied by severe cognitive loss.

Neurological Symptoms of Increased Intracranial Pressure

In addition to the focal effects of a tumor, there will be effects caused by an increase in intracranial pressure. This can arise from adding mass to the brain, obstructing the flow of cerebrospinal fluid (CSF) in the ventricles or swelling of the brain. The effects of this pressure may be headache, vomiting, or papilloedema of the eye. Papilloedema is common in cases of temporal tumors and may not appear with prefrontal disorders (Bannister, 1973). The effect of the papilloedema is to interfere with sight in the visual periphery. There may be a general loss of vision in later stages. It is important not to confuse this symptom with visual symptoms arising from a cerebral lesion.

Related Disorders

Most brain abscesses arise as a result of an infection spreading to the brain, often from disorders of the lung. They begin as an area of generalized inflammation and progress to a walled-off, localized pocket of pus within the brain (Bannister, 1973). The abscess can gradually expand, destroying and compressing brain tissue as it grows (Robbins, 1974). It may present symptoms similar to those of a tumor; at first, it looks more like an astrocytoma, and later, like a glioblastoma. There is usually a history of an infection, although it may have been several months prior to the onset of the symptoms.

Other disorders which may present symptoms similar to tumors will be discussed later. These include aneurysms and subdural hematomas.

HEAD TRAUMA

The effects of head trauma may vary considerably, depending on the strength of the trauma, the resilience of the head injured, and the relative movements of the injured head and injuring object. Not all head traumas will produce significant neuropsychological deficits. Some will cause permanent and severe deficits.

Concussion

A concussion has occurred when a patient loses consciousness due to a blow on the head. If the trauma is limited to a concussion, there may be minor neuropsychological symptoms. These are limited to the focus of the injury and to the opposite side of the head as a result of contrecoup. The *contrecoup* disorders result from a thrust of the opposite side of the brain against the irregularities and contours of the skull (Courville, 1942).

The effects of a concussion are focal in the injured hemisphere; they are more diffuse in the area of the contrecoup. The severity of the deficit is related to the length of time the patient was unconscious (Klonoff and Paris, 1974; Dailey, 1956). The focal deficit rarely takes on the character of a highly limited disorder, as may be seen in tumors. Generally, the overall impairment is less. The amount of impairment seen depends on the length of time before the subject regains consciousness. Immediately after the patient regains consciousness, there may be generalized losses in cognitive skills (Becker, 1975) and in memory functions (Brooks, 1976). The focal symptomology will only clearly appear after the subject regains awareness and is able to show sustained attention and effort. Early testing of a trauma patient may serve to establish a baseline against which recovery can be measured.

Contusion

Two types of contusion can be identified (Robbins, 1974). A small object hitting against the head may cause bleeding in the brain directly under the site of impact; however, when the head is hit by a large object, the skull tends to move away from the object faster than the brain does. This results in a separation between brain and skull at the point opposite the site of injury. A tearing of blood vessels interconnecting the brain and the meninges may then occur. This causes the major effects of the contusion in the contrecoup area.

The neuropsychological deficits caused by contusion will be more severe than concussion in the area of bleeding, causing a stronger focal deficit. It will be accompanied by a less-focal deficit opposite the contusion. The amount of injury varies greatly. Milder contusions result in many intact behaviors, while more-severe contusions may cause relatively widespread depression of ability. These deficits generally involve higher cognitive functions more than basic sensorimotor functions (Reitan and Fitzhugh, 1971).

Lacerations

A laceration occurs when there is an interruption in the continuity of the brain tissue (Robbins, 1974). This can happen in severe contrecoup injuries or through penetration of the skull and brain tissue by an object such as a bullet. This latter disorder is called a *penetrating head wound* or *open head trauma*. The extent of injury caused by an open head wound may vary considerably depending upon the extent of penetration by the object. A minor penetration may cause few symptoms. A more severe penetration can cause death.

The neuropsychological deficit associated with a closed head laceration tends to be similar to that already described for contusion. But it is greater in severity and may show more precise localization. There are usually secondary deficits opposite the laceration.

Open head traumas may show up as very precisely limited disorders characteristic of the path of the penetrating object. If this is limited enough, the generalized disorder may be very slight. In sensory areas, the destruction of tissue can cause the loss of sensation or clear suppressions. An open head trauma may cause very severe results if there is a hemorrhage of a major artery. Hemorrhage will be discussed along with disorders of the vascular system of the brain. An open head wound is also subject to abscess formation and subsequent progressive destruction.

Whether an injury is a contusion or a laceration, it can cause permanent damage to the brain and result in a scar. These scars are highly irritative and may cause epilepsy (discussed in detail later). There may be long-term deficits, usually those dependent on the area of the injury. The more severe the initial laceration or contusion, the more obvious and severe these behavioral consequences may be.

Hematoma

As a result of head injury, blood vessels may be disrupted, producing pools of blood within and between the meninges. Of most interest to the neuropsychologist is the *subdural hematoma*. The acute form arises as a result of a laceration which allows blood and cerebrospinal fluid to accumulate in the subdural space. This follows the head injury directly and is generally dealt with during the medical treatment. Consequently, it is not usually seen by neuropsychologists.

The chronic form of hematoma is associated with closed head trauma. It is caused by the rupture of small blood vessels at the site of the injury or the contrecoup. These vessels slowly leak blood into the subdural space, accumulating over time into a significant encapsulated mass (Auld et al., 1965). This has the effect of compressing the brain, acting much as would a meningioma. In one obvious diagnostic form, two subdural hematomas will form, one opposite the other. The secondary effects of head trauma may also be seen. However, since a hematoma may take many months to form, such trauma signs may not be present. The hematoma may then be misdiagnosed as a tumor if the patient's history is not closely examined. In older people, subdural hematomas can arise from very mild head traumas.

VASCULAR DISORDERS

In considering disorders of the vascular system, it is necessary to be familiar with the major arterial supplies of the brain. The major blood supply to the brain is supplied by the right and left internal carotid arteries, and the two vertebral arteries. The two vertebral arteries join together at the level of the pons to form the basilar artery. The basilar artery divides into the left and right posterior cerebral arteries. The left carotid artery divides into the left anterior cerebral and left middle cerebral arteries. The right internal carotid artery similarly divides into the right anterior cerebral artery and the right middle cerebral artery. The areas of the brain served by each of these major arteries can be seen in Figure 6-1.

The two anterior cerebral arteries are connected by the anterior communicating artery. The two posterior cerebral arteries are connected by the posterior communicating arteries to the internal carotid artery on the same side of the brain. These cross-brain connections, forming the circle of Willis, allow intact blood vessels to take over for injured blood vessels. However, this pattern of cerebral arteries is not the same in all persons, and parts of the system are missing in some people. Thus, occlu-

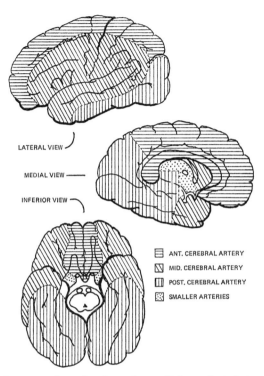

LATERAL VIEW

MEDIAL VIEW ———

INFERIOR VIEW ⌐

⊟ ANT. CEREBRAL ARTERY

◪ MID. CEREBRAL ARTERY

▥ POST. CEREBRAL ARTERY

▦ SMALLER ARTERIES

Figure 6-1. Areas within the lateral, medial, and inferior (basal) surfaces of the brain served by the major cerebral arteries.

sion of the upper basilar artery will be normally compensated for. But this will not happen if the posterior communicating artery does not exist.

Symptoms of Arterial Disruption

Disruptions of each of the major arteries cause characteristic symptoms according to the area served by each artery (*see* Fig. 6-1). Disorders of the internal carotid rarely affect the anterior cerebral artery because of the blood which can be supplied through the anterior communicating artery. Consequently, disorders of the internal carotid artery are generally equivalent to those of the middle cerebral artery (Silverstein and Hollin, 1965).

Disorders of the middle cerebral or internal carotid on the

left side involve the areas of the brain responsible for both expressive and receptive speech; disorders of these arteries can thus cause serious speech deficits. Deficits on the right side involve those areas responsible for spatial, rhythmic, and music skills and identification of complex and unusual visual and auditory patterns. Thus, disorders of either of these arteries have striking cognitive effects.

On both sides, the respective middle cerebral artery serves all the major sensory and motor areas. Thus, there will be motor, tactile, auditory, and visual deficits from disorders of these arteries. Disorders involving branches of the middle artery will generally cause some subset of these disorders.

A branch of the internal carotid artery, the ophthalmic artery, serves as the blood supply to the retina. Thus, some disorders of the internal carotid can result in complete blindness in one eye. This can never be associated with a simple disorder of one middle cerebral artery.

Disorders of the anterior cerebral artery may cause motor or sensory symptoms involving the leg, but not the rest of the body. Since parts of the prefrontal lobe are served by the anterior cerebral artery, they may also be mental symptoms characteristic of prefrontal disorders.

Disorders of the posterior cerebral artery are infrequent. They can be characterized by visual field loss (Mones, Christoff, and Bender, 1961) and even complete loss of sensory functions on one side, if the branch to the thalamus is affected. Visual agnosia may also be seen without loss of vision, especially on the left side. Interruption of the blood supply to the medial-basal temporal lobe may cause memory disorders consistent with those areas (Perez, Rivera, Meyer, Gay, Taylor, and Mathew, 1975).

Basilar artery disorders may have similar effects as the posterior cerebral arteries, if the posterior communicating artery on either side is missing. The deficits may be bilateral. In addition, it may give rise to disorders of the cerebellum, as described in Chapter 2.

Infarction

Infarctions result from an inadequate blood supply to an area of the brain, causing tissue death from lack of oxygen.

This can occur to the brain as a whole, as in severe heart failure, or in one of the major arteries or their branches.

Infarction may be a result of the blockage, *occlusion,* of a vessel, causing no blood flow through the vessel. Occlusions may be caused by a clot, usually a blood clot, lodging in a vessel. The middle cerebral artery on the left side is the most common reported site for such a disorder (Bannister, 1973). The area of the brain in which this occlusion occurs depends on clot size: If it is large, it may lodge in one of the major arteries; if it is smaller, it will lodge in one of the branches of the major arteries.

Infarction due to occlusion is often precipitated by arteriosclerosis. Fat deposits build up along blood vessel walls, reducing the size of the cerebral arteries. This condition is progressive and tends to become worse as a person grows older. Arteriosclerosis itself restricts blood supply to the brain and results in inadequate oxygenation of the brain tissue. This produces a general decline in brain-based abilities of a diffuse nature (Perez et al., 1975; Vitale et al., 1974).

As a result, it is common in major infarctions to see a severe, focal area of deficit combined with a general depression in abilities of a diffuse nature. In the common middle cerebral artery infarction of the left brain, this is generally accompanied by severe motor and tactile symptoms as well as aphasia. Infarctions commonly cause highly lateralized deficits when comparing performance and verbal IQs.

Historically, infarctions are easily differentiated from tumors, because of their sudden onset. The degree of disability caused by any infarction depends upon the general status of the cerebrovascular system and the collateral blood vessels available (Robbins, 1974). In turn, these factors help affect the neuropsychological expression of the deficits, as well as the possibility of rehabilitation. The more general the effects, the less positive the prognosis.

Gradual obstruction of a vessel, it should be noted, may not produce an infarction. In fact, if an occlusion develops over a long period of time, its eventual course into full occlusion may have little or mild effects, due to the formation over time of alternate blood sources for the affected tissue. Such a process depends on the general health of the cerebrovascular system.

Hemorrhage

Hemorrhage results from the disruption of a blood vessel, causing the spilling of blood in the cerebral tissue. The most common cause of hemorrhage is a combination of hypertension and arteriosclerosis (Robbins, 1974). Such hemorrhages are usually massive and often cause death. Prognosis for these disorders is poor.

Neuropsychologically, the hemorrhage is seen as a large area of destruction, usually involving suppressions and highly lateralized test results. As in the case of infarction, this may be superimposed against a pattern of diffuse deterioration in both hemispheres.

Aneurysms

Aneurysms represent weak areas in the walls of an artery that cause the artery to balloon, creating a space-occupying disorder. The weakness may be the result of a congenital disorder or of any processes which weaken the arterial walls. On the neuropsychological exam, aneurysms are seen as highly localized disorders without general effects on the brain as a whole. Consequently, the Impairment Index seen in such disorders is low, in the range of 0.4 to 0.6 (borderline condition).

Aneurysms can produce more significant disorders when they begin to hemorrhage. Such bleeding may be minor or a complete rupture. The minor bleeding will cause more severe neuropsychological results than seen with simple aneurysms, including suppressions and extreme depressions of localized abilities. However, the overall effect of the aneurysm on the brain as a whole is not greatly increased. When the aneurysm ruptures completely, the pattern is that of the severe hemorrhage described above.

Most aneurysms (about 50%) occur in the middle cerebral artery (Chusid, 1970). When symptoms of an aneurysm appear in a young adult or child, this is usually the result of a *congenital vascular anomaly*. These represent defects in the vascular walls present from birth. These vascular anomalies may remain undetected, or may begin to cause symptoms due to such factors as high blood pressure, as might any aneurysm.

EPILEPSY

At present, it is not possible to infer epilepsy from neuropsychological results. Epilepsy is often a secondary disorder caused by the irritation of other lesions. There is also a large class of epilepsies which are of unknown origin and labeled *idiopathic.* Matthews and Klove (1967, 1968; Klove and Matthews, 1966, 1969, 1974) have established that epileptic disorders with known causes show more severe deficits than those with unknown causes, as has Tarter (1972). In each case, the neuropsychological results seem to be measuring the underlying brain dysfunction rather than the epilepsy itself.

There are several major forms of epilepsy. *Temporal lobe epilepsy* is associated with disturbances of consciousness in which the person may compulsively perform highly organized acts, such as making a bed (Hansotia and Wadia, 1971). This may also be associated with emotional disorders and feelings, because of its common focus in the anterior temporal lobe (Garvin, 1953). Temporal lobe epilepsy with unknown causes generally shows normal neuropsychological behavior overall, although the pattern may suggest a temporal lobe focus. When there is a known cause, testing does indicate brain dysfunction in the temporal lobe area.

Petit mal epilepsy is accompanied by a loss of consciousness. The patient does not fall, but may pause and stare. Afterwards the patient may go on as if nothing had happened. Neuropsychological results here are similar to those found in temporal lobe epilepsy.

Grand mal epilepsy generally has an aura which warns the patient of a seizure. Generally, the type of aura is related to the focus of the seizure. The patient then becomes unconscious, falls to the ground, and often has a general convulsion. The patient's breathing may cease, and there can be foaming at the mouth or biting of the tongue. Generally, the neuropsychological deficits in major motor seizures are the most severe (Matthews and Klove, 1967).

Other forms of epilepsy include *reflex* and *sensory epilepsy;* the epilepsy is set off by a sensory event (Daube, 1965) and *jacksonian epilepsy,* where convulsions radiate from one small part of the body to the entire body.

Identification of neuropsychological factors that predict epilepsy has not yet been found. Some research on this topic is available (Dodrill and Wilkus, 1976). More research attempting to identify these neuropsychological components is continuing at present.

ALCOHOLISM

Chronic alcoholics of ten or more years have been reported to have significantly impaired neuropsychological abilities (Page and Lindin, 1974). The deficits appear to fall into three major categories. First, tests reflecting frontal lobe skill are generally down significantly (Chandler, Vega, and Parsons, 1973; Plutchik and DiScipio, 1974; Talland, 1959; Tarter, 1973, 1975). Secondly, there are disorders of emotion and memory. These are similar to those caused by limbic lobe disorders (Cermak, Butters, and Goodglass, 1971; Meissner, 1967; Talland, 1960; Tarter, 1973, 1975). Finally, there are a number of deficits characteristic of right brain disorders. These include a loss of spatial skills reflected in low scores on the performance tests of the Wechsler Adult Intelligence Test. Deficits are also seen on the Tactual Performance Test and Seashore Rhythm Test. There are also deficits on tests requiring drawing, such as the Bender-Gestalt or Benton Visual Retention Tests. There are also left-sided motor deficits (Page and Lindin, 1974; Tartar and Jones, 1971). The deficits are more severe, depending on how long a patient has been an alcoholic and how much alcohol s/he has consumed.

GENERALIZED DISORDERS

There are a number of neurological disorders resulting in generalized deterioration of brain function. One such disorder, arteriosclerosis, has already been discussed. Other major causes include brain atrophy, infectious diseases, and the presenile dementias, Alzheimer's and Pick's diseases.

Atrophy

Atrophy of the brain refers to the reduction of the size of the cerebral hemispheres, which may be caused by a number of processes, including aging. Atrophy is usually accompanied by enlargement of the ventricles, which act to partially fill the space left by the atrophy.

A number of studies have reported an association between intellectual deterioration and atrophy (Blessed, Tomlinson, and Roth, 1968; Gosling, 1955; Kaszniak et al., 1975; Kiev, Chapman, Guthrie, and Wolff, 1962; Matthews and Booker, 1972). However, there is a great deal of variation in the effects of atrophy on a single subject. In some cases, significant atrophy may result in little or no dysfunction, while in others minimal atrophy will produce striking deterioration.

One factor that may affect the relationship between atrophy and intellectual deterioration is the rate at which the atrophy proceeds. As was noted in the section on tumors, the effect of a lesion becomes more severe as the rate of growth of the lesion increases. Until recently, no determination of the rate of change in atrophy could be determined, since this would have required repeated pneumoencephalograms, a potentially dangerous and very painful process. Now, however, the introduction of the CAT scan provides a safe and quick method to make these determinations. As a consequence, it is likely that our knowledge of the effects of atrophy should increase dramatically over the next few years.

Infectious Disorders

A variety of infectious disorders may result in diffuse symptoms. The major disorders in this category are meningitis and encephalitis. *Meningitis* is due to an infection of the meninges. The disease may cause fever, vomiting, drowsiness, headache, or loss of consciousness. If not treated properly and promptly, death may occur. The intellectual deficits associated with meningitis are seen most often in children. Many patients receive proper treatment, and there is no permanent intellectual decline (Kaszniak, 1977).

Encephalitis is due to an infection of the brain caused by a virus or other disease agent. There are several different forms of encephalitis, including forms secondary to other infections. Some survivors of encephalitis later develop Parkinson-like symptoms (see the section below on Parkinson's disease).

Encephalitis presents symptoms similar to those of meningitis. As with meningitis, children are usually more seriously affected than adults.

Some brain infections may result in a focal rather than a diffuse impairment of the brain. These disorders generally form brain abscesses which were discussed earlier.

Alzheimer's Disease

Alzheimer's disease is the major cause of organic mental changes in the elderly (Rosenstock, 1970; Barrett, 1972). It is marked by a gradual loss of memory and disturbances in speech and spatial orientation in its early stage. This is followed by the disorientation of time and place. Finally, there is a total degeneration of personality and intellectual functions (Alzheimer, 1969; Bowen, Hoehn, and Yahr, 1972; Rosenstock, 1970; Sim and Sussman, 1962; Wilkins and Brody, 1969). Scores across all tests are generally low, with WAIS scores in the 60s or less. The Impairment Index is 1.0. Early forms of the disorder are marked by both short- and long-term memory loss (Miller, 1973) and a general lowering of all other scores.

Pick's Disease

Pick's disease is characterized by general atrophy as in Alzheimer's, but the major effects appear to involve the frontal and temporal lobes (Constantindis, Richard, and Tissot, 1974; Mitsuyama and Takamatsu, 1971). The course of the disease starts with memory and intellectual disturbance. There are also lapses in social conduct with either apathy or overactivity. In the later forms, the patient is reduced to mutism with all movement stereotyped and complete lack of cognitive behavior. The mutism is more characteristic of Pick's disease than it is of Alzheimer's. Like Alzheimer's, the disorder is marked by severe depression in neuropsychological tests. In a few early cases, the frontotemporal focus can be identified.

HYDROCEPHALUS

Hydrocephalus is the pathological enlargement of the brain's ventricles; it places pressure on and compresses brain tissue. It can arise out of a blockage in the ventricular system, called *obstructive hydrocephalus*. Hydrocephalus may result from a rise in the pressure of the cerebrospinal fluid, in which case it is called *communicating hydrocephalus*. A third form, *normal pressure hydrocephalus*, may occur without a blockage or rise in pressure. As yet, the reasons for normal pressure hydrocephalus are unclear. In infants, hydrocephalus may cause an enlargement of the head and compression of the brain, sometimes reducing it to a thin sheet on top of an enormous fluid balloon. Such cases often result in severe retardation, although the effects are inconsistent from child to child.

Hydrocephalus in the adult will generally show a diffuse picture, with generalized impairment relative to the degree of growth of the ventricles. No localizing signs will be found on the neurospychological tests. Motor disorders are often prominently seen, as well as visual problems.

PARKINSON'S DISEASE

Seven different forms of Parkinson's disease are currently recognized. All are caused by a disturbance of the extrapyramidal system and involve the biochemical balance of the brain. However, all researchers do not agree on the mechanisms (Robbins, 1974). All do not classify these seven disorders as Parkinson's disease, although they have similar symptoms.

The primary form of Parkinson's disease is *idiopathic*. At present, there is no known reason for its onset, which usually occurs after the age of fifty. *Postencephalitic* Parkinson's is an aftereffect of encephalitis, usually occurring earlier in life than primary Parkinsonism and generally progressing more slowly. This form is responsible for most cases of Parkinson's disease before the age of fifty. *Latrogenic* Parkinsonism is caused by antipsychotic medications, the phenothiazines. This form is usually reversible after the patient discontinues the drug or the patient's dosage is lowered. However, it can be permanent. *Juvenile* Parkinsonism generally occurs in young adults and is caused by a degeneration of the liver (Wilson's disease). Three additional forms of Parkinsonism can occur as a result of any neurological disorder involving the midbrain or basal nuclei (Duvoisin, 1976).

The course of Parkinson's disease reflects five stages. Initially, symptoms are usually mild and unilateral. There is often a tremor in the affected limb at rest. In the second stage the patient's overall pattern of movement is slow. The patient walks stooped over. The next stage includes a pronounced gait disturbance, a tendency to fall, and a generalized disability. In the fourth stage, the patient is significantly disabled; in the last, totally disabled.

Drawings on the neuropsychological test generally show a significant tremor in Parkinson's disease. The patient's writing and drawing tend to be very small in an attempt to correct for the tremor, *micrographia*. While the patient's IQ tends to be normal, the score on the Category Test tends to be down significantly (Reitan and Boll, 1971). Overall measures of motor and somatosensory control are down, and performance on tests generally sensitive to brain dysfunction is impaired. In the later stages of this disorder, all scores may be down, except for tasks such as vocabulary.

MULTIPLE SCLEROSIS

Multiple sclerosis (MS) is a degenerative disease of the myelin sheath covering nerve axons. It causes interferences in communications between cells. It primarily attacks the spinal cord and the brain stem. The sensory and motor symptoms arising from the disorder are often inconsistent, and the patient may have periods of exacerbation and remission. In multiple sclerosis, the verbal is significantly higher than the performance IQ. There is usually motor and tactile dysfunction, seen as low scores on such tests as Finger Tapping, the Tactual Performance Test, and tests of sensory deficits.These deficits can often be lateralized, but not necessarily in a consistent manner. There may be a mild cognitive deficit, with the patient showing a borderline score on the Category Test. Usually, no auditory deficits are seen, but visual disorders caused by involvement of the optic nerve may be present (Goldstein and Shelly, 1974; Matthews et al., 1970; Reitan et al., 1971; and Robbins, 1974).

Multiple sclerosis patients also show a typical elevation on the MMPI of the hypochondriasis and the hysteria scales (Hy, Hs) with depression being significantly lower. This is the typical conversion "V" on the MMPI profile characteristic of hysterical disorders. The examiner must be careful in this disease not to mistake the inconsistent deficits and the MMPI pattern as a hysterical disorder rather than MS (Cleeland et al., 1970).

CHRONICITY

The further delayed a test is from the actual time of injury to the patient, the less severe the results are likely to be on the neuropsychological exam. Most general indicators of brain injury, such as the Category Test, Trail Making Test, and the Impairment Index, will improve, although the performance will be distinguishable from normal performance (Fitzhugh et al., 1961, 1962). The specific, severe effects of the injury will also be less clear. The difference between the injured and intact side of the brain will diminish or may even disappear. Differences in the performance and verbal IQ's become much less predictable, and the two IQs will often be relatively equal.

Lateralizing signs will often be slight, although the pattern of the results will remain the same as after the injury. This, of course, does not hold for all injuries: Some patients, especially the older or more severely injured, may show little change in their test results, an obviously poor prognostic indication.

Generally, a chronic disorder can be diagnosed by the lack of severe signs on the generalized tests and the overall equality of the two brain hemispheres, despite evidence of a focal lesion involving one hemisphere. In some cases, a mild disorder, such as an aneurysm, will yield much the same pattern as the chronic picture of a more serious disorder. Although some disorders may be revealed by the presence of some acute signs, e.g. a speech deficit or loss in a measure that should have recovered, a thorough history is often needed to make a final determination.

Chapter 7

NEUROPSYCHOLOGICAL DIAGNOSIS
WITH CHILDREN

THERE HAS BEEN a great deal of controversy regarding the effects of brain injury on children. Some theorists emphasize the plasticity of the child's brain: the ability of uninjured areas to take over the functions of injured areas. Consequently, the effects of brain injury are expected to be less severe in children. Others have emphasized the importance of basic, early learning on development of later skills. Thus, brain injuries in children produce not only direct effects caused by lesions in a given area, but also affect the development of later cognitive skills.

The evaluation of children who have undergone hemispherectomies, complete removal of one cerebral hemisphere, has provided important research in this controversy. The research has indicated that the removal of one hemisphere in a young child, even if it is the language-dominant hemisphere, results in less speech impairment than is seen in adults who have the same hemisphere removed (Annett, 1973; Basser, 1962; Bruell and Albee, 1962; Geschwind, 1972; Hebb, 1942; Lansdell, 1969; Milner, 1974; Smith, 1975, 1976). These studies have demonstrated that it is possible for one side of the brain to take over the functions of the other side.

Researchers have also noted that children who have received hemispherectomies rarely obtain full scale IQs above the low 80s, some twenty points below what is expected of the normal population (Milner, 1974), although some cases with IQs well above normal have occasionally been reported (Smith, 1976). McFie (in DeRenzi and Piercy, 1969) has reported that children with hemispherectomies are impaired in both the skills mediated by the injured and by the intact hemisphere. It has been suggested that the impairment of the abilities related to the intact hemisphere may be due to the sacrifice of those skills in order to allow the takeover of the functions of the impaired hemisphere.

More recent research has established that the takeover phe-

148

nomenon is the exception rather than the rule in childhood injuries. Takeover by the opposite hemisphere appears to occur only in very young children with large lesions that involve a substantial part of one hemisphere, but leave the opposite hemisphere intact (DeRenzi and Piercy, 1969; Reed and Reitan, 1969). As Strich (in DeRenzi and Piercy, 1969) has observed, such lesions are rare in children with injuries discovered at or shortly after birth. As a result, the importance of this takeover phenomenon is generally not as applicable to a clinical population as it is to a surgical population.

The alternate theory suggests the effects of a brain injury appear to be most severe in younger children. Boll (1976) found that children with brain damage at the age of five to seven were generally less impaired than children with brain damage at the age of two to four. In turn, each of these groups showed fewer deficits than children with injuries during the first two years of life (Boll, 1976; Dikmen, Matthews, and Harley, 1975). The older the age at which the child is injured, the more the deficits resemble those of the adult (Reed et al., 1965; Reed and Reitan, 1969).

In early childhood injuries, the basic functional systems fail to develop, interrupting the development of more complex abilities (Luria, 1966). In the adult who has already established the major functional systems, brain injury only affects those abilities directly associated with the injured area. In addition, the adult is able to compensate by the use of alternate functional systems, as may an older child. Thus the child with early brain injury will often show a generalized deficit in abilities regardless of the primary locus of the injury.

These results have several implications for diagnosing injuries of early childhood. A level-of-performance approach is an inadequate diagnostic approach with children. The general decline in scores seen with injured children may be indistinguishable from other conditions, such as mental retardation or developmental delay. Injuries in diverse areas may cause generalized depression of scores. Only through an analysis of the pattern of the scores can the presence and localization of a brain injury be inferred. The identification of the basic deficits underlying the general loss of ability is important, both for localizing the circumscribed disorders and in planning rehabilitation programs.

The present chapter will first examine some of the tests used in children's evaluations and then present some of the deficit patterns seen with neurological disorders common to children.

SINGLE DIAGNOSTIC TESTS

Spatial Tests

Most of the spatial tests described in Chapter 4 are also available in forms for children. The test itself may be changed, as in the case of Block Design, or children's normative data employed, as in the case of the drawing tests. These spatial tests have been found to be effective in differentiating normal and brain-injured groups. However, their prediction rate is not high enough for individualized diagnosis (Reitan, 1974b).

Of the drawing tests available for adults, the Benton Visual Retention Test and the Bender-Gestalt have been used widely with children. Canter (1976) and his associates have employed the background interference procedure with the Bender-Gestalt in child populations. As with the adult research, there have been a number of positive studies (Adams and Canter, 1969; Adams, Kenny, and Canter, 1973; Benton, 1963, 1974; Benton, et al., 1967; Canter, 1976; Kenny, 1971; Koppitz, 1958, 1962, 1964; McConnell, 1967) as well as negative studies (Chorost, Spivack, and Levine, 1959; Friedman, Strochak, Gitlin, and Gottsegen, 1967; Shaw and Cruickshank, 1956). Studies attempting to relate visual-motor performance to reading achievement have generally failed, with few correlations exceeding 0.4 (Friedrich and Fuller, 1974; Giebink and Birch, 1970; Smith and Keogh, 1962; Thweatt, 1963; Welcher, et al., 1974; Wetzel, Welcher, and Mellitis, 1971). In many respects, the results from these studies are similar to the results seen in studies with adults.

From the research, it can be concluded that the spatial tests are almost as effective with children as they are with adults, when children's normative data is employed. However, none of these tests provide enough accuracy for use as a single screening test, although inclusion of spatial skill measures would appear to be an important part of any test battery for children.

Verbal Tests

Many aphasia tests have been adapted for children as well as adults. In general, these tests are identical to the adult versions, except that simpler items are included for younger children. The effectiveness of a given item depends upon a child's age, grade level, and training. For example, a test for writing skills cannot be employed until the child is taught to write. Consequently, a pathological dysgraphia cannot be diagnosed in younger children. Such problems limit the localizing value of many tests in younger children. In a number of children, there is often the problem of determining whether the child performs poorly because of inadequate schooling, due to educational or personal problems, or because of a brain injury.

The *Illinois Test of Psycholinguistic Abilities* was devised by Kirk, McCarthy, and Kirk (1961, 1968) as a method of evaluating verbal deficits in children. The research on this test, however, has not been encouraging. In general, subtests purporting to identify specific deficiencies have been found to be very unreliable (Burns and Watson, 1973; Waugh, 1975). The subtests do not appear to measure separate abilities as suggested by the authors, nor have remediation programs derived from the pattern of subtest scores proven to be successful (Waugh, 1975). At best, this test appears to yield only a measure of general verbal skills (Hallahan and Cruickshank, 1973).

The *Frostig Test* was originally developed to aid in the diagnosis of neurologically handicapped, learning-disabled children (Frostig, Lefever, and Whittlesey, 1961). This study reported a failure to discriminate between learning-disabled and normal children in terms of scores on specific subtests, although learning-disabled children demonstrated more subtest scatter. While the measure of scatter could discriminate at a reasonable level between children who were fully normal and children with severe deficits, the test was ineffective with children who fall in between these extremes.

In addition, the Frostig subtests have been found to measure general verbal skills rather than specific deficits. Black (1974a) found that when the IQ was controlled, the Frostig failed to relate to academic achievement. Others have concluded that the profile analysis used with the Frostig was ineffective, because of the unreliability of the subtests and their tendency to measure the same underlying factor (Hammill et al., 1970; Sabatino et al., 1974). After an extensive review of the research on the Frostig, Hallahan and Cruickshank (1973) concluded that "extreme caution should accompany use of . . . (the Frostig) . . . to differentiate specific aspects of a child's perceptual functioning" (p. 87).

With both the Frostig and the Illinois Test of Psycholinguistic Abilities, careful consideration should be given before using any of the rehabilitation tasks accompanying the tests. In both these tests, the training tasks tend to provide specific practice on the type of items the evaluation test includes. Consequently, evaluation after rehabilitation only demonstrates that a child can be taught to do the test, not gain a generalized skill that will aid the child in other areas (Hallahan and Cruickshank, 1973). (The requirements for designing effective rehabilitation programs are discussed in Chapters 9 and 10.)

WECHSLER INTELLIGENCE SCALE FOR CHILDREN (WISC)

This test represents the children's version (ages six to fifteen) of the Wechsler Adult Intelligence Scale. Originally introduced by Wechsler (1949), the test has been substantially revised (Wechsler, 1974). The newer version of the test, the Wechsler Intelligence Test for Children-Revised (WISC-R), has supplanted the WISC to a large extent. However, almost all the published research in neuropsychology has been with the WISC. The WISC-R tends to give somewhat lower IQs than the WISC, because the WISC-R normative data indicates that children today show stronger skills than their counterparts in 1949.

The WISC and WISC-R have the same subtests as the WAIS, except that the items have been made simpler. In addition, one new subtest has been added, Mazes. This test requires the child to use a pencil to draw a pathway through printed mazes that increase progressively in difficulty. The scale scores, verbal IQ (VIQ), performance IQ (PIQ), and full-scale IQs are calculated in the same manner as on the WAIS. However, Digit Span is not included when figuring the verbal IQ. Excellent age-norms are provided for determining the child's scale scores (Wechsler, 1974).

Reitan (1974b) has reported that brain-injured children show more of an overall decrease on the WISC IQs than on any other measure. The WISC subtests are, in general, much more sensitive to early brain lesions than the WAIS subtests are to lesions in adults. Reitan has listed the WISC subtests in terms of sensitivity to brain injury: Mazes, Object Assembly, Similarities, Information, Coding (Digit Symbol), Vocabulary, Picture Arrangement, Comprehension, Block Design, Arithmetic, Picture Completion, and Digit Span. The order of sensitivity is nearly the reverse of that found with adults. Other studies have reported similar findings (Boll, 1974; Reed et al., 1965).

Differences between the performance and verbal IQs are less important in children. If the verbal IQ exceeds the performance IQ by twenty-five or more points, then brain damage may be indicated (Gubbay, Ellis, Walton, and Court, 1965; Holroyd and Wright, 1965; Rourke and Telegdy, 1971; Rourke, Young, and Flewelling, 1971). Investigators working with epileptic children have not found the PIQ-VIQ difference to be diagnostic (Hartlage and Green, 1972; Rourke, Dietrich, and Young, 1973). Overall, it appears that very large differences in favor of the verbal IQ are diagnostically significant. However, smaller differences or differences in favor of the performance IQ are common in both normal and brain-injured populations. Differences in favor of the performance IQ are especially common in cultural groups that do not speak standard English at home, e.g., American Indian or Chicano populations.

HALSTEAD-REITAN TESTS FOR CHILDREN

There are two versions of the Halstead-Reitan Neuropsychological Battery for Children. The Halstead Neuropsychological Test Battery for Children is designed for patients aged nine to fourteen, while the Reitan-Indiana Neuropsychological Test Battery for Children is designed for children between five and eight years, although it has been used with children as young as two years (Klonoff and Low, 1974; Reitan, 1959c; Reitan and Davison, 1974). Normative data for these tests may be found in Klonoff and Low (1974), Spreen and Gaddes (1969), and Hughes (1976).

Halstead Battery for Children

This battery uses many of the same tests as does the adult battery, although several of the tests have been simplified for children. The battery includes a shorter version of the Category Test. The Trail Making Test has fifteen rather than twenty-five circles. On Speech Sounds Perception, the patient must choose from three rather than four alternatives. The Tactual Performance Test uses a six- rather than ten-figure form board. As with the adult battery, the instructions are given so that the child clearly understands what is to be done (Reitan and Davison, 1974).

In some older children, there is an inability to read, making it difficult for the child to do the Speech Sounds Perception Test, even when the child's ability to discriminate phonemes is intact. Matthews (1974) has suggested using the *Boston University Speech Sound Discrimination Picture Test* (Pronovost and Dumbleton, 1953) in such situations. This test consists of thirty-six cards, each showing three subsets of pictures, e.g. a cat and a bat in one picture, two cats in the second, and two bats in the third. The subject listens to a tape recorder instructing him/her to point to the pair indicated by the tape. Matthews (1974) has also suggested using this test with younger children not yet able to read.

Reitan-Indiana Children's Battery

This battery consists of several tests from the adult battery, modified for young children, as well as a number of newly developed tests (Reitan, 1959c; Reitan and Davison, 1974). The modified tests include children's versions of the Category Test, Tactual Performance Test, Aphasia Exam, Perceptual Exam, and the Finger Tapping Test. The new tests include the Marching Test, Color Form Test, Progressive Figures Test, Matching Pictures Test, Target Test, and Individual Performance Tests (Reitan, 1959c).

The *Marching Test* was included as a test of gross motor control. The child must connect a series of circles with a crayon in a given order with the right hand and left hand alone. In a second procedure, the child must reproduce the examiner's finger and arm movements. The examiner alternates his movements between the right and left hands, marching his fingers away from the child.

The *Color Form Test* provides a measure of flexibility and abstraction (Reitan and Davison, 1974). On this test the child must connect colored shapes, first by color and then by shape. This color-shape alternation is similar to the letter-number alternation seen on the Trail Making Test. The *Progressive Figures Test* attempts to measure similar abilities. The subject must connect several figures, each consisting of a small shape contained within a large shape. The subject connects the figures first by noting the inside shape on the first figure, which indicates which outer shape to look for. For example, if a triangle were enclosed within a square, the subject would progress to a triangle which enclosed another shape. The shape within the triangle would then indicate the next item. This test is somewhat more difficult than the Color Form Test.

The *Matching Pictures Test* requires subjects to match figures at the top of a page with figures at the bottom of the page. At first, the figures at the top and the bottom are identical and easy to match. Later, the subject must match such items as a candle and a light.

The *Target Test* requires the patient to reproduce a visually presented pattern after a three-second delay. The pattern involves connecting some of the dots on a nine-dot (three by three) grid. The reproduction is done on a smaller version of the grid which the subject is given. Items become more complex as the test progresses. This test measures visual memory, as well as visual-spatial skills.

The *Individual Performance Test* includes several measures of visual-spatial skills. First, the subject must match several

"Vs" by the size of the angle at the vertex of each V. A second task involves the matching of different complex figures. A third test requires the subject to draw a series of concentric squares. The last task involves copying a six-pointed star made up of two triangles. In each of the drawing tasks, the subject is told how the figures were constructed and asked to draw them in a similar manner.

Validation Studies with the Children's Batteries

The children's batteries have received less experimental verification than the adult Halstead-Reitan. The studies which have been completed are quite positive in evaluating the effectiveness of the tests (Boll, 1974b; Boll and Reitan, 1972, 1973; Klonoff and Low, 1974; Klonoff, Robinson, and Thompson, 1969; Reitan, 1974a and b). For example, Klonoff and his associates (1969) reported hit rates ranging from 80 percent in three-year-olds to 96 percent in eight-year-olds, using the battery as a whole. Klonoff and Low (1974) reported overall hit rates of 80 percent in normal children and 75 percent in brain-injured patients under the age of nine. With children over nine years, they reported a hit rate of 90 percent in normal and 80 percent in brain-injured children. Each of these studies used discriminative analysis to determine hit rates.

As was seen with the WISC, the tests most sensitive to brain injury in adults are not the tests most sensitive in younger children. Of the younger children's tests, the most sensitive are measures of tactile perception, the Progressive Figures Test, the Marching Test, and the Color Form Test. The Category Test, the most sensitive of the adult tests, is only moderately effective. Of all the tests the Tactual Performance Test was the least effective, especially the Location score (Reitan, 1974b).

In older children, the most effective tests were the Trail Making Test, name writing speed, motor skills, and the Speech Sounds Perception Test. The least effective were measures of tactile sensitivity and the Tactual Performance Test (Boll, 1974). In both younger and older children, the overall WISC measures and many of the WISC subtests were as effective as the Halstead-Reitan tests. In adults, the Halstead-Reitan tests are usually found to be more sensitive than most of the WAIS measures.

DIAGNOSIS OF BRAIN INJURY IN CHILDREN

Unlike adults, brain-injured children may have had little or no opportunity to show that they are capable of normal levels of performance. As a consequence, while the level of performance deficits may be associated with brain injury, they may also be caused by a number of other factors, such as low intelligence, developmental delays, and cultural differences. Under these circumstances, a pattern-of-performance approach offers a much more effective and accurate method of diagnosing brain injury in children. Level-of-performance indicators should be used only to establish the severity of a condition that is identified by other methods.

LATERALIZATION AND LOCALIZATION

The procedure used in lateralizing and localizing brain injuries in children is identical to that used with the adult. However, several additional factors need to be recognized. First, major localized lesions are much less common in children than in adults. Many disorders of early childhood are much more likely to produce diffuse disorders.

Second, all deficits from chronic childhood disorders are subsequently affected by later training. Since schools and parents tend to concentrate on teaching verbal rather than spatial skills, a mixed pattern of recovery may be seen. In these children, consistent sensory or motor deficits are more helpful in diagnosing the correct lateralization than are cognitive deficits.

Third, the age at which the injury has occurred affects the pattern of deficits. The older a child is when injured, the nearer the pattern will approach those seen in adults. Earlier injuries tend to produce severe deficits on such measures as Vocabulary, Comprehension, Information, and Achievement Tests, the adult "hold" tests. To a certain extent, there may be more "takeover" of functions in younger children, depending on the factors discussed at the beginning of this chapter. In these cases, the cognitive symptoms will be bilateral and the overall IQ generally low.

Sensory and motor signs are again effective in helping to establish laterality.

Fourth, the neuropsychologist must be careful to judge the performance of each child against appropriate normative samples. Scores on all of the tests discussed, including motor and sensory exams, change with age. Symptoms which are pathognomic signs at one age may represent normal performance at a younger age. Consequently, the use of inadequate norms can produce incorrect conclusions.

Finally, it is important to differentiate between the factors that are the direct results of brain injury and those that are secondary results caused by the emotional and behavioral problems a child may develop. For example, a child with a severe verbal deficit may fail to have established the ability to follow instructions. This, in turn, can cause a number of apparent deficits across all tested skills. Behavioral and emotional problems can similarly interfere with the child's performance. Often the diagnosis of the extent of a child's basic deficits must await rehabilitation programs to treat deficits in these basic areas.

Overall, these factors cause the results from children to be much less precise, even when the lesion itself is closely circumscribed. Thus, the neuropsychologist must depend on an analysis by the weight of the total evidence. Such an analysis is extremely important for the proper treatment of the child.

NEUROLOGICAL DISORDERS IN CHILDREN

Except for some of the disorders of old age, most of the neurological disorders seen in adults may be seen in children, although such problems as tumors or cerebrovascular disease are rare. There are, however, several disorders which are seen and diagnosed primarily in children.

Birth Trauma

Birth trauma is a general term referring to many disorders that can affect a child before, during, and immediately after birth. In general, a diffuse brain injury of any kind before a child acquires speech can produce symptoms similar to those to be described. The causes of birth trauma include head trauma, genetic disorders, anoxia, encephalitis, meningitis, and nutritional deficiencies or other metabolic disorders that began in the child or in the pregnant mother.

Reed and Fitzhugh (1966) found in these cases that there was significant impairment in tasks demanding stored memory, such as Vocabulary or Achievement Tests, rather than in those demanding immediate, adaptive ability, such as the Tactual Performance Test. The most severely impaired score is the full-scale IQ on the WISC (Reitan, 1974b). Sensory and motor signs are usually present bilaterally. It is not unusual for these children to be mixed dominant: Left-handers in this group are often right brain dominant for speech (Milner, 1975).

In these disorders, the underlying deficits are usually quite basic, involving perceptual input and the integrative functions of the secondary areas. As the child grows up, the test scores generally fall farther and farther behind those of the child's age-group. If s/he is tested as an adult, there is clear evidence of a failure to establish the higher cognitive skills of the tertiary areas (Luria, 1966).

Turner's Syndrome

This is a genetic disease that has received attention from neuropsychologists. The patient in these cases is always female. She shows deficits in intelligence (Money, 1964), with especially poor performance on Block Design and Object Assembly. There are also deficits on the Bender-Gestalt, the Benton Visual Retention Test and map reading, as well as evidence of construction apraxia (Alexander and Money, 1966; Money, Alexander, and Erhardt, 1966; Money and Granoff, 1965). The patient may show superior reading and verbal abilities compared to spatial abilities (Money et al., 1965). Money (1973) has suggested that in the main, this disorder is similar to a lesion of the right parietal area in the adult. When a female child presents the pattern of a localized right parietal disorder of long standing without appropriate physical findings, or history, referral to a skilled physician knowledgeable in genetic disorders should be made.

Learning Disabilities

The area of learning disabilities has begun to attract a great deal of attention within neuropsychology. Many definitions of learning disabilities have stressed the role of cerebral dysfunction. For example, Hallahan and Cruickshank (1973) have written that "the problems of a great majority of children described as 'learning disabled' . . . are fundamentally based in neurological function or dysfunction." Although others have disagreed with this idea (Ross, 1976), an overwhelming amount of evidence has shown that as a group, youngsters identified as learning disabled show a significant number of neurological and neuropsychological deficits (Benton, 1964; Black, 1976; Bowley, 1969; Clements, 1966; Cohn, 1961; Cole and Kraft, 1963; Crinella, 1973; Denhoff, Hainsworth, and Hainsworth, 1972; Eisenson, 1968; Gaddes, 1968; Gubbay et al., 1965; Hartlage, 1973; Hertzig et al., 1969; Hinton and Knights, 1971; Kinsbourne and Warrington, 1963; Pontius, 1973; Reitan and Boll, 1973; Rourke et al., 1973; Walker, 1965).

Although such studies do not establish that *all* learning-disabled children have neurological deficits, the research clearly indicates that a significant percentage of learning-disabled children have patterns of deficits identical to those expected in certain types and loci of brain injury (Rourke, 1975). Rourke's (1975) review of the clinical research has established that such children can be identified through neuropsychological evaluation. In addition, it is believed that learning-disabled children can benefit from remedial programs based on such evaluations (Golden, 1977).

The deficits shown by learning-disabled children vary considerably, though the overall test patterns of these children have many factors in common. First, the overall level of performance is good in these children. One does not see the general loss of skills associated with early, diffuse brain trauma.

Second, the pattern of results implies a focal lesion somewhere in the child's brain. As a rule, this lesion involves the left hemisphere, but only because teachers and parents are much more likely to refer the child with left hemisphere language problems than the child with right hemisphere disabilities.

Third, the cognitive deficits are accompanied by appropriate motor or sensory deficits consistent with the focal area of the brain involved in the hypothesized lesion. This is an important consideration, since these lateralizing motor and sensory deficits establish that there is more involved than just a cognitive disorder. Otherwise, there is a tendency to assume every time there is a deficit, e.g. in reading, there must be a brain lesion. This avoids the fallacious circular reasoning that all deficits must imply a lesion, and a lesion is the cause of all deficits.

Finally, it must be recognized that, just because a child has or had a neurological problem, this does not mean that any or all of the deficits shown by the child are the result of the neurological disorder. The deficits must be consistent with the cause and locus of the lesion before such a conclusion can be reached. There is too often a tendency to use a history of a neurological problem or an electroencephalograph (EEG) abnormality to explain away what are actually emotional or behavioral problems.

Once a neurologically handicapped, disabled child has been identified, it is important to specify the areas in which the child is impaired, as well as the areas of strength that the child possesses. This information can then be used to set up individualized rehabilitation and educational programs for such children (see Chapter 9).

Cerebral Palsy

Cerebral palsy refers to brain lesions, usually during the first years of life, resulting in motor disorders. It is not a single disorder but represents lesions in widely different parts of the brain, including the cerebral hemispheres, brain stem, and cerebellum. The disorders of muscle control can range from very slightly impaired control to conditions where there is no effective control of the limbs.

There are five major types of cerebral palsy, although mixed types are not uncommon. These types include patients with tense, contracted muscles; uncontrolled movement; rigid muscles; poor sense of balance; and tremor. All types may or may not include cognitive impairment. If such cognitive deficits are present, they may implicate any area of the brain. Although neuropsychological techniques and evaluations as described in this book have not been used extensively with cerebral palsied children and adults, they are potentially valuable in isolating specific dysfunctions that might further handicap the cerebral palsied patient, or in pointing out strengths valuable to the patient. Some rehabilitation techniques devised in neuropsychology (*see* Chapter 10) are also potentially valuable to these individuals.

There are some problems involved in testing the cerebral palsied patient. In many cases, motor disorders can be quite serious, making it difficult for the patient to complete the tests requiring motor manipulation. As noted in the discussion of adults with peripheral movement problems, such patients can be tested by substituting tests of spatial, verbal, and other cognitive skills, which do not require extensive motor responses. In addition, some tests may be adapted to eliminate the motor component. In each of these cases, the neuropsychologist should be careful in the interpretations assigned to test results under these conditions (*see* Chapter 3).

CONCLUSIONS

The diagnosis and evaluation of children has much in common with adult neuropsychology. The examiner must be aware of the differential effects of brain injury on children, as well as different instruments that must be employed; however, the processes involved in reaching decisions are identical. As we have seen, child neuropsychology is a less-developed field than adult neuropsychology. The full development of diagnostic approaches with children remains a major research task within clinical neuropsychology.

Chapter 8

CASE EXAMPLES OF NEUROPSYCHOLOGICAL DIAGNOSIS

A S CAN BE SEEN from the preceding chapters, a great number of decisions must be made in the neurodiagnostic process. Test results must be analyzed for the effect of many interacting variables. Although many of the rules which govern this process can be specified, extensive experience is necessary with patients and test protocols before the process may be completely learned. The cases in this chapter have been chosen both to illustrate some of the principles and procedures discussed in the last four chapters, as well as some problems in diagnosis. Brain damage ranges for the tests used are indicated in Table 8-I.

CASE 1: F.R.

F.R. was a sixty-six-year-old, right-handed male with a seventh-grade education. He was referred for neuropsychological testing

TABLE 8-I

BRAIN DAMAGE RANGES FOR NEUROPSYCHOLOGICAL TESTS

Test	Brain Damage Range
Category Test*	> 51 errors
Tactual Performance Test (Total Time)*	> 15.7 minutes
Memory*	< 6 blocks
Location*	< 5 blocks
Rhythm*	> 5 errors
Speech Perception*	> 7 errors
Trail Making Test (Part A)	> 39 seconds
Trail Making Test (Part B)	> 91 seconds
Finger Tapping (dominant hand)*	< 50
Finger Tapping (nondominant hand)	< 46
Impairment Index†	> 0.4

* These norms were adapted from Reitan (1959); Halstead (1947); and Russell, Neuringer, and Goldstein (1970).

† The Impairment Index is the number of key tests in the brain-damaged range divided by 7. The key tests are indicated by preceding stars in the above table. For finger tapping, the hand with the poorest performance was used in the Index.

163

because of a gradual loss of sensation in his right side over the preceding three weeks. The neuropsychological exam was part of a more extensive neurological investigation.

Table 8-II presents the patient's test results. As can be seen from general indicators, the patient's performance was quite impaired. He missed 120 items on the Category Test. He was unable to place all ten blocks of the Tactual Performance Test on any of the trials: He failed to remember the location or shape of any of the forms on the Tactual Performance Test.

TABLE 8-II

RESULTS FOR F.R.

(Male, sixty-six, right-handed seventh-grade education)

Wechsler Adult Intelligence Scale		Tactual Performance Test	
Information	7	Left	10:00 (2 blocks in)
Comprehension	7	Left	10:00 (2 blocks)
Arithmetic	6	Left	10:00 (2 blocks)
Similarities	6	Memory	1
Digit Span	2	Location	0
Vocabulary	6		
Digit Symbol	0	*Trail Making Test*	
Picture Completion	6		
Object Assembly	3	Part A	84 seconds
Block Design	3	Part B	discontinued
Picture Arrangement	6	*Category* (errors)	120
Verbal IQ	81		
Performance IQ	79	*Finger Agnosia*	
Full-scale IQ	79	Right (errors)	9
Peabody Picture Vocabulary		Left (errors)	0
IQ	88	*Fingertip Number Writing*	
Speech Perception (errors)	36	Right (errors)	11
		Left (errors)	5
Rhythm (errors)	13	*Tactile Form Recognition*	
Finger Tapping		Right (errors)	0
Right	0	Left (errors)	1
Left	37	*MMPI:*	normal
		Impairment Index	1.0

Aphasia symptoms: dysnomia, spelling dyspraxia, dysgraphia, dyslexia, dyscalculia, dysarthria, construction dyspraxia.
Dominance: right hand, right foot, left eye.
Suppressions: right hand, right ear.

He earned an Impairment Index of 1.0, indicating all tests on which the index is based were impaired. He also showed severely depressed performance on the Wechsler tests most sensitive to brain damage, the Digit Symbol and Digit Span Tests.

In examining the scores for laterality, several are outstanding. The right-hand tapping was highly impaired, compared to the left hand. The right hand was also more impaired on all tests of tactile sensitivity (Finger Agnosia, Fingertip Number Writing, Tactile Form Recognition). The patient was unable to do the Tactual Performance Test with his right hand. He also showed reliable suppressions on the right hand and in the right ear. Trails A was slow, but the patient was unable to finish Trails B. Both the speech perception and rhythm tests were down severely. The patient had numerous signs of aphasia. All of these signs indicate left brain involvement.

However, not all the scores were consistent with this lateralization. The patient was severely depressed on the WAIS Object Assembly and Block Design. He showed overall impairment on the Tactual Performance Test with no improvement across trials. F.R. demonstrated severe construction dyspraxia when attempting to draw a Greek cross. Finally, the expected difference in the performance and verbal IQs that should accompany a severe lateralized left brain deficit was missing. All of these signs suggest the possibility of right brain involvement as well.

Overall, it must be recognized that the lesion in the left hemisphere is clearly more severe. It also appears to be localized in the left temporoparietofrontal area. There is not a complete loss of speech skills, however, which suggests that the parietal involvement may be limited. It should be observed that the patient's WAIS scores on Vocabulary, Comprehension, and Similarities Tests suggest relatively good communication for a subject with little education.

It is likely, given this evidence, that there is possibly a fast-growing tumor in the left frontotemporoparietal area. This is based on the localization of the deficit, the severe effects overall, as well as the suppressions and complete loss of motor movement in the right arm. A secondary possibility would be a hemorrhage. Both of these possibilities, however, fail to account for the right brain disorder. The right brain deficits discussed above imply a clear focal deficit in the right posterior parietal lobe. Although a tumor may cause secondary pressure effects, it is unlikely that such effects would yield results indicating a circumscribed lesion. A second hemorrhage might be postulated, but the data do not fit such a case. Alternatively, an aneurysm would probably produce less dramatic results. Another likelihood would be a second tumor, one that was smaller than the first but still expanding at a fairly fast rate. Considering the overall pattern of results, the possibility of such an incipient tumor appears the most likely. The presence of multiple tumors suggests that the source is likely tumors metastasized from elsewhere in the body.

Neurological Report

Initially, an angiogram indicated only the left frontotemporo-parietal tumor. It was presumed to be metastatic because the patient had a prior history of lung cancer. After the neuropsychological report was finished, a CAT scan was requested that confirmed the presence of the second, right parietal tumor, which was, at that point, considerably smaller than the left hemisphere tumor. In the following weeks, the right parietal tumor expanded rapidly giving clearer signs. The patient was given radiological therapy in hopes of slowing the growth of the tumors.

CASE 2: M.M.

M.M. was a thirty-eight-year-old, right-handed male who was complaining of severe headaches and vomiting. The initial diagnosis was a probable tumor, but this had not yet been confirmed. Neuropsychological testing was requested as part of the diagnostic process. M.M.'s results are reported in Table 8-III.

M.M.'s score on the Category Test was normal, although just below the cutoff point. His scores on the Tactual Performance Test, Location, and Trails B were all within the normal range. There was a normal performance on all the tests developed by Halstead. The only deficit on the WAIS was a low score on Digit Span, possibly due to the patient's tendency to be distracted easily. Overall, the performance was so good as to argue against any kind of tumor or space occupying disorder.

TABLE 8-III
RESULTS FOR M.M.
(Male, thirty-eight, right-handed, twelfth-grade education)

Wechsler Adult Intelligence Scale		*Tactual Performance Test*	
Information	9	Right	3′ 35″
Comprehension	14	Left	2′ 57″
Arithmetic	13	Both	1′ 23″
Similarities	9	Memory	7
Digit Span	7	Location	5
Vocabulary	12		
Digit Symbol	14	*Category* (errors)	48
Picture Completion	10	*Trail Making Test*	
Block Design	12		
Picture Arrangement	10	Part A	27″
Object Assembly	11	Part B	50″
Verbal IQ	104		
Performance IQ	114	*Speech Perception* (errors)	5
Full-scale IQ	109	*Rhythm* (errors)	2
Impairment Index	0	*Tapping Test*	
		Right	54
		Left	50
Aphasia symptoms: none.			
Sensory symptoms: none.			

Neurological Report

The neurological tests were completed on this patient, including CAT scan. All tests were normal. The final diagnosis was one of severe depression with hypochondriacal symptoms. The patient was referred for psychiatric treatment.

CASE 3: P.S.

P.S. was a twenty-two-year-old, right-handed female with one year of college. The referral was for assessment of residual brain damage after a car accident that had happened five months prior to the testing. The patient had been at home for three and one-half months after being discharged from the hospital.

The results for P.S. are listed in Table 8-IV. The overall IQ showed a great drop from the intelligence levels expected of a normal college student. The Category Test score was borderline,

Clinical Neuropsychology

TABLE 8-IV

RESULTS FOR P.S.

(Female, twenty, right-handed, one year college)

Wechsler Adult Intelligence Scale		Tactual Performance Test	
Information	8	Right	10′ 10″
Comprehension	7	Left	6′ 30″
Arithmetic	7	Both	5′ 00″
Similarities	10	Memory	8
Digit Span	4	Location	7
Vocabulary	7		
Digit Symbol	6	Category (errors)	52
Picture Completion	9	Rhythm (errors)	10
Block Design	5		
Picture Arrangement	4	Speech Perception (errors)	4
Object Assembly	7		
Verbal IQ	86	Tapping Test	
Performance IQ	76		
Full-scale IQ	81	Right	41
		Left	25

Peabody Picture Vocabulary		
Test (IQ)	67	Trail Making Test

	Part A	36″
Tactile Form Recognition	Part B	252″

Right (errors)	1	Finger Agnosia	
Left (errors)	0		
		Right (errors)	4
Grip Strength		Left (errors)	3

Right (kg)	21	Fingertip Number Writing	
Left (kg)	16		
		Right (errors)	3
Impairment Index	.72	Left (errors)	0

Aphasia symptoms: mild dysnomia, right-left disorientation, reversal of key drawings, mild construction dyspraxia.

but indicative of brain dysfunction. The overall Tactual Performance Test time was well into the brain-injured range, as was the Impairment Index, Location score, and the Trail Making Test (Part B). All of these indicators suggested that there was moderate brain dysfunction remaining.

A number of signs pointed to a right brain focus. On the WAIS, the performance score was ten IQ points below the verbal score. The patient's lowest scores were on Digit Span (where digits backward was much worse than digits forward), Picture Arrangement, and Block Design. The Rhythm Test was significantly impaired, while the Speech Sounds Perception Test performance was normal. The left hand was considerably reduced (39%) in tapping speed compared to the right hand, although both hands were slow. There were signs of left-hand deficits on Fingertip Number Writing, while the right-hand performance remained normal. The left hand was also some 24 percent weaker than the right hand, although both were considerably below the mean for college women on our instrument (45 kg). P.S. also had mild construction dyspraxia, including a reversal of her key drawing on the aphasia test.

There were a number of good right brain scores as well: The left hand on the Tactual Performance Test performed quite well compared to the right hand; the Trail Making Test (Part A) was within normal limits; the memory score of the Tactual Performance Test was quite good; and the left hand on the Tactile Form Recognition (astereognosis) test was normal.

There were also signs of left brain involvement. P.S. showed several aphasia symptoms, although none of them were severe. Her receptive vocabulary, as measured by the Peabody Picture Vocabulary Test, was also down considerably. This suggested a problem in attaching names to pictures. The decrease in the verbal IQ from her expected level was also indicative of left brain involvement. She missed one item on the right hand of the tactile form recognition test. There was a slight impairment of the right hand on the Tactual Performance Test as compared to the left hand. The Finger Agnosia score suggested somewhat more impairment on the right hand than the left hand, although the difference was not large enough to suggest any localization. Trails B was severely impaired, compared to Trails A, which was normal.

In conclusion, then, the overall pattern of results indicates diffuse brain impairment. However, there was a more severe focal area in the right frontotemporal area. This was seen through the greater impairment in left finger tapping than on the left-hand Tactual Performance Test. There were relatively good scores on Object Assembly and the sensory tests. There were also good scores on Trails A and the Memory score of the Tactual Performance Test. There was only mild construction dyspraxia and good learning across trials on the Tactual Performance Test. All of these argue against a primary focus in the parietal area. In addition, the severe impairment in Rhythm and Picture Arrangement (the lowest WAIS score) and Digits backwards argue for an anterior right brain focus.

In the left brain, the deficits were primarily in the parietal area. The right hand of the Tactual Performance was worse than expected when compared to the Finger Tapping Test. There were mild dysphasia symptoms, tactile errors, and both expressive and receptive vocabulary problems. Auditory reception was normal on Speech Sounds Perception. The severe deficits on Trails B suggested a difficulty in handling verbal symbols. The relatively good Category Test argues against a focus in the left frontal lobe. Indeed, the Category Test is normal for a person with an IQ score of 81. It is likely that the primary focus of the head injury was either in the right anterior or left posterior areas with the countrecoup effects responsible for the deficits in the opposite hemisphere.

Neurological Report

The neurological report noted that P.S. was struck above the right eye during a car accident. She has severe surface lacerations in that area and the right side of her face with no other external evidence of trauma.

CASE 4: K.L.

K.L. was a right-handed, twenty-six-year-old male with a twelfth-grade education. Much of this time was spent in special education. The history indicated learning problems throughout his life. His problems were reported to have become more severe in recent times, resulting in a diagnosis of hydrocephalus. This was corrected through a ventricular shunt. He was referred for a program to help control his behavior and aid his learning.

K.L.'s results can be seen in Table 8-V. These results indicate a low level of performance. His IQ scores are in the range characteristic of mental retardation. Trails B was discontinued at ten minutes because of the subject's inability to understand what he was to do. The Tactual Performance Test overall and

TABLE 8-V

RESULTS FOR K.L.

(Male, twenty-six, right-handed, twelfth-grade education)

Wechsler Adult Intelligence Scale		Tactual Performance Test	
Information	7	Right	10′ (1 in)
Comprehension	4	Left	10′ (6 in)
Arithmetic	4	Both	10′ (3 in)
Similarities	4	Memory	3
Digit Span	6	Location	0
Vocabulary	5		
Digit Symbol	0	Category (errors)	126
Picture Completion	6	Speech Perception (errors)	24
Block Design	1		
Picture Arrangement	4	Rhythm (errors)	11
Object Assembly	2		
Verbal IQ	70	Wechsler Memory	55
Performance IQ	52	Finger Tapping	
Full-scale IQ	60		
		Right	17
Peabody Picture Vocabulary		Left	15
Test (IQ)	66		
		Grip Strength	
Tactile Form Recognition		Right (kg)	18
		Left (kg)	16
Right (errors)	0		
Left (errors)	1	Fingertip Number Writing	
Trail Making Test		Right (errors)	8
		Left (errors)	9
Part A	261″ (2 errors)		
Part B	discontinued at 600″		
Impairment Index	1.0		

Aphasia: dysnomia, dysarthria, spelling dyspraxia, dysgraphia, dyslexia, severe construction dyspraxia.

Suppressions: tactile (right and left), visual (right and left), auditory (right and left).

the Memory and Location scores were impaired. He earned an overall Impairment Index score of 1.0.

An analysis of the WAIS scores indicate that he scored low on everything. He had particular trouble with those tests requiring motor coordination. His lowest scores were the Digit Symbol and Block Design, suggestive of right brain damage (as does his low performance IQ). This interpretation must be considered cautiously in light of his motor speed scores on the Halstead. He was able to tap only seventeen times with his right hand and fifteen times with his left hand, about 33 percent of normal. His strength was also reduced considerably in both hands. There were no indications of lateralization on these measures.

He was impaired on all the complex tests within the battery: Rhythm, Category, Speech Perception, Tactual Performance Test, Trails A and B, the Stroop Color and Word Test and the Wechsler Memory Test. He did not appear to be more severely depressed on one kind of skill as compared to another. The impairment appeared to be generalized.

The patient also displayed a number of bilateral sensory symptoms on Finger Agnosia and Fingertip Number Writing. He had sensory suppressions on both hands, in both visual fields, and in both ears. It is likely that the suppression scores reflected the subject's overall cognitive problems, as it is rare to get bilateral suppressions in all modalities. The patient demonstrated signs of severe aphasia although he was able to communicate and apparently able to understand simple commands. He also demonstrated severe construction dyspraxia.

The overall picture is one of general depression in all skills in both the right and left hemispheres with more motor than cognitive impairment. Assuming the cause is unknown, the patient's age would be taken into account, which makes cerebrovascular problems of a diffuse nature unlikely. There would be three possible causes: a large tumor growing at the level of the thalamus and compressing the brain as a whole, hydrocephalus, or diffuse early brain injury. Because of the patient's age, a large tumor would be unlikely although tumors have been reported in individuals this young. The severity of the deficits suggest a continuing disorder. Thus, the more likely diagnosis would be hydrocephalus, which had recently become more severe, causing the deterioration seen on the tests.

In writing the report on this patient, the neuropsychologist was struck by the lack of recovery after the treatment of the hydrocephalus. (A shunt is supposed to act to lessen the ventricular pressure, thus relieving most of the acute effects of the disorder.) The motor symptoms remained quite severe, as did the overall performance deficits. The patient's performance indicated confusion, as seen in the aphasia and sensory and nonverbal deficits. It was suggested in the report that the shunt might not be working and should be reevaluated.

K.L. also had low scores on Vocabulary and other "nonsensitive" tests. This is suggestive of a chronic disorder, likely from early childhood. Such results are also seen in severe degenerative disorders, but that is not a viable possibility at the age of twenty-six.

Neurological Report

The patient was referred back to the neurosurgeon who had previously installed the shunt in the patient. He found that the shunt was no longer operational, causing a return of the acute symptoms of hydrocephalus. A second operation corrected this problem.

CASE 5: P.A.

P.A. was a sixty-three-year-old, right-handed male who carried a diagnosis of Parkinson's disease. The patient was referred for neuropsychological testing to evaluate his current functioning.

P.A.'s results are presented in Table 8-VI. All the general indicators for brain dysfunction were down considerably, as can be seen in his scores on the Tactual Performance, Trail Making, and Category Tests, and the Impairment Index. As is typical of many cases of Parkinsons, his full-scale IQ was within the normal range (93) with no evidence of lateralization.

His performance on the WAIS was somewhat inconsistent. His lowest performance scores were Block Design and Digit Symbol. All the performance scores were down, compared to his verbal scores. However, the decrease was not any more than would be expected by the patient's age, which was reflected in his equal verbal and performance IQs. The low score on the verbal subtests were information and arithmetic. This does not suggest any lateralized deficit to either side.

The patient showed a normal Trails A, but was considerably impaired on Trails B. He was also extensively impaired on the

TABLE 8-VI

RESULTS FOR P.A.

(Male, sixty-three, right-handed, twelfth-grade education)

Wechsler Adult Intelligence Scale		*Tactual Performance Test*	
Information	6	Right	15′ (3 in)
Comprehension	9	Left	15′ (0 in)
Arithmetic	7	Both	15′ (1 in)
Similarities	9	Memory	3
Digit Span	9	Location	0
Vocabulary	10		
Digit Symbol	5	*Category* (errors)	120
Picture Completion	9		
Block Design	4	*Speech Perception* (errors)	14
Picture Arrangement	6	*Rhythm* (errors)	14
Object Assembly	7		
Verbal IQ	94	*Trail Making Test*	
Performance IQ	92	Part A	32″
Full-scale IQ	93	Part B	480″
Finger Tapping		*Tactile Form Recognition*	
Right	51.2	Right (errors)	0
Left	39.6	Left (errors)	0
Finger Agnosia		*Suppressions*	0
Right (errors)	0	*Impairment Index*	1.0
Left (errors)	3		
Fingertip Number Writing			
Right (errors)	5		
Left (errors)	6		

Aphasia: micrographia, dysarthria, dysgraphia, slight construction dysproxia.

Rhythm Test (his score is essentially chance) and was moderately impaired on Speech Sounds Perception. His Category score was severely impaired.

On the Tactual Performance Test, P.A. showed somewhat better performance with his right than with his left hand. The overall performance was very poor, however. Even though he worked with the left hand second, he was unable to get a single block in. The Memory and Location scores were also severely depressed. He was impaired on the left hand of the finger tapping test, while the right hand was essentially normal. In fact, his right hand score was quite good for a man of sixty-three. On the Finger Agnosia Test, he showed a deficit lateralized to the left hand. On Fingertip Number Writing, however, there were generally equal errors on both hands. There were no signs of suppressions.

The patient had some central dysarthria with difficulty pronouncing such words as "Massachusetts." He also showed some dysgraphia. His handwriting and drawings were all extremely small in an attempt to make them accurate. Nevertheless, he demonstrated a very small tremor. There were also some very mild signs of construction dyspraxia.

P.A. showed a generalized disorder affecting most of the tests sensitive to brain damage. The major signs of the disorder were motor and generally lateralized to the right brain. However, there were speech and cognitive symptoms present indicating involvement of both hemispheres, although the WAIS scores were within normal limits. There was particularly impaired performance on the Category Test and Trail Making Test (Part B), both of which imply a frontal disorder. The patient showed a slight tremor, as well as micrographia. This is a pattern typical of Parkinson's disease, although the pattern of the sensorimotor results appears somewhat less severe than might be expected given the cognitive deficits.

Neurological Report

In discussing these results with the physician, he indicated that the patient's motor symptoms were previously more severe but they had been helped by the use of L-dopa. In many patients, L-dopa acts to improve the sensorimotor deficits without necessarily improving cognitive skills (Marsh and Kravitz, 1971). This patient is a good example of how such chemotherapy may affect the neuropsychological results.

CASE 6: C.C.

C.C. was a seven-year-four-month-old child who was right-handed and referred for testing after a shunt to relieve hydrocephalus had been placed in his brain several months earlier.

The referral question was whether the child would be capable of continuing in normal classes or should be placed in special education. His tests results are presented in Table 8-VII. The patient achieved a somewhat higher verbal IQ on the WISC-R (94) than his performance IQ (84). His verbal IQ was raised considerably by the child's one high score (12) on Comprehension. This suggested that his IQ before the hydrocephalus may have been somewhat higher. This was further confirmed by the Peabody Picture Vocabulary Test on which he earned an IQ of 114. His Finger Tapping scores were normal for his age (using the norms of Spreen and Gaddes, 1969). He made several errors on the Finger Agnosia task, with some lateralization to the left hand. He also made two errors on the Fingertip number writing, both on the right hand. His scores on the Tactual Per-

TABLE 8-VII

RESULTS FOR C.C.

(Male, seven years, four months, right-handed, first grade)

Wechsler Intelligence Scale for Children (Revised)		Tactual Performance Test	
		Right	5'28"
Information	9	Left	3'40"
Similarities	9	Both	2'42"
Arithmetic	7	Memory	4
Vocabulary	8	Location	3
Comprehension	12		
Digit Span	6	Finger Tapping	
Picture Completion	7	Right	34
Picture Arrangement	9	Left	32
Block Design	7		
Object Assembly	7	Wide Range Achievement Test	
Coding	8		
Mazes	9	Reading (grade)	1.2
Verbal IQ	94	Spelling (grade)	1.3
Performance IQ	84	Arithmetic (grade)	1.0
Full-scale IQ	87	Finger Agnosia	
Peabody Picture Vocabulary Test (IQ)	114	Right	1
		Left	3
Matching V's (seconds)	38"	Fingertip Number Writing	
Matching Figures (seconds)	32"	Right	2
		Left	0

Aphasia symptoms: severe dysarthria, construction dyspraxia.

formance Test were all normal for a seven-year-old, as were his scores on two visual matching tasks.

On the Wide Range Achievement Test, he scored somewhat below expectations for his current grade level. He earned scores indicating early first-grade placement, although the school year was near completion. However, this was not that surprising, considering he had missed a great deal of school time while sick and in the hospital.

The patient's most severe symptom was central dysarthria. This was evident both talking to C.C. and on his test scores. No other aphasia symptoms were seen.

Overall, C.C. did extremely well on the measures of brain dysfunction, although there was a clear depression in his WISC-R scores due to the hydrocephalus. He appears to have recovered well, however, and his skills for future learning appear to be intact. Consequently, the school was advised that he would need special help both to catch up in areas he had missed while out of school and to work on the expressive speech deficit. It was felt that he was capable of doing work commensurate with his grade placement and did not need to be placed in a special education class.

Neurological Report

At present, one year later, he is progressing well, and no problems have been reported by the family at check-ups. No further neurological deficits have developed.

CASE 7: L.J.

L.J. was brought in by her mother to help her with learning problems. She was reported to have had grand mal seizures about three times a month. She had been on Dilantin® for three years, although it did not fully control the seizures. At the time of the exam, she was nine-years-three-months old and was completing the fourth grade. Her scores are reported in Table 8-VIII. The diagnosis of seizures was made by the family physician on the basis of the mother's description of the child's behavior.

L.J. earned a verbal IQ of 124, indicating superior verbal in-

TABLE 8-VIII

RESULTS FOR L.J.

(Female, nine, right-handed, fourth grade)

Wechsler Intelligence Scale for Children (Revised)		*Tactual Performance Test* (6 figures)	
		Right	1'02"
Information	15	Left	25"
Similarities	17	Both	16"
Arithmetic	6	Memory	6
Vocabulary	16	Location	6
Comprehension	16		
Digit Span	16	*Speech Perception* (errors)	6
Picture Completion	14	*Trail Making Test*	
Picture Arrangement	13		
Block Design	9	Part A	27"
Object Assembly	11	Part B	50"
Coding	9		
Mazes	14	*Category* (Errors)	50
Verbal IQ	124	*Finger Tapping*	
Performance IQ	108		
Full-scale IQ	123	Right	38
		Left	35
Peabody Picture Vocabulary Test (IQ)	110	*Bender-Gestalt* (errors)	0

Peabody Individual Achievement Test

Mathematics (grade)	4.9
Reading Recognition	6.2
Reading Comprehension	9.2
Spelling	3.4
Information	4.7

Aphasia: none, except mild construction dyspraxia.
Sensory symptoms: none.

telligence. Her performance IQ was somewhat lower, but still above average. Her only serious specific deficit was in arithmetic, a subject she apparently disliked and refused to study. On the Peabody Individual Achievement Test, she earned scores at or above grade level on all subjects except spelling, where she was about one year behind. Her reading comprehension placed her at the ninth grade, quite advanced for her grade.

On the Halstead tests, all of her scores were excellent and well within the normal range for a nine-year-old. Her Tactual Performance Test was excellent. Her tapping scores (36 and 33) were slightly above average for her age. There were no sensory deficits in any modality. The Aphasia Test was completely normal. She did show a very mild construction dyspraxia when drawing a cross, but her Bender-Gestalt was done perfectly, indicating no serious problems in this area.

Clearly, the above results are consistent with a normal or above-normal youngster. There were no indications on the tests whatsoever indicative of any brain pathology and certainly none indicative of grand mal seizures. As seen in the last chapter, patients with grand mal seizures generally display quite significant impairment.

Neurological Report

As a result of these findings, she was referred to a neurologist for an EEG. (It was not clear if any EEG had been done previously. In any case, one was not available.) The EEG also proved to be normal. The neurologist then agreed to take her off the Dilantin. A behavioral program was introduced for the "seizures" and the school learning problems. Within two months from the start of the program, all the seizures had been eliminated. The school indicated that it no longer had any trouble with her behavior or learning ability.

CASE 8: B.A.

B.A. was a forty-three-year-old, right-handed man with a twelfth-grade education. He was referred for determination of disability caused by an accident to his neck. His results are listed in Table 8-IX.

The patient scored in the above average range on the WAIS, with the verbal some ten points higher than the performance IQ. His lowest scores were on Digit Symbol and Picture Arrangement, while he earned a 17 on Arithmetic.

On the dysfunction sensitive tasks, he scored in the normal range on Category, but was clearly impaired on the Tactual Performance Test total time (over twenty-five minutes). His Location performance was normal. Trails B was barely into the brain-damaged range, while Trails A was somewhat more severely impaired. The Impairment Index was normal.

On the Tactual Performance Test, there was a deficit in both

TABLE 8-IX
RESULTS FOR B.A.
(Male, forty-three, right-handed, twelfth grade)

Wechsler Adult Intelligence Scale		*Tactual Performance Test*	
Information	12	Right	9'43"
Comprehension	14	Left	10'04"
Arithmetic	17	Both	5'37"
Similarities	10	Memory	9
Digit Span	13	Location	7
Vocabulary	12		
Digit Symbol	9	*Trail Making Test*	
Picture Completion	9	Part A	55"
Block Design	11	Part B	101"
Picture Arrangement	11		
Object Assembly	12	*Category* (errors)	30
Verbal IQ	118		
Performance IQ	108	*Speech Perception* (errors)	2
Full-scale IQ	114	*Rhythm* (errors)	2
Finger Tapping		*Finger Agnosia*	
Right	43	Right (errors)	2
Left	36	Left (errors)	2
Grip Strength		*Fingertip Number Writing*	
Right (kg)	53	Right (errors)	1
Left (kg)	45	Left (errors)	0
Wide Range Achievement Test		*Impairment Index*	0.3
Reading (grade)	15.9	*Tactile Form Recognition*	
Spelling (grade)	12.4		
Arithmetic (grade)	10.8	Right (errors)	0
		Left (errors)	0

Aphasia: none.
Suppressions: left visual field.

the right and left hands but it was more pronounced in the left hand. Both finger tapping scores were down, but the left was 16 percent slower than the right. Grip strength was also impaired on the left hand. It is possible that the deficit on Trails A and B came from a combination of the motor and visual deficits present.

The visual deficit involved substantial loss of peripheral vision in both visual fields. Although he could see things on which he focused, his visual field was considerably reduced. The patient compensated by head movements, but tended to look to the right if forced to fixate. This resulted in many left-sided errors with double simultaneous stimulation. It is possible that this may have reflected a mild degree of unilateral spatial neglect.

The Speech and Rhythm tests were finished without trouble. No aphasic deficits were found. The Wide Range Achievement Test showed that the patient continues to show academic skills at a level commensurate with his education.

This patient presents an interesting set of deficits. He has visual deficits in both visual fields, perhaps suggesting bilateral occipital lobe involvement. He also shows bilateral motor and kinesthetic deficits. There are, however, no cognitive deficits accompanying these symptoms. It is clear that a number of disorders can be ruled out. Head trauma, degenerative disorders, or tumors could not cause these results without cognitive deficits as well.

The only vascular lesion which could produce visual deficits bilaterally would be in the basilar artery, as it is the blood supply for both posterior cerebral arteries, which, in turn, bring blood to the two occipital lobes. Such a deficit is rare, because the two posterior arteries are also served by the internal carotid arteries through the two posterior communicating arteries. However, a significant minority of people are born without posterior communicating arteries. This appears to be the only viable hypothesis that can explain the current results.

An occlusion of the basilar artery can also account for the motor-kinesthetic deficits since another major branch of the basilar artery system serves the cerebellum. Deficits of the cerebellum can account for these additional symptoms. Basilar disorders also cause deficits of memory, because branches serving the limbic area of the brain are occluded. This disorder would be seen primarily as problems in learning or new long-term memory.

In light of the above results a delayed testing on some of the Wechsler Memory Scale Items as suggested by Milner (1975), was included. Although the patient had a normal short-term memory, he was greatly impaired on the delayed memory task with interpolated activity. This was a further confirmation of the diagnosis of basilar artery occlusion.

Neurological Report

The neurological report indicated agreement with this diagnosis, as did the history of the disorder which was provided.

CASE 10: S.B.

S.B. was a nine-year-old, left-handed male in the fourth grade when he was referred because of severe learning problems. The initial history (taken by the referring organization for whom we consult) indicated no known neurological problems, but that there was a suspicion of possible brain damage. His protocol is listed in Table 8-X.

S.B. showed an extremely poor overall performance on the Wechsler Intelligence Scale, earning a borderline 75 IQ on the performance tests and a 67 on the verbal tests. Although this appears to suggest little lateralization, an inspection of the performance subtests indicates that two tests sensitive to left brain disruption (Coding, the children's version of Digit Symbol and Picture Arrangement) were pulling the performance score down. If performance IQ is calculated only on the basis of Block Design, Object Assembly, Picture Completion and Mazes, S.B. earned a performance IQ of 101, indicating normal performance.

Inspection of the verbal scores show lower test results on Information, Comprehension, and Vocabulary, almost a classic pattern of a child with an injury before the first or second year of life. This was especially significant, since the child also showed mixed dominance. The grade-level scores on the Peabody Individual Achievement Test also indicated this severe verbal deficit, as did the presence of dyslexia, dysarthria, dysgraphia, and left-right confusion.

Left brain deficits were also seen in the low finger tapping score for the right hand (36% below the dominant left hand) and the extremely poor performance on Part B of the Trail

TABLE 8-X

RESULTS FOR S.B.

(Male, nine, left-handed, fourth grade)

Wechsler Intelligence Scale for Children (Revised)		*Tactual Performance Test* (6 figures)	
		Left	7'52"
Information	4	Right	4'57"
Similarities	6	Both	3'08"
Arithmetic	5	Memory	4
Vocabulary	4	Location	2
Comprehension	4		
Digit Span	8	*Trail Making Test*	
Picture Completion	9	Part A	42"
Picture Arrangement	3	Part B 600" (discontinued)	
Block Design	9	(Older Children's Version)	
Object Assembly	9		
Coding	2	*Finger Tapping*	
Mazes	14	Left	39
Verbal IQ	67	Right	25
Performance IQ	75		
Full-scale IQ	69	*Name Writing*	
		Left	37"
Peabody Individual Achievement Test		Right	21"
Mathematics (grade)	1.1		
Reading Recognition (grade)	1.5	*Grip Strength*	
Reading Comprehension (grade)	1.9		
Spelling (grade)	1.4	Left (kg)	15
General Information (grade)	2.2	Right (kg)	15
Category (errors)	121		
(Older Children's Version)			

Sensory symptoms: Finger agnosia—left (3 errors), Tactile Form—left (2 errors).
Suppression: right hand, right face.
Aphasia: spelling dyspraxia, dyslexia, dysarthria, left-right confusion, dysgraphia.
Dominance: left-handed, no established eye and foot dominance.

Making Test (children's version). There were two suppressions, both tactile, on the right hand and right face. However, not all the scores lateralized to the left brain. The right-hand performance on the Tactual Performance Test is as good as the left hand performance. The hands were equally strong. There were two minor sensory deficits on the left Finger Agnosia and left Tactile Form Recognition Tests. The dominant left hand was extremely slow in name writing, compared to the nondominant right hand. The overall Tactual Performance Tests scores were also slow. Both Memory and Localization were down as well, although only slightly (Spreen and Gaddes, 1969).

Overall, the results appear to imply a focal, destructive lesion in the left parietal or parietotemporofrontal area. The speech symptoms, suppressions, lateralized differences on the Trail Making and Finger Tapping Tests all suggest such a locus. The injury appears to be chronic, as there is no severe deficit on the Tactual Performance Test or most of the sensory tests which would be associated with a current lesion in that area. In addition, the WISC-R scores and the mixed dominance clearly imply an old lesion.

It is interesting in this case to note that, although the child appears to have attempted to become right dominant, this change has been only partial and highly incomplete. The left hand is faster than the right on finger tapping; it is not any stronger nor better on the Tactual Performance Test. In addition, the overall pattern of deficits suggest a clear focus. This should not have been so clear if verbal functions switched successfully to the right hemisphere. It must be concluded that the focal lesion was not large enough to cause the take over of the verbal functions by the right hemisphere.

It is also evident from the child's Category score (barely above chance) that he has failed to develop many higher cognitive skills. (We also administered several other tests, designed for younger children, to see the level of his higher cognitive skills. He scored at the level of a two- or three-year-old.) This is consistent with Luria's (1966) hypothesis that basic verbal symbolic skills are necessary for the development of higher cognitive skills.

Neurological Report

After seeing these results, the history was redone and it was discovered that the child had had surgery for the removal of a brain tumor while still an infant. Hospital records, which were, unfortunately, incomplete, indicated that the tumor was in the general area indicated by our results.

CONCLUSION

As can be seen from these few case studies, neuropsychological techniques can be a powerful addition to neurological procedures in the diagnosis of brain dysfunction. However, it can also be seen that such diagnosis involves the consideration of many interacting variables. Full competence with such procedures can only come through proper supervised training and an extensive working knowledge of neurophysiology, neuropsychology, and neuropathology.

Chapter 9

THE REHABILITATION PROCESS

RELATIVELY LITTLE RESEARCH has focused on the rehabilitation process, in comparison to the extensive interest in diagnostic problems. Primarily within the past decade, a literature has developed in psychological and neuropsychological rehabilitation. The first part of this chapter deals with the research that has identified factors affecting the success of rehabilitation with the brain injured in general. The second part will deal with the theoretical and practical basis for setting up and evaluating a neuropsychological rehabilitation program.

PATIENT FACTORS

There have been many attempts to identify the patient characteristics and environmental circumstances that might help predict rehabilitation outcome. These factors include the age of the subject at the time of the injury; premorbid IQ status; general health; social environment; the extent, etiology, and site of the lesion; time since the lesion; dominance; motivation; emotional reactions of the patient and extent of the patient's cognitive deficits (Bardach, 1971; Darley, 1975; Kutner, 1971; Lewinsohn, 1973; Luria, 1963, 1970).

Age

In general, rehabilitation research has indicated that the younger the person is when injured, the greater the probability s/he will recover (Adler and Tal, 1965; Aita and Reitan, 1948; Boyle and Scalzitti, 1963; Bruell and Simon, 1960; Teuber, 1975; Vignolo, 1964). Several factors are likely to be involved in this finding: Older patients may do less well because of a higher incidence of general brain deterioration, a lack of financial and personal resources, and less expectations for recovery by both the patient and rehabilitation staff.

Premorbid IQ

Generally, the more intelligent and capable the person before the brain trauma, the more extensive the expected recovery. This

186

may be a result of having more cognitive resources available after the injury, compared to the person who started with few intellectual resources. This level of abilities directly after an injury has been found to correlate with final recovery level (Keenan and Brassell, 1974).

General Health and Brain Integrity

The person's physical health and the overall integrity of the brain are significant factors in rehabilitation. The patient with severe medical problems generally is not ready to be rehabilitated (Lehmann et al., 1975b; Sterling, 1967). General measures of brain integrity, such as an intelligence test or the Trail Making Test, serve as good prognostic measures for success (Meier, 1974).

The ability of tests to predict prognosis is based on several factors. First, good scores imply that the lesion is relatively localized and that there is good perseveration of basic skills that can be used in the rehabilitation process. As more basic skills are impaired by a lesion, the overall prognosis is lower. In general, prognosis is based on the presence of alternate areas of the brain which are intact and able to help reformulate the functional systems disrupted by a brain injury. In making a prediction for a specific patient, the nature of the remaining strengths must be assessed to see if they are capable of playing the necessary roles in the disrupted functional systems.

Social Environment

Although rehabilitation is often thought a process involving only the patient and therapist, the reactions of the patient's family and relevant others are significant in determining prognosis. The family can provide support and motivation for the patient or sabotage recovery through indifference or reinforcement of the disability (Archer, 1964; Berlin, 1974; Boone, 1967; Hirschenfang, Shulman, and Benton, 1968; Lehmann, DeLateur, Fowler, and Warren, 1975a and b; Menolascino and Eaton, 1967).

Concern about the family's role may lead to therapy for the family, who may feel guilt because they believe the patient's injury is their fault or because of negative feelings towards the patient. Therapy may help to alleviate any sense of helplessness or guilt the family might feel, enabling them to interact with the patient more positively. It may also motivate the patient, because the family is expressing interest in his or her recovery in a demonstrable manner. Also, the family can help by providing additional therapy that an institution may not have the resources to provide.

Motivation

Since rehabilitation requires a great deal of effort and cooperation on the part of the patient, the patient's motivation is a key factor in successful programs (Anderson, Bourestom, and Greenberg, 1970; Fogel and Rosillo, 1969, 1971a and b; Rabinowitz, 1961; Wepman, 1953). The patient may be motivated in a number of ways: by initial success in rehabilitation programming, by social rewards, by development of a personal relationship between the therapist and patient, and by general methods of operant conditioning (Belmont, Benjamin, Ambrose, and Restuccia, 1969; Gudeman, Golden, and Craine, 1977; Ullmann and Krasner, 1967).

Emotional Problems

This is the area in which both clinical and counseling psychology have been most heavily involved. The emotional problems a patient may exhibit after a brain injury include denial of the disorder, depression, aggression against the staff or the patient's family, a loss of self-concept, and a loss of initiative (Aita and Reitan, 1948; Bell, 1972; Blackman, 1950; Fogel and Rossillo, 1971a; Foxx and Azrin, 1972; Hollon, 1973; Hyman, 1972; Kamin, Llewellyn, and Sledge, 1958; Merskey and Woodforde, 1972; Nemiah, 1964; Rosillo and Fogel, 1970, 1971; Shaffer, 1973; Vineberg and Willems, 1971; Wanderer, 1974).

The treatment of emotional, behavioral, and motivational problems is closely interrelated. In picking out a suitable therapy, it is important to consider the subject's overall condition. Brain-injured patients may be highly intelligent, successful people in their own field and may react negatively to techniques treating them as patients somehow less than equal to the therapist. Alternatively, the patient may have little ability to understand anything but the most basic reinforcers. It is imperative that the diversity of this population be recognized and that therapeutic techniques be modified to fit these considerations.

Dominance

As was reported in Chapter 3, left-handed individuals are more likely to be mixed dominant. In mixed dominance, abilities are partially represented in both hemispheres rather than being lateralized. Because of this, such individuals tend to be more successful in recovering from localized injuries (Luria, 1963, 1970; Smith, 1971; Subirana, 1958). It has been speculated that this situation allows such individuals to transfer functions from one hemisphere to the other with less difficulty.

Time Since Injury

It has been reported that therapy soon after an injury results in more recovery (Darley, 1975). It is likely that at least part of the reason for this finding is the effect of spontaneous recovery, strongest during the initial period after an accident and usually complete within six to twelve months (Sarno and Levita, 1971; Thomsen, 1975; Vignolo, 1964). Spontaneous recovery itself is probably due to reorganization within the brain and to the improvement in brain integrity. This is due to recovery and to a lessening of secondary effects, such as higher intracranial pressure.

THEORETICAL FACTORS IN NEUROPSYCHOLOGICAL REHABILITATION

Luria (1963) has suggested when one area of the brain is destroyed, it interrupts the functional systems dependent on that area. Recovery of any lost abilities depends upon reformulation of the functional systems responsible for those abilities. The reformulation may take place in one of three ways. First, another area may substitute for the lost area. This is more likely in situations where both hemispheres of the brain may be involved in a task. For example, both parietal lobes can be involved in spatial tasks. Consequently, loss on one side can be compensated for by increasing the participation of the opposite parietal lobe in the appropriate functional system. One can also involve new areas of the brain by providing an alternate method of doing a task.

Second, the task may be done by involving more basic systems of the brain. For example, the patient may have injury to the motor speech areas and be unable to say the letter *p*. However, such patients are often able to still do the more basic motion of blowing through pursed lips. Starting at this point, such a response may be shaped into saying *p*.

Finally, a functional system may be reformed by including higher centers of the brain. For example, a subject with lesions in the motor area may be unable to tap his finger on command. If the patient is told to tap out his age, the patient is able to do this since this task involves the higher cortical centers to a greater extent.

The emphasis in each of these situations is that the overt behavior is maintained, although the manner in which the brain executes the behavior has changed. The formation of an effective new functional system depends upon the integrity of the areas which must form the new functional system. Consequently, the neuropsychologist must be interested not only in what deficits are present but what strengths are present as well.

Whichever mechanism may be operating in a given case, it is the job of the rehabilitation neuropsychologist to provide training that enables the brain to efficiently form the most workable alternative functional system. The major technique is providing a situation in which the brain receives accurate feedback on its performance. This feedback allows the brain to assess the accuracy of its attempts to reformulate the functional system. The tasks must be designed so that the feedback is clear. The lack of clear feedback is one factor limiting the spontaneous improvement that a subject makes without therapy.

Role of Neuropsychology

It is important to recognize the role that neuropsychology can play in the complete rehabilitation process. Neuropsychological rehabilitation is directed toward the redesign of basic functional systems, rather than the direct restoration of "everyday" behavior. In essence, the neuropsychologist attempts to design rehabilitation techniques which will prepare the patient to maximally benefit from training given by physical therapists, occupational therapists, speech pathologists, and other rehabilitation workers.

Neuropsychology attempts to look at the functioning of the brain as a whole. Too often, treatment of the brain-injured patient is piecemeal, directed towards the observable symptoms, rather than the underlying, basic deficits. Little consideration is given for the interrelationships of the symptoms. In treating the basic deficits, neuropsychological rehabilitation helps reformulate the functioning of the brain as a whole, rather than providing training for overt symptoms.

As a consequence, neuropsychological rehabilitation does not replace the rehabilitation effort of other professions, but rather supplements and complements those efforts. Neuropsychological rehabilitation cannot only aid in the patient's readiness to respond to other treatments, but can also be used to select the treatment procedures within other areas that would be most effective with the patient. The neuropsychological theory of brain function can also provide a system coordinating the treatment of a patient with the individual rehabilitation professions.

A program of rehabilitation based on the theoretical considerations discussed above had several advantages. First, the program takes advantage of modern, neuropsychological methods of investigating deficits due to brain injuries. These methods allow the neuropsychologist to identify the basic deficits underlying the symptoms of brain dysfunction. Treatment of the basic functions, rather than their behavioral symptoms, allows for more generalized rehabilitation effects. This treatment is potentially less time-consuming, as the staff and patient energy is used more effectively.

This does not mean that other rehabilitation methods are ineffective or valueless. It is likely that many of the programs currently in use do achieve results. However, the question is not one of effectiveness, but of optimal improvement in the patient. The treatment of the patient's basic deficits offers the opportunity to provide this maximal treatment in the brain-injured patient. Only through the careful consideration of the deficits and strengths of a patient and a recognition of the functional organization of the brain can a fully optimal program of rehabilitation be designed for the individual patient.

PLANNING THE REHABILITATION PROGRAM

Examination

The aim of the neuropsychological examination in rehabilitation planning is to fully document the deficits and strengths of the individual patient. The content of the exam is identical to the exam designed for accurate diagnosis, since both require a full understanding of the effects of a neurological disorder.

The relationship of the diagnostic process to the information needed in rehabilitation offers a check for the interpretation of the neuropsychological results. If the basic deficits and strengths have been properly analyzed, it should be an easy process to predict the locus of the neurological disorder, as well as some information about the disorder itself. If these diagnostic conclusions are inconsistent with the actual neurological disorder, it is likely that the test results have not been properly interpreted. Such a check can help avoid erroneous conclusions about the patient's status.

In addition to evaluating the status of the patient's cognitive abilities, it is also necessary to evaluate the patient's emotional status. As can be seen from the research reviewed at the beginning of this chapter, the client's emotional status can significantly effect the efficiency of rehabilitation programs. In some cases, emotional problems are so severe as to preclude a successful program. In many cases, treatment of the emotional disorder is necessary either as a prelude to treatment or as an integral part of the treatment.

Assessments of the patient's emotional status may be made through a combination of an instrument, such as the MMPI, supplemented by a clinical interview. In addition, it is often valuable to interview the nursing staff, if the patient is in the hospital. Interviews with the family may indicate emotional changes that may have accompanied the patient's neurological disorder.

Priorities

After the patient's individual results have been thoroughly analyzed, it is necessary to assess the effects of the findings on the patient's life and family. In many institutions, social workers are responsible for assessing these environmental conditions. If that is the situation, the social worker should be thoroughly aware of the neuropsychological results and their implications, so that the kind of information necessary may be collected. After the environmental and individual test data have been gathered, initial recommendations may be prepared indicating areas in which the patient's deficits exist and the nature and importance of those deficits. This information can be used to determine the priority in working with the patient in any given area.

Several considerations help to set the priorities. The major goal is the organization of the program so that maximal performance levels may be achieved by the patient with a minimum expenditure of staff and patient effort. Beginning therapy in an area dependent upon skills which have not yet been trained is an inefficient approach. Putting a patient with a low motivation in a program that requires great effort is also valueless, until the motivational problems have been treated.

It is important at this point to determine which deficits, if any, may be due to the emotional disorders the patient may be showing. In order to do this, it is necessary for the psychologist to have a good working knowledge of what disabilities can be expected from the client's neurological disorder, considering the health of the patient and the criteria discussed throughout this book. It requires a full integration of the neurological and psychological data. This is important, since deficits which are due to the patient's emotional reaction may be very resistant to normal rehabilitation treatment. While severe cases of this phenomenon may be relatively rare, it is important that they be recognized.

It is also necessary to assess the importance of the deficits to the patient's life. Some deficits will be more relevant to a patient's occupation or more important psychologically to the patient. For example, the author's group had one patient whose motor strength and coordination tested as normal but who felt he was weak and impaired, compared to his former status. Although he had many more severe problems, the author and cohort found assigning him a strength-building program aided considerably in getting his cooperation and making him feel therapy was important.

Finally, the neuropsychologist needs to consider in which areas progress can be made most successfully. Early and obvious success in a rehabilitation program can be a powerful reinforcer to the patient and his family. This is a considerable aid in enlisting the patient's full effort in the rehabilitation program.

After the process of assigning priorities and goals for the rehabilitation program is completed, it is necessary to integrate this report and findings with the therapists responsible for the rehabilitation program. Depending on the settings, this may include the patient's family, physician, or other rehabilitation workers. This step is important, because a successful program requires the full cooperation and understanding of all those involved. In most institutions, there are few neuropsychologists who direct rehabilitation work with patients. Direct patient contact is usually through speech, occupational, vocational and physical therapists, and institutional aides. Consequently, the success of a program depends upon the full understanding and efforts of these rehabilitation professionals.

Some of the reasons for family participation were noted early in this chapter. This is very significant in the case of children; parents usually welcome both an understanding of their child's condition and an opportunity to become part of the treatment program.

After feedback has been received on the initial report, changes are made to adapt the program to input from others involved in the rehabilitation program. It is important that the neuropsychologist remains involved with the case through this process; this is the stage where, traditionally, most responsibility for implementation passes to others. The reasons for staying involved are many: The rehabilitation process is involved with too many variables to have an initial program remain fully accurate for a significant length of time. These factors may include initially slower progress than expected in an area, incorrect specification of the nature of the basic deficits, lack of support for the program from the family, and changes in the patient's neurological status. The neuropsychologist is also needed for proper and continuous evaluation of the training programs.

TASK CONSTRUCTION

There are four major considerations in the design of a rehabilitation task: (1) It should include the impaired skill that one is trying to reformulate. All other skill requirements in the task should be in areas with which the subject has little or no trouble. (2) The therapist should be able to vary the task in difficulty from a level which would be simple for the patient to a level representing normal performance. (3) The task should be quantifiable so that progress may be objectively stated. (4) The task should provide immediate feedback to the patient. (5) The number of errors made by the patient should be controlled.

The first requirement of including the specific skill to be taught is relatively clear. This skill should be the central problem involved in the task, with no other skills tapped that are difficult for the patient. Unfortunately, in actual practice many rehabilitation tasks do not meet this requirement. In some cases, this is simply due to a failure to understand the nature of the patient's deficits. In other cases, it reflects the lack of analysis of the skills demanded by a given task.

The task should be constructed so that it may not be done in an alternate manner without the skill demanded by the rehabilitation plan. For example, tasks teaching sequencing of a set of items in a logical manner often become memory tasks for the order of several often-repeated items. A task requiring the patient to tell a story suggested by a scene may be done only by describing the things in the scene rather than telling a story.

Almost any task imaginable can be turned into a rehabilitation task, although initial ideas must often be modified to fit the individual client's needs or the requirements set forth in this chapter. The rehabilitation literature itself is filled with many ideas for tasks that can be adapted into the approach advanced here. The diagnostic tests themselves can suggest ideas for tasks, as can the experimental literature on testing the brain-injured patient cited in Chapter 2. One caution should be advanced: Material from standardized tests used to evaluate the patient is usually not good task material; it eliminates that test as an evaluator of the patient's condition. This makes it more difficult to distinguish between *task-specific learning,* which does not generalize to other conditions, and *basic skill learning,* which generalizes, since the test used to measure the skill on a test battery is also used for the specific training.

The second requirement for the rehabilitation task is that it can be modified in terms of difficulty. Diller (1976) has presented a useful survey of ways in which a task can be varied so as to change its difficulty. These include the following: (1) speed of presentation of items; (2) number of items presented at a time; (3) sensory modality in which the problem is presented; (4) number of spatial dimensions (one versus two versus three); (5) concreteness; (6) size; (7) color; (8) familiarity; (9) complexity; (10) speed of response required; (11) duration of effort required; (12) amount of information from alternate sensory modalities; (13) requirements for the correct answer, slowly raising the criterion; and (14) the amount of extra information given the subject.

All of these dimensions are not relevant to all rehabilitation tasks, but all are useful at sometime. Which dimension is relevant for a given task is a matter of judgment of the patient's capabilities and the importance of the dimension to the rehabilitation goals. For example, a given spatial deficit may only be seen in complex figures. To vary the items by the size of the figure, then, might be irrelevant in this situation; varying the complexity within three dimensions would be most useful. If the nature of the basic deficit and the goals of the rehabilitation program are clear, the way in which the task should be varied is usually clear.

A task may also be changed in level of automaticity (Luria,

1963). A complex thought process can be broken into simple steps a patient may follow. This is useful for frontal disorders, where the subject is unable to appreciate a complex process, but is able to follow a series of simple instructions. Alternatively, a normally automatic process, e.g. walking, can be changed into a higher-level prefrontal process when lower brain centers, like the basal ganglia, are injured. Instead of walking, the patient can carefully match his/her steps to lines on the floor, a voluntary, conscious process.

The third requirement is that the task be quantifiable. This yields an objective measure of the progress the patient is making. This information can be used to evaluate the effectiveness of a task and provide the patient with a measure of progress, usually by showing a graph of the patient's improvement. These measures are a significant part of the overall program to insure maximum progress. Often the measurement reflects the level of the task the patient reaches on a given day.

The final requirement for the rehabilitation task is feedback. There are two primary types of feedback in the rehabilitation task: *internal feedback* inherent in the tasks themselves and *external feedback* on the patient's accuracy. Internal feedback comes from within the task. Usually the patient receives information from two sources: from an impaired source, due to the brain injury, and from an unimpaired source. For example, a patient who has trouble naming an object when seeing it but not when feeling it might be given the object in both sensory modalities. The information from the tactile modality allows the patient to name what he is seeing. With progress, the unimpaired feedback is reduced, perhaps by using more complex figures which are difficult to identify by tactile feedback alone, and the patient slowly learns to use and rely more on the impaired modality, sometimes without even realizing what is happening. Theoretically, this process may begin to involve the unimpaired part of the brain in the completion of the task in the impaired sense.

External feedback comes from sources outside of the task. This is usually from a therapist or sometimes from a machine which monitors the patient progress. Usually this feedback advises the patient whether his attempt to solve the rehabilitation task has been successful. It is important that the meaning of this feedback be specific. For example, if the patient was doing a task in which s/he could fail by either getting the wrong answer or being too slow, feedback indicating "wrong" would not be specific: The patient would not know if the answer was simply wrong or the speed too slow. This error is a common one in unstructured rehabilitation tasks. The subject may be making errors in a variety of modalities, e.g. input, motor error, motor-kinesthetic error, associative error, and so finds it difficult to turn the feedback into behavioral change. The obvious answer to this problem is to judge the patient on only one measure at a time. Usually a dimension like speed of response can only be used after accuracy of response is assured. When only one dimension is used, the feedback takes on more meaning and is more effective.

The final issue when designing a task is the relative number of errors that the patient will make. Tasks can be set up so that the task gets difficult so slowly that the patient makes few or no errors, *errorless learning*, or in such a manner that the patient makes a large number of errors. Generally, an approximation of the errorless learning approach is probably best. Too many errors indicate that a task is progressing in difficulty too fast. No errors at all, however, may indicate that the task is progressing too slowly. A few errors may indicate a reasonably designed task progressing at an optimum rate. This approach allows the patient to generally get positive feedback, an important motivational situation. It also shows the patient that progress is being made and that therapy is achieving the goals it promises. This feedback is often important to the therapist as well.

THERAPY APPROACHES

One type of rehabilitation task must deal with the emotional needs and problems of the patient and family. These can be severe, as brain injury often leads to extensive disruption of a patient's life, finances, marriage, and family. It is important that the family and patient, as much as possible, understand the nature of the patient's deficits, the likelihood of recovery, and the nature and length of the rehabilitation program. The type of therapy for emotional and behavioral disorders depends on the age of the patient.

With children, the best approach appears to be behavioral in nature. Emotional/behavioral disorders in children often stem from cognitive deficits making it difficult for them to understand their environment. In children, there is a preponderance of diffuse deficits particularly affecting the ability of the child to integrate information and understand the complexities of social interactions. Thus, in their attempts to get attention and regard from others, they often fall into stereotyped activity. Misbehavior and hyperactivity may be behaviors gaining attention for the child. When the child is unable to conceive any alternate way to get these same rewards, it is not surprising that this behavior dominates the child's way of interacting with the world.

It is often the case that the child's parents, siblings, schoolmates, and teachers force the child into such an offensive position as well. The child is punished for failing: It's often reported that the brain-injured child is "stupid," "lazy," or "just doesn't try," both by teachers, parents, and other significant people in the child's environment. Playmates may not like the child because s/he is clumsy, socially inappropriate, or just different. As a result, the child is forced into being friends with other children whose emotional and social problems may be expressed in "acting out" and other antisocial behaviors.

Behavior modification can also provide a standard and predictable world which the child is able to comprehend. The child is able to learn that there are alternate routes for reinforcement, as well as routes which bring immediate and reliable punishment. In this kind of environment, many of these children react quite positively. This is also a useful situation for parents who previously did not know what to do because the child was "brain damaged" or "hyperactive" and "couldn't help it." In the author's experience, there are very few children who do not improve in such a situation or who are organically incapable of normal behavior.

With adults or older children, an attempt is made to explain their situation: what has happened to them; what caused it, in detail if they wish to know and are able to understand; and what can be done about it. If some injuries are expected to be permanent, the patient is informed of that. Too high expectations are often a cause of adverse reactions to therapy and rehabilitation by the patient. The therapeutic situation then becomes a process of getting the patient to realistically accept his/her situation and motivate him/her to aid in those tasks and areas where help can be offered.

One prime goal is to get the patient in a job which will be found to be interesting and within the patient's limitations. Make-work jobs should be avoided, because most patients, except those very severely injured, are quite capable of recognizing such situations.

In some cases, family therapy has been found useful; members of a family may express themselves and understand one another. Such group therapy should come, usually, after individual sessions, so that the therapist has an understanding of the patient. Allowing a patient to be in a family therapy situation must depend on the patient's readiness to handle any problems that may arise in therapy.

Some patients are referred for standard psychotherapies when the original neuropsychological counseling indicates a severe emotional problem. In making such referrals, we attempt to match the patient's levels and patterns of abilities with a therapy appropriate for that patient. Some therapies are too difficult for many of the moderately or severely injured patients or inappropriate for their present problems. Group therapy is often used to allow the patient to see that others have similar problems. Often, the patients of a carefully chosen group can provide aid and support for one another. However, group therapy should only follow initial individual counseling to insure that the group experience would be valuable both to the patient and the group .

EVALUATION

Evaluation is an important aspect of rehabilitation therapy that has been largely ignored. One problem with evaluation is the complexity of the processes which are involved: Each patient has different problems, priorities, and goals. As a result, studies involving groups of patients getting a particular treatment versus those who do not get the treatment are difficult to interpret. Diller et al. (1974) have noted in an excellent study that different patients gained different skills from a single task depending on the nature of the patients' underlying deficits. This makes group evaluation difficult. Consequently, an individualized or single-subject approach to evaluation would appear most reasonable (Gudeman et al., 1977).

Single-subject designs have been developed in recent years as a technique for the evaluation of behavioral therapy (Sidman, 1960). These techniques offer powerful experimental approaches to the complex question of individual rehabilitation. In addition to these techniques, more global measures designed for an assessment of the overall effectiveness of the ideas and principles presented in a program have been added. Finally, an evaluation procedure for day-to-day progress relevant to the ongoing course of therapy is described.

Multiple Baseline (Single-Subject) Designs

This design is based on the assumption that factors affecting general recovery, improvement of the physical condition or general motivation, will affect all impaired abilities equally. As a consequence, improvement on one skill for which there is no training given can act as a baseline for a skill in which treatment is given. For a rehabilitation technique to be classified as successful, it must show more improvement in the trained than in untrained tasks. Usually, several skills for which training is planned but not yet begun are used to give independent estimates of the spontaneous rate of improvement.

After the initial task has been in progress long enough to establish effectiveness, the patient begins another task. This task is measured against all the remaining, unused tasks. In this way, skills not yet learned can serve as baselines for preexisting skills. More than one task can begin at any one time as long as there remains at least one baseline task.

An example may make this rehabilitation process clearer. It is found that a patient is deficient in five areas: A, B, C, D, and E. It is decided that the patient needs to start immediately with tasks A and B. The level of the patient is measured on all five tasks in which the rehabilitator plans to work with the subject. (The procedure for this is discussed in the next section.) Later the patient is measured on all skills. If it is found that skills A and B increase more than skills C, D, and E, then the program has been successful. At this time, the program can start with tasks C and D. A month later the subject is reevaluated on all the tasks. More improvement on tasks A, B, C, and D would be expected than on E. At this time, task E could be started.

An alternative way of analyzing each skill would be to compare the improvement on each task during the training period against improvement during the no-training period. This is not as effective a design in an experimental sense but offers additional information. These techniques have the advantage that the patient serves as his or her own control group. Thus we are able to measure the patient against an individualized rather than group rate of recovery.

Baseline Determination for Tasks

It is relatively easy to design baseline measures for tasks. After the task has been constructed, new but similar items—using different materials—should be constructed. Items should reflect each major level of difficulty in the task. Two to three items from each level are usually appropriate. The patient is then tested on each item without feedback or training to determine the patient's baseline level.

Testing should take place at least twice, on two different days, in order to determine if familiarity with the material without feedback is alone adequate for improvement. If significant changes are seen from one day to the next, further baseline days should be gathered until a stable baseline is reached (usually defined as the subject no longer making any significant improvement). This is done for all the tasks on which the patient will be trained.

Day-to-Day Measures

The day-to-day evaluation is based on the highest level or score the patient achieves in each training session with a task. This progress should be graphed so that the patient and the therapist can be aware of the progress the patient is making.

Global Measures

The global measures are the neuropsychological tests given at the beginning of the rehabilitation program. They should be readministered at the end of the rehabilitation program or at the point where the major goals of the training program have been achieved. One can look at several measures here. Overall performance across tests is one measure of change, but suffers in that it does not control for spontaneous recovery. A second method is to look at changes in specific tests theoretically related to the areas that have been worked on, as measured against tests in areas where there has been no training (control tests). If the control tests are in areas that were not impaired in the first place, the results are questionable. There is a tendency for the subject's high scores to go down and the low scores to go up because of statistical error, or regression to the mean. However, if the measurement is against impaired but untrained areas, the comparison is meaningful.

Global scores may also be used to compare treated and untreated groups or groups receiving different types of treatment. Since most treatment is likely to produce some positive results no matter what is done, simply through motivation and effort, the comparison of alternate treatment programs, e.g. individualized versus group programs, is the stronger demonstration of the effectiveness of any approach.

TASK ADMINISTRATION PROCEDURES

In most cases, more than one task is usually designed for a given area to insure that training is not task specific. The decision on the number of tasks usually involves an assessment of the importance of the skill and the specificity or generality of the contexts in which the skill will be needed by the patient.

At the initial training session, baselines are determined for all tasks to be used in the rehabilitation program. If further tasks are later added to the program, baselines are established for these as they are developed. Baselines may indicate that a task is too simple or too hard; the patient may finish all or none of the items. If this occurs, the task must be revised to include less- or more-difficult levels.

After the baseline period is completed, regular training sessions should begin. These should be daily or as frequent as possible. If the patient is living at home, the family should be given the responsibility for completing some of the training tasks. Tasks should begin at the highest level the patient was able to perform perfectly during the baseline period.

The patient should proceed to higher training levels as each level is completed. Completion means getting all items correct at the training level at least two sessions in a row, although this criterion can be changed for a given task, depending on the judgment of the therapist.

After the patient has completed all levels of a task, the baseline items are again administered to see whether there is a carry-over to other items. If the patient can solve all the baseline items, the therapy proceeds to the next planned task. If the patient fails the baseline items, it is usually necessary to add more items to the task for additional training, or to reject the task as a whole and plan new tasks to train on the desired skill.

In between the beginning and the end of a training task, the day-to-day data may be analyzed to check the patient's progress and the task itself. A long period without improvement suggests that the task level is too difficult for the patient. Alternatively, if the patient progresses at a rapid rate with little effort, the tasks are likely too easy. Both of these conditions require changes in the rehabilitation task or programs.

After completion of the entire rehabilitation program, or after every three months or so, the full set of baseline tasks should be readministered to record the patient's progress. Re-administration of the neuropsychological test battery should come after six to twelve months of work, in order to assess the long-term change. At this time, a new rehabilitation program may be designed or the patient terminated.

The length of the rehabilitation program varies considerably, depending on the severity of the deficits. Most of the information is directed toward patients with severe problems, since these are the patients who most need long-term help of the kind described in this chapter. The techniques are appropriate for patients with mild disorders, but the length of therapy is not as extensive. Depending on severity, maximum gain can usually be achieved for most patients in a period of two to eighteen months.

Chapter 10

REHABILITATION TECHNIQUES

A S OBSERVED in the last chapter, there are numerous techniques that can be adapted for the treatment of specific brain disorders. There is no specific task applicable to all persons with a given problem, since each individual has a different pattern of overall strengths and weaknesses. It is important in the design of the individual rehabilitation program to take these factors into account, if the maximally effective rehabilitation program is to be designed.

Despite this, it is possible to discuss general approaches to individual deficits that can be modified to fit the overall pattern of skills displayed by each patient. Each can be adapted in terms of how instructions are presented, the rate at which the tasks progress, and the kind of material used. Consequently, the following suggestions can only be considered guidelines. It is not within the scope of this chapter to consider techniques devised by such areas as physical and occupational therapy and speech pathology. The emphasis will be on techniques developed out of a theoretical basis consistent with Chapter 9.

MOTOR DISORDERS

These disorders can arise out of a number of different lesions in the brain. This includes disorders of the secondary and primary areas of the frontal lobes, as well as disorders of kinesthetic feedback from lesions of the parietal lobe. Disorders of the brain stem, cerebellum, and extrapyramidal system may also cause significant movement deficits. In choosing the proper rehabilitation technique, it is necessary to discriminate among these problems.

Biofeedback Techniques

The use of biofeedback for the treatment of motor disorders is a relatively new development. The early controlled research, however, has been very supportive, indicating a growing future for these techniques (Blanchard and Young, 1974). The basic

206

procedure involves the placement of electrodes on the disturbed muscle, transmitting impulses to an electromyograph (EMG). The EMG measures and records changes in the electrical activity of the muscle. The electrical activity in the muscle increases as the muscle contracts and decreases as it relaxes. Thus, biofeedback can provide a sensitive measure of the activity within a muscle.

Biofeedback procedures are used for rehabilitation by displaying the information from the muscle to the patient, usually as an auditory or visual signal that changes as the muscle activity changes. This allows the patient to devise strategies by which s/he can control the muscle activity. The task may be varied in two major ways. First, the criterion for a successful performance can be changed. At first, the amount of change necessary can be very minimal. This is extended in small steps as the patient progresses. Usually, the patient should be able to make reliable changes at a given level before moving to a higher level.

The difficulty of the task can also be manipulated by changing the sensitivity of the EMG. Lowering the sensitivity causes the EMG to require a greater change in muscle activity, in order to get any change in the feedback. This can be used effectively to fade out the dependence for EMG feedback and make the patient more dependent on his/her own sensory feedback. At the end of a successful program, the patient should have independent control of the muscle and the limb. However, recovery may only be partial in some cases, depending on the extent of the injury.

Biofeedback can be a useful technique for those patients with involvement of the somatosensory pathways or the parietal lobe. Many of the studies which have been reported have used patients with infarctions of the middle cerebral artery, which usually include both motor and somatosensory deficits. The patients had often attempted and failed with other motor therapies (Basmajian, Kulkulka, Narayan, and Takebe, 1975; Simard and Ladd, 1971; Taft, Delagi, Wilkie, and Abramson, 1962).

A second type of patient for whom these techniques may be useful is one who has suffered complete destructions of the sensorimotor areas of one hemisphere, although the other hemisphere is intact. In these patients, there is a need for the intact hemisphere to take over the control of the ipsilateral arm and leg. Theoretically, biofeedback should be an efficient and useful tool in such a process.

Another technique needing more attention is the use of bio-feedback in the movement disorders of children. Children with early brain injury may develop a number of disorders character-istic of somatosensorimotor deficits ranging from clumsiness to paralysis. The feedback can be given to a child in either audi-tory or visual signals and modified into forms suitable for a child of a given age. The modification of the feedback can be made into a game for many children.

The procedures described above have been altered to treat other motor deficits. Cleeland (1973) has described a procedure for treating patients with torticollis. *Torticollis* is a spasm of the neck muscles causing a sudden rotation of the head. It is gener-ally an intractable disorder, responding poorly to both medica-tion and surgical intervention (Bannister, 1973). It has been speculated this is a disorder of kinesthetic feedback, although the actual etiology remains unknown. Cleeland (1973) found that the condition could not be treated by EMG feedback alone. However, a combination of a shock which began and ended with the spasm and continuous EMG biofeedback was found to be successful with some patients. Research in this area is in a developmental stage, but there seems to be strong clinical evi-dence of the potential of biofeedback in these problems.

The Cleeland study appears to use a procedure similar to the technique described by Luria (1963). Luria has reported that the extra feedback from a muscle caused by pain, electrical stimulation, or intense pressure aids in the training of a patient with somatosensorimotor deficits. It is possible that the presence of pain either enhances the somatosensory feedback being re-ceived or that receptors normally carrying pain impulses are be-coming involved in carrying kinesthetic impulses. In either case, it appears that these procedures do add extra effectiveness to therapy of otherwise untreatable disorders.

Involvement of Higher Cognitive Skills

Luria (1963) has found that disorders of the pathways involved in the extrapyramidal tract, such as Parkinsonism, might be partially aided by making the task a more complex, cognitive task rather than an automatic motor skill. Luria has suggested painting lines on a floor and asking the patient to walk carefully from line to line rather than across the floor. In this situation, he says, much of the gait disturbance is eliminated. To make this task useful to the patient, a procedure would have to be developed by which the lines would be faded out, perhaps by periodically eliminating one or two of the lines until they are all eliminated. Whether this procedure would have any general applicability is as yet unclear.

Gross Motor: Finer Control

Biofeedback techniques are most applicable to establishing control over moving a muscle but not for establishing the accuracy of gross motor movements. Since such finer control is absolutely essential, restoration of movement must be followed by further procedures designed to aid in the restoration of accuracy.

There are several major steps in this process. First, there is a need to establish movements with one hand. This can be done in a variety of ways. The patient may be asked to imitate gross motor movements done by the examiner, who varies them from the simple, requiring only one movement, to those which are complex and involve several, unrelated movements. Another task might include the copying of large drawings on a blackboard. Achievement could be measured by the accuracy of the drawings to the models. More complex figures could then be attempted by the patient. After accuracy has been established, then speed can be worked on. It is important to note that all of these gross motor accuracy tasks involve visual coordination as well. If there exists a significant visual problem, it is necessary to work on that deficit either concurrently or before initiating these programs.

Once a patient has achieved success with visual feedback, it is often useful to have the patient do a series of tasks without visual aids to help in the development of the patient's internal sense of his/her own body schema. These tasks can start off simply by having the patient, with his/her eyes closed, keep an arm in a given position for longer and longer periods of time. More complex tasks include matching the position of one arm to the position of the second arm placed for the patient by the examiner. Finally, the patient can be required to place each arm singly or together in a given position from rest by verbal command. It is often important for the subject to develop these skills, since many tasks in work situations, running machines, trucks, and assembly lines, require gross motor movements while the client's visual attention is directed toward other events. Because this deficit is minor, it may not be observed in an ordinary examination to see if a patient is ready to go back to work. In the author's practice, he has treated several patients with this deficit after they had failed at work which they had been given. In many cases, the referral indicated the employers thought there was an emotional problem, since the patient had been declared ready to return to work.

If a patient is to be returned to a job using these skills, some specific training should be suggested, even if this is only a return to a former job that the patient supposedly knows well. This is an important step in coordinating the rehabilitation program with returning the patient to work.

Fine Motor Techniques

A common deficit after sensorimotor injury is a loss of fine motor skills. It is important in treating such disorders to begin at a simple level, so that the patient is able to succeed with few problems. Involvement of the patient in more complex tasks, even those made up of a series of relatively simple movements, may retard the success and effectiveness of the training, because of the number of variables the patient has to manipulate in order to do what is required.

In general, fine motor programs should change over several major steps: (1) making simple single movements successfully and reliably on command, e.g. making one twist of a screw, moving a finger; (2) combining sequentially the same movement repetitively until the sequence is smooth, e.g. twisting a screw into a nut; (3) combining sequentially different simple movements, such as picking up a peg and placing it in a pegboard; (4) coordinated, simple movements in both hands simultaneously; (5) continued repetitive movements with both hands; (6) alternating coordinated movements between the two hands; and (7) complex fine motor tasks, playing a musical instrument the patient may have known, sculpture, painting, and other similar skills selected for the patient's interest in them.

In addition to these major levels of a program, it is also possible and useful to vary a number of alternate dimensions within each level. The first of these is size: In any task which involves manipulation of objects it is useful to start with larger, easier-to-grasp objects and then progressively shrink the size of the object. A second dimension which is important is shape: Objects of different shape require somewhat different grasping and handling skills. It is useful for the patient to work with a wide variety of shapes. The next dimension is speed. This is obviously important, but it is necessary not to emphasize it until accuracy at the tasks over a variety of stimuli has been achieved. Finally, it is useful to develop the simpler skills without visual feedback. An ability to do simple motor movements without watching is important for day-to-day activities.

The tasks used at each level of the program may vary considerably, using different materials and assessment procedures. Among those tasks that might be considered are movement tasks of the hands and fingers without any other material, usually imitating the trainer, nuts and bolts, pegboards, building tasks, sorting tasks of chips or matches changed in lengths, hand puppets, and pantomime. For younger patients, educational games sold by toy stores can often be adapted into the kind of task required. For patients previously interested, carpentry tasks, sewing, knitting, typing, writing, drawing, painting, and other similar skills may be adapted into the program.

The area of fine motor skills, because of its pervasive importance in everyday activities, offers a nearly infinite number of tasks that can be adapted to the needs and interests of the individual patient. As long as the basic levels are followed without progressing too quickly, the task used does not seem to matter. As there is a tendency for many motor skills not to generalize as well as might be expected, it is important that the patient is exposed to many different stimuli and demands within an overall program.

In addition to the tasks described here, Luria (1963) has suggested that additional performance may be developed by involving higher cognitive skills. Rather than asking a patient to tap his finger, for example, the patient may be asked to tap out his age in years. This involves processes other than simple motor skills and may aid in the reorganization of the underlying functional system.

Avoidance Conditioning

This technique takes advantage of two processes: motivation and the use of a more basic functional system. This task causes movement by applying a shock to a paralyzed limb. This is effective because shock avoidance depends upon a much more basic, involuntary functional system than that mediated by the frontal motor areas. In addition, it provides motivation for the patient to move the arm, which might not have been previously present. Several studies have reported successful results with this technique on patients who have been unimproved by more standard approaches (Halberstam, Zaretsky, Brucker, and Guttman, 1971; Ince, 1969). Such techniques, however, are not used in general unless more benign approaches have failed.

Epileptic Seizures

Epileptic seizures, often involving the motor system, are a common secondary result of many brain injuries as well as a primary, idiopathic disorder. A subset of seizures can be identified which are set off by well-defined stimuli, such as certain acoustic, visual, or tactile stimuli. A series of studies over the past decade (Forster, Hansotia, Cleeland, and Ludwig, 1969; Forster, Klove, Peterson, and Bengzon, 1965; Forster, Booker, and Gascon, 1967;

Forster and Campos, 1964) has reported that the individual with such problems can be extinguished, using classical extinction procedures so that the sensory stimuli no longer evoke the seizure.

Other researchers (Johnson and Meyer, 1974; Sterman, McDonald, and Stone, 1974) have attempted to teach patients how to modify their brain rhythms to affect the incidence and severity of seizures. While some successes have been reported using biofeedback of brain waves, the value of this area is unclear at the current time. Consequently, such procedures are usually only indicated when traditional medical treatments have failed or as adjuncts to medical treatment.

VERBAL FUNCTIONS

Because of the importance of verbal functions in everyday life, a tremendous amount of rehabilitation interest has been focused on verbal disorders. As has been seen in earlier chapters of this book, verbal disorders represent widely different underlying deficits in which the expression in terms of observable behavior may be difficult to distinguish.

Disorders of the Temporal Lobe

Disorders of the primary area of the left temporal lobe can result in pure word deafness. The patient is able to hear but not to understand speech sounds. Depending on the severity of the loss, this can be a difficult deficit to rehabilitate. The most efficient way to attempt rehabilitation is to involve the use of another functional system to assist and compensate for the problem. This usually involves the teaching of lipreading to the person. This method allows the right hemisphere to take over some of the speech decoding function. It is useful to begin with common words which can be pronounced by the trainer, simultaneously seen by the patient, and then repeated by the patient. Then the trainer may switch to words with less-concrete representations, e.g. verbs and nouns like *liberty*, and eventually eliminate all visual representations entirely. Difficulty may be changed by varying the number of syllables in a word.

When the disorder is in the secondary temporal area, the loss is more serious, since there is a deficit in the phonemic structure of all verbal processes. Such a disorder may be reflected as a deficit in speaking, reading, and writing, as well as hearing. It must be recognized in such situations that the basic deficit is the analysis of phonemes and all resources should be concentrated in this area.

Several techniques can be employed in the loss of phonemic hearing; all are dependent on any intact areas in the left secondary temporal lobe taking over the lost functions or in the transfer of some of the functions to the intact right hemisphere. The first techniques associated pictures of objects which begin with a certain sound, for example, *t*, with the written representation of the word and the oral presentation of the word. The attempt is to get the subject to say the initial phoneme. In more severe cases, the trainer may help the patient express the sound by molding the mouth and lips and allowing the person to feel the air flow at the larynx so that it can be imitated. The purpose of this technique is to involve other areas of the brain in improving functioning of the damaged system.

It is important that each basic English phoneme be highly practiced before moving on to longer words or fading any of the visual aids. The development of phonemic understanding after a severe lesion is slow and very difficult (Luria, 1963). It should be found, in cases where this process is successful, that subsequent retraining in areas like reading or writing should be quick, unless the lesion extends into areas of the brain outside of the temporal lobe.

The training tasks as outlined above are highly dependent on the ability to speak. If there is a serious motor speech deficit as well, it may be better at first to have the patient point to a letter representing the sound, out of several similar letters, or select a picture of an object beginning with the same sound as the sound being taught.

After the initial training and the relearning of the phonemic structure of words and language, the patient can work on naming objects and words presented to him or her. If there remains a speech problem caused by the phonemic disability, the patient may be aided by pronouncing his own words on a tape which s/he must later decode by listening to the words on the tape. This helps to make the patient more aware of his/her own pronounciation deficits, compared to what is expected or heard from others. This technique can also be used for patients tending to mumble or slur words because of carelessness or minor motor disability.

Temporo-Occipital Dyslexia

This form of reading disability is known as *pure dyslexia,* since a lesion limited to this area will produce no other deficits. This deficit may be a major cause of specific reading disabilities in children. Since the deficit is limited to verbal-auditory associations, training can best accomplish its goal by teaching auditory-tactile relationships, relating phonemic sounds to plastic or sand-paper letters that in turn, can be associated with their visual equivalents. As the child progresses, the intermediate tactile step can be faded out.

It should be emphasized that this technique is clearly inappropriate for secondary temporal or parietal injuries. Techniques like this can be effective only with specific brain deficits. Similarly, intensive drilling in phonetics which is suggested for the temporal deficit is not appropriate for the temporo-occipital deficit; if both areas are involved, restoration of reading may take strong training in phonetics as well as the temporo-occipital procedures.

Verbal-Spatial Deficits

Lesions of the parietal lobe may cause deficits in the understanding of relations and words denoting relationships, especially prepositions. Treatment of this disorder is usually through concrete, spatial representation of the word meaning, allowing involvement of the frontal and right parietal areas. For example, the patient may be taught the various meanings of the word *below* by pictures representing the concept the subject must identify and then by manipulating objects to represent the concept. In early rehabilitative stages, it might be necessary for the patient to imitate the therapist's actions in order to produce the required answer. Eventually, such help must be faded out.

Grammatical and word relationships can also be taught in a diagramatical process. In each case, the concept must be expressed so that it can be understood without recourse to verbal explanations. When such deficits appear in isolation, they are usually quite amenable to treatment. When they are part of a more global aphasia, the prognosis depends on the nature of the primary deficit.

Categorization Deficits

In categorizing tasks, there are several basic dimensions which can be varied: the number of categories, abstractness of each category, degree of generation of categories, and speed of categorization. The number of categories is determined by the kind of objects or words to be categorized and the number of categories demanded for a successful performance. Generally, tasks are begun, asking for only two categories and extending this over the tasks up to about seven different categories of objects. Abstractness is an important dimension because it gives many patients a great deal of trouble. Early tasks should deal with very concrete, clear, and specific ideas, e.g. cats, circles, or birds. Initial categories should never overlap, e.g. categories of cats, dogs, and animals, although this may be done later as more abstract demands are made on the patient. Categories such as "living things" should also be delayed until the end of training, since that would require a subject to see as alike such diverse things as plants, animals, insects, and people.

The generation of categories involves either the patient generating the categories or having them given by the therapist. At first, categories should always be given to the patient. In more complicated tasks, the patient may be given some categories and expected to generate other categories. Slowly, the number of categories the patient generates should increase, until it is no longer necessary to give the patient any categories. Speed of categorization is another important variable, since this skill is used often in everyday life. However, it should not be emphasized at all until all other objectives of the program have been met.

Although the categorization process is intrinsically a verbal process (Luria, 1966), it is possible to present verbal items, words, or nonverbal items, usually pictures. Since the handling of each kind of item involves different functional systems, it is necessary to work with both kinds of items. Generally, patients with right hemisphere deficits will have more trouble with the nonverbal items, while the left hemisphere injured patient will show more trouble with verbal items. Overall, the worst deficits across items will be seen in the left hemisphere injured patient. As much as possible, training should start with the easier type of item for the patient.

When pictures are used, it is necessary to consider closely the visual complexity of the pictures. The greater the number of elements contained in a picture, the more difficult it will be for the patient. Similarly, the less concrete the word used, the more difficult the task. Words used should be familiar and easy to define.

As with all other tasks, it is important to concentrate on only one dimension at a time in moving to more difficult tasks. Since categorization is so difficult a task for many patients and because of the ease in which trainers can find themselves varying the dimensions involved at the same time, extra caution needs to be taken in designing these tasks.

Sequencing Deficits

Sequencing deficits can arise out of a number of basic disorders: (1) a verbal inability to link objects by a logical story, (2) an inability to keep sequences organized spatially, and (3) a disorder of memory. The memory and spatial deficits will be discussed later. The verbal deficit is an inability to make a story out of a picture or to see the role of a single unit within a temporal event. Usually, these deficits are seen in frontal disturbances although they may also be associated with some severe parietal injuries.

The basic training for the verbal deficit consists of two parts: (1) observing the actions and possibilities within the single picture or frame and (2) fitting a series of pictures within a reasonable story line. The first goal requires the subject to examine the contents of a picture, the relationship of the objects within the picture, and to speculate on the possible antecedents and consequences of the actions of the picture. It is typical of the brain-injured patient to either concentrate on describing one or more of the objects within the picture or omitting any information on the relationship of the parts or a past or present for the picture.

The training task should encourage the patient to develop such information by providing the kind of questions or program the patient should be asking of himself. It is often useful to do some of the steps for the patient, gradually turning over more and more responsibility. These tasks are difficult to measure, for it is necessary for the patient's responses to be judged on quality, as well as quantity. The evaluation should be set up to insure maximum feedback on what is wrong and right. In the beginning, the pictures that the patient describes should be simple, so that the feedback can be clear and useful to the patient.

The second step in developing sequencing is to give the subject a series of pictures, starting with two, that can be arranged in only one logical, sequential manner. It is the patient's responsibility to put the pictures in the correct order. The task may be judged on a right or wrong basis, or simply on the amount of time to get the correct answer. (Incorrect sequences are rejected, or the patient is asked "how else could that be arranged?") It is usually useful to have the patient explain the story by which the pictures are linked, so that the patient and the examiner may examine the logic the patient has used.

Kinesthetic Speech Deficits

Kinesthetic speech deficits result from the inability of the patient to locate his tongue or lips accurately to produce speech sounds. In these disorders, the patient has a great deal of trouble with series of sounds produced with similar muscular motions. Training in this area generally involves feedback to the patient, so the patient may relearn control of the vocal apparatus. This can be done through feedback from the trainer but is probably most effectively done through the patient's own visual feedback, using a mirror, and auditory feedback, listening to what one said. Training should begin with saying clearly separate phonemes and then concentrating on saying similarly pronounced phonemes. Attention should also be addressed to tongue and lip movements as necessary.

Motor Speech Deficits

Lesions of the motor speech area may completely paralyze the speech apparatus. In less-severe cases, however, there may be the ability to say simple phonemes, but the loss of the ability to say complex words. It may also be characterized by perseveration; the patient has difficulty switching from one sound to another.

In the more severe cases, speech may be started by taking advantage of more basic behaviors. For example, although unable to say the letter *p*, the patient usually can blow out a match. This blowing behavior can then be shaped into the letter *p*. Activities such as this, taking advantage of what the patient can do, can help lead to the reacquisition of speech. It also helps here to allow the patient to see his mouth movements (Luria, 1963). In some cases, it may be necessary to restore the use of vocal muscles. Such activities as gum chewing or playing a harmonica may aid in exercising tongue and lip muscles and breathing habits.

A recent research project has suggested taking advantage of the intact right hemisphere's musical skills to begin speech again. This *melodic intonation therapy* attempts to embed short phrases and sentences in simple, nonlinguistic-oriented melody patterns allowing the patient to speak again (Albert et al., 1973; Sparks, et al., 1974).

In less-severe cases, the patient has difficulty stringing sounds together without perseveration. In these cases, the introduction of a second element in the sequence may aid in the speech process. For example, the patient could be taught to say a syllable after he squeezed his fist or blinked an eye. This makes the task a more complicated cognitive task and helps the prefrontal area take over for the injured motor areas. With such techniques, a patient may be able to restore reasonable speech. With training, the time between syllables can be reduced, as well as the smoothness of the speech restored. The amount of restoration possible in each case depends on the extent of intact tissue (Luria, 1963).

Memory Functions

The loss of verbal memory can lead to a great number of obvious symptoms. The basic rehabilitation strategy is building upon the abilities of the brain as a whole to take over memory functions. The patient is started with simple memory problems, one unit, and worked up to remembering six or seven units of information. It is also possible to work on the memorization of stories, as well as verbal association. In each case, the basic rehabilitation plan involves practice on many items of increasing complexity.

Items may also be made more difficult by varying the relationship between the items to be memorized. The less the relationship between the items, the harder it is to remember. For example, the series "cat, dog, bird" is easier to remember than the series "castle, measles, and bark."

Memory items can also be varied by the amount of time the items are presented. Standard memory drums or *tachistoscopes* can be used for this purpose. They allow a patient to see an item for times ranging from less than one-half second to several seconds or more. Initially, the items are presented slowly with the time reduced as training advances.

Finally, such procedures can be changed by the amount of time allowed to elapse between giving the items to be remembered and the recall of the items. In more difficult trials, the time between recall and exposure can be filled by irrelevant activities. It is this task which most closely approximates the situation in the real world.

Writing Disorders

Writing disorders are often secondary to motor or phonemic disorders. In such cases, any training for writing must follow the appropriate training for the primary deficits. When the basic problem is motor, writing training generally involves many of the stages seen in teaching a young child the appropriate motor movements. Useful texts in these cases are those allowing the subject to copy an already-formed letter which is slowly faded out as the person progresses. Such texts allow the patient to progress as slowly or quickly as necessary. In addition, the patient can see immediately how well he or she is doing, as measured against the examples. In many cases, this can yield rapid results. In some patients, it may be necessary to retrain the relationship between the phonemic sound and its visual representation. In these cases, the patient works on giving the appropriate sound for a given letter or writing the letter or letters when given a sound. This training may also be valuable in some reading disorders as well.

The last two tasks are also useful for children with frontal disorders which interfere with the child's ability to learn to read and write. Such children need a highly structured, overpracticed learning situation emphasizing the basic phonemic relationships until they become automatic. It is often seen that the frontal and diffusely injured child, as well as other brain-injured children, are moved ahead in these skills before the basics have been overlearned as much as necessary for successful completion of later tasks. A normal child might use other skills to compensate for moving ahead too fast; the child with brain injuries may not have other skills on which s/he can depend when the basic skills are not learned sufficiently well.

Reading Disorders

A number of reading disorders have already been discussed; however, the treatment of visual-letter agnosia, a result of secondary left occipital disorders, has not been examined. In this disorder the patient, while able to see, may lose the meaning of letters and be unable to discriminate them, visual-letter agnosia. One way to work on this deficit is to have the patient construct and name letters. Forming them out of sticks helps the patient appreciate the construction of the letters and their relationship to visual images (Luria, 1963).

In less-severe forms of secondary occipital disorders, the patient may be able to appreciate letters and objects, but only one at a time. Consequently, the patient's reading will be very slow. Teaching such a patient to see each word as a single unit rather than as a collection of words, *sight-reading*, can be valuable, since s/he can process the single word units in the time taken to process single letters.

In disorders of the right occipital lobe, the phenomenon of visual inattention may be seen: The patient will ignore the entire left half of a page. For such patients, an anchor or arrow at the left hand margin is sometimes useful in telling the patient where to start each line. It is very important in the case of such patients to make them aware of their disability, so that active scanning can be initiated to overcome the deficit. A potentially useful device for such patients is a box which gives off irregular beeps (Hurlburt, 1975). At each beep, the patient is taught to examine his behavior to see if the left visual field is being ignored. In this way, the patient may be taught to automatically take cognizance of the left visual field.

Another reading disorder can be caused by a right spatial deficit. The patient has trouble staying on the line being read. This deficit is easily handled by providing a card that can isolate the line the subject is reading. The major training in such cases is for the spatial disability to be discussed below.

Mathematical Disorders

These disorders, arising as a result of left parieto-occipital deficits, come as a result of the patient not understanding the spatial nature of the mathematical operations and symbols. Consequently, rehabilitation must emphasize teaching the spatial nature of the operations. It is important to relate numbers to the quantitities they represent, as well as to concretely demonstrate the meaning of mathematical operations. For school children with these disabilities, as well as adults with severe losses of skills, it is also important to teach the memorization of basic multiplication, addition, and subtraction tables.

Other Training Tasks for Verbal Disorders

In some cases with serious losses of reading, writing, or speaking skills, no rehabilitation program is successful in bringing back the lost skill. In such cases various alternate skills such as sign language (Eagleson, Vaughn, and Knudson, 1970; Glass et al., 1973) or braille may be taught. In each of these cases, the emphasis of the rehabilitation would be in developing fine motor and somatosensory skills.

SPATIAL SKILLS

As we have already seen, there are a number of important verbal skills and movement skills that depend on basic spatial orientation. Visual-motor tasks rely considerably upon basic spatial abilities.

Basic Visual-Spatial Orientation

The most basic visual-spatial tasks are the perception of line, angle, and orientation. Thus, the most basic tasks in this area deal with the matching of lines drawn at different angles with other lines drawn at a variety of angles. Alternately, two lines forming an angle can be matched against a number of similar elements. (This task is borrowed from one of the tests on the Reitan-Indiana Neuropsychological Battery for Children.) The task can be made more difficult by making the items and choices more similar and by increasing the number of choices. The patient needs to be able to do these simple matching tasks before s/he can try more difficult, construction tasks.

Another basic deficit involves secondary visual problems. This is similar to the visual-letter agnosia but is an agnosia for objects. As with visual-letter agnosia, it is helpful for the patient to construct objects to conceptualize their structure, as well as to rely more on the capacities of the left hemisphere and right visual field. This deficit, in its more severe forms, can be very difficult to deal with. In some cases, the patient must be taught to deal with the deficit by scanning his or her visual field carefully before making decisions.

Visual scanning of the environment may be taught by giving the patient pictures in which the specific objects must be found. Initially, the patient may be asked to pick out one object, and later many. The complexity of the pictures can be varied from simple to highly complex. The basic measure (since nearly all patients are successful at the task) is time, with a goal of reducing the time to normal levels. In later tasks, the therapist can have a patient scan his environment for objects.

After these basic skills have been established, along with fine and gross motor skills, the patient can practice at a number of construction tasks. This includes such tasks as block construction and also toothpick construction and any similar tasks one can develop. The tasks may be begun at a very simple level using few and building up to more pieces. The constructions themselves can vary in complexity, as the designs or objects reproduced grow more complicated.

Alternatively, Diller et al. (1974) have presented a training task by which the patient is aided on the task by cues which are slowly decreased in value. On a block design task, the cues consisted of nine levels going from those which conveyed little or no help to those which provided everything except the very final stage of the answer. For example, the cues included an outline of the final figure, indications where each block went and indications of the orientation and color of the block that went in each space. As the patient progresses, the more informative cues are eliminated until the patient is able to do the task without cues.

Orientation in Space

A second type of disability is the inability to locate oneself in space. Teaching in this area may involve such tasks as mazes, both visually guided and without vision, map reading, and locating oneself in a neighborhood or ward.

Maze learning is a useful orientation task, since the patient may be asked to rotate the way in which the maze is done. Once the patient has shown the ability to do a visually guided maze, the maze can then be rotated, and the patient must solve the maze as rotated. The complexity of the maze may be changed by altering the number of turns in the maze. The angle of rotation may also be changed to demand more spatial transformations.

After a visually guided maze has been successfully done, a maze done by touch alone is useful, since this can be done without visual feedback. Thus, the tactile maze demands more of a purely spatial transformation and is consequently somewhat harder than a visual maze, whether on paper or a stylus maze board. The basic task construction is the same.

A third stage is a human maze in which the subject must orient himself within a mazelike structure, much as was done representationally in the paper and tactile mazes. A similar task may be done by teaching the patient to negotiate the hospital or local neighborhood, requiring the patient to go to a given place from different starting points and when traveling in different directions.

Map reading is also a useful task for these deficits since the patient must use the concept of direction. In this task, the patient should show how to get from a variety of places to other spots on the map, specifying the directions and turns that are required. Adjusting the orientation of the map allows the patient to make basic spatial transformations.

Spatial-Frontal Disorders

Spatial disorders due to frontal lesions reflect an inability to properly program incoming stimuli (Luria and Tsvetkova, 1964). These subjects do not have difficulty with reproducing simple drawings but are severely impaired when the task requires analysis and breakdown into a series of simpler procedures. These patients must be taught either a sequence of behaviors which are generally useful, or specific techniques for handling particular types of problems. The breakdown of tasks into basic steps as demonstrated by Diller and his associates (1974) offers an ideal training task for these patients. This process is basically one of taking a higher cognitive skill and making it into a series of more basic, automatic skills.

SELECTING REHABILITATION TECHNIQUES

In this chapter, possible rehabilitation techniques or approaches which may be used with a given deficit in an individual program were discussed. Hopefully, it is clear to the reader that our suggestions represent only a fraction of the possible techniques that may be needed in regularly setting up such programs. The author's own experience has been that, with each new patient, the unique pattern of results on the diagnostic evaluation often demands, as well as suggests, new rehabilitation techniques that had not previously been included in the program. Consequently, it is important that a rehabilitation neuropsychologist carefully avoid being too dependent on a technique or set of techniques, to the extent that the techniques become the answer to all rehabilitation problems.

BIBLIOGRAPHY

Adams, J.: An Investigation of School Children on Canter's Background Interference Procedure for the Bender-Gestalt. Unpublished masters thesis, University of Iowa, 1966.

Adams, J. and Canter, A.: Performance characteristics of school children in the BIP Bender Test. J Consult Clin Psychol, 33:508, 1969.

Adams, J., Kenny, T. J., and Canter, A.: The efficacy of the Canter Background Interference Procedure in identifying children with cerebral dysfunction. J Consult Clin Psychol, 40:489, 1973.

Adler, E. and Tal, E.: Relationship between physical disability and functional capacity in hemiplegic patients. Arch Phys Med Rehabil, 46:745, 1965.

Aita, J. A., Armitage, S. G., Reitan, R. M., and Rabinowitz, P.: The use of certain psychological tests in the evaluation of brain injury. J Gen Psychol, 37:25, 1947.

Aita, J. A. and Reitan, R. M.: Psychotic reactions in the late recovery period following brain injury. Am J Psychiatry, 105:161, 1948.

Aita, J. A., Reitan, R. M., and Ruth, J. M.: Rorschach's Test as a diagnostic aid in brain injury. Am J Psychiatry, 103:770, 1947.

Ajax, E. T.: Acquired dyslexia. Arch Neurol, 11:66, 1964.

Albert, M. L., Reches, A., and Silverberg, R.: Hemianopic colour blindness. J Neurol Neurosurg Psychiatry, 38:546, 1975.

Albert, M. L., Sparks, R. W., and Helm, N. A.: Melodic intonation therapy for aphasia. Arch Neurol, 29:130, 1973.

Alexander, D. and Money, J.: Turner's syndrome and Gerstmann's syndrome: Neuropsychologic comparisons. Neuropsychologia, 4:265, 1966.

Allen, R. N.: The test performance of the brain injured. J Clin Psychol, 3:225, 1947.

Alvarez, R. R.: Comparison of depressive and brain injured subjects on the Trail Making Test. Percept Mot Skills, 14:91, 1962.

Alzheimer, A.: On a peculiar disease of the cerebral cortex. Arch Neurol, 21:109, 1969.

Andersen, A. L. and Hanvik, L. J.: The psychometric localization of brain lesions: The differential effect of frontal and parietal lesions on MMPI profiles. J Clin Psychol, 6:177, 1950.

Anderson, T. P., Bourestom, N., and Greenberg, F. R.: Rehabilitation Predictors in Completed Stroke: Final Report. Minneapolis, American Rehabilitation Foundation, 1970.

Annett, M.: Laterality of childhood hemiplegia and the growth of speech and intelligence. *Cortex, 9:*4, 1973.

Archer, R. W.: The role of the parents in the treatment of cerebral palsy. *Rehabilitation, 49:*25, 1964.

Archibald, Y. M., Wepman, J. M., and Jones, L. V.: Performance on nonverbal cognitive tests following unilateral cortical injury to the right and left hemisphere. *J Nerv Ment Dis, 145:*25, 1967.

Armitage, S. G.: An analysis of certain psychological tests used for the evaluation of brain inury. *Psychol Monogr, 60:*277, 1946.

Arrigoni, G. and DeRenzi, E.: Constructional apraxia and hemispheric locus of lesion. *Cortex, 1:*170, 1964.

Auld, A. W., Aronson, H. A., and Gargans, F.: Aneurysm of the middle meningeal artery. *Arch Neurol, 13:*369, 1965.

Avakian, S. A.: The applicability of the Hunt-Minnesota Test for organic brain damage to children between the ages of ten and sixteen. *J Clin Psychol, 17:*45, 1961.

Ayers, S. J., Templer, D., and Ruff, C. F.: The MMPI in the differential diagnosis of organicity versus schizophrenia: Empirical findings and a somewhat different perspective. *J Clin Psychol, 31:*685, 1975.

Bachrach, H. and Mintz, J.: The Wechsler Memory Scale as a tool for the detection of mild cerebral dysfunction. *J Clin Psychol, 30:*58, 1974.

Balasubramanian, V. and Ranamurthi, B.: Stereotaxic amygdalotomy in behavior disorders. *Confin Neurol, 32:*367, 1970.

Balthazar, E. E.: Cerebral unilateralization in chronic epileptic cases: The Wechsler Object Assembly Subtest. *J Clin Psychol, 19:*169, 1963.

Balthazar, E. E. and Morrison, D. H.: The use of Wechsler Intelligence Scales as diagnostic indicators of predominant left, right and indeterminate unilateral brain damage. *J Clin Psychol, 17:*161, 1961.

Bannister, R.: *Brain's Clinical Neurology,* 4th ed. London, Oxford U Pr, 1973.

Bardach, J. L.: Psychological factors in the handicapped driver. *Arch Phys Med Rehabil, 52:*328, 1971.

Barnes, G. W. and Lucas, G. J.: Cerebral dysfunction vs. psychogenesis in Halstead-Reitan Tests. *J Nerv Ment Dis, 158:*50, 1974.

Barrett, R. E.: Dementia in adults. *Med Clin North Am, 56:*1405, 1972.

Basmajian, J. V., Kukulka, C. G., Narayan, M. G., and Takebe, K.: Biofeedback treatment of foot-drop after stroke compared with standard rehabilitation technique: Effects on voluntary control and strength. *Arch Phys Med Rehabil, 56:*231, 1975.

Basser, L. S.: Hemiplegia of early onset and the faculty of speech with special reference to the effects of hemispherectomy. *Brain, 85:*427, 1962.

Basso, A., DeRenzi, E., Faglioni, P., Scotti, G., and Spinnler, H.: Neuropsychologic evidence for the existence of cerebral areas critical to the performance of intelligence tasks. *Brain, 96:*715, 1973.

Beaumont, J. G.: Handedness and hemispheric function. In Dimond, S. J. and Beaumont, J. G. (Eds.): *Hemisphere Function in the Human Brain.* New York, Wiley, 1974.

Beaumont, J. G.: The validity of the Category Test administered by on-line computer. *J Clin Psychol, 31:*458, 1975.

Beaumont, J. G. and Dimond, S. J.: Clinical assessment of interhemispheric psychological functioning. *J Neurol Neurosurg Psychiatry, 36:*445, 1973.

Becker, B.: Intellectual changes after closed head injury. *J Clin Psychol, 31:* 307, 1975.

Becker, J. T. and Sabatino, D. A.: Frostig revisited. *J Learn Disabil, 6:*180, 1973.

Bell, D. S.: Speech functions in the thalamus inferred from the effects of thalamotomy. *Brain, 91:*619, 1968.

Bell, D. S.: Group therapy of epilepsy. *Rehabilitation, 67:*31, 1972.

Belmont, I., Benjamin, H., Ambrose, J., and Restuccia, R. D.: Effect of cerebral damage on motivation in rehabilitation. *Arch Phys Med Rehabil, 50:*507, 1969.

Belmont, I., Handler, A., and Karp, E.: Delayed sensory motor processing following cerebral damage. II. A multisensory defect. *J Nerv Ment Dis, 155:*345, 1972.

Bender, L.: *A Visual Motor Gestalt Test and Its Clinical Use.* New York, Am Orthopsychiatry, 1938.

Bender, M. B., Postel, D. M., and Krieger, H. P.: Disorders of oculomotor function in lesions of the occipital lobe. *J Neurol Neurosurg Psychiatry, 20:*139, 1957.

Bennett, A. E.: Mental disorders associated with temporal lobe epilepsy. *Dis Nerv Syst, 26:*275, 1965.

Benson, D. F.: Psychiatric aspects of aphasia. *Br J Psychiatry, 123:*555, 1973.

Benson, D. F., Segarra, J., and Albert, M. L.: Visual agnosia—prosopagnosia. *Arch Neurol, 30:*307, 1974.

Benson, D. F. and Wier, W. F.: Acalculia: Acquired anarithmetica. *Cortex, 8:*465, 1972.

Benton, A. L.: A visual retention test for clinical use. *Arch Neurol Psychiatry, 54:*212, 1945.

Benton, A. L.: A multiple choice type of the visual retention test. *Arch Neurol Psychiatry, 64:*699, 1950.

Benton, A. L.: Development of finger-localization capacity in school children. *Child Dev, 26:*225, 1955.

Benton, A. L.: The function of the "Gerstmann syndrome." *J Neurol Neurosurg Psychiatry, 24:*176, 1961.

Benton, A. L.: The visual retention test as a constructional praxis test. *Confin Neurol, 22:*141, 1962.

Benton, A. L.: *The Revised Visual Retention Test.* New York, Psychol Corp, 1963.

Benton, A. L.: Developmental aphasia and brain damage. *Cortex, 1:*40, 1964.

Benton, A. L.: Construction apraxia and the minor hemisphere. *Confin Neurol, 29:*1, 1967.

Benton, A. L.: Right-left discrimination. *Pediatr Clin North Am, 15:*747, 1968.

Benton, A. L.: Differential behavioral effects in frontal lobe disease. *Neuropsychologia, 6:*53, 1968.

Benton, A. L.: Development of a multilingual aphasia battery: Progress and problems. *J Neurol Sci, 9:*39, 1969.

Benton, A. L.: Abbreviated versions of the visual retention test. *J Psychol, 80:*189, 1972.

Benton, A. L.: Visuoconstructive disability in patients with cerebral disease: Its relationship to side of lesion and aphasic disorder. *Doc Ophthalmol, 34:*67, 1973.

Benton, A. L.: *The Revised Visual Retention Test,* 4th ed. New York, Psychol Corp, 1974.

Benton, A. L.: Psychological tests for brain damage. In Freedman, H. I., Kaplan, H., and Sadock, B. J. (Eds.): *Comprehensive Textbook of Psychiatry/II.* Baltimore, Williams & Wilkins, 1975.

Benton, A. L., Elithorn, A., Fogel, M. L., and Kerr, M.: A perceptual maze test sensitive to brain damage. *J Neurol Neurosurg Psychiatry, 26:*540, 1963.

Benton, A. L. and Fogel, M. L.: Three dimensional constructional praxis. *Arch Neurol, 7:*347, 1962.

Benton, A. L., Hannay, J., and Varney, N. R.: Visual perception of line direction in patients with unilateral brain disease. *Neurology, 25:*907, 1975.

Benton, A. L. and Hecaen, H.: Stereoscopic vision in patients with unilateral cerebral disease. *Neurology, 20:*1084, 1970.

Benton, A. L., Levin, H. S., and Van Allen, M. W.: Geographic orientation in patients with unilateral brain disease. *Neuropsychologia, 12:*183, 1974.

Benton, A. L., Spreen, O., Fargman, M. W., and Can, D. L.: Visual retention test. Administration C: Norms for children. *J Special Educ, 1:* 151, 1967.

Benton, A. L. and Van Allen, M. W.: Prosopagnosia and facial discrimination. *J Neurol Sci, 15:*167, 1972.

Ben-Yishay, Y., Diller, L., Gerstman, L., and Haas, A.: The relationship between impersistence, intellectual function and outcome of rehabilitation in patients with left hemiplegia. *Neurology, 18*:852, 1968.

Berg, E. A.: A simple objective technique for measuring flexibility in thinking. *J Gen Psychol, 39*:15, 1948.

Berlin, I. N.: Minimal brain dysfunction. *JAMA, 229*:1454, 1974.

Billingslea, F. Y.: The Bender-Gestalt: A review and a perspective. *Psychol Bull, 60*:233, 1963.

Bisiache, A. and Faglioni, P.: Recognition of random shapes by patients with unilateral lesions as a function of complexity, association value and delay. *Cortex, 2*:101, 1974.

Black, F. W.: Memory and paired associate learning of patients with unilateral brain lesions. *Psychol Rep, 33*:919, 1973.

Black, F. W.: Patterns of cognitive impairment in children with suspected and documented neurological dysfunction. *Percept Mot Skills, 39*:115, 1974a.

Black, F. W.: The cognitive sequelae of penetrating missile wounds of the brain. *Milit Med, 139*:815, 1974b.

Black, F. W.: The utility of the Memory for Designs Test with patients with penetrating missile wounds of the brain. *J Clin Psychol, 30*:75, 1974c.

Black, F. W.: The utility of the Shipley-Hartford as a predictor of WAIS full scale IQ for patients with traumatic head injuries. *J Clin Psychol, 30*:168, 1974d.

Black, F. W.: Use of the MMPI with patients with recent war-related head injuries. *J Clin Psychol, 30*:571, 1974e.

Black, F. W.: Unilateral brain lesions and MMPI performance: A preliminary study. *Percept Mot Skills, 40*:87, 1975.

Black, F. W.: Cognitive, academic and behavioral findings in children with suspected and documented neurological dysfunction. *J Learn Disabil, 9*:182, 1976.

Blackburn, H. L. and Benton, A. L.: Simple and choice reaction time in cerebral disease. *Confin Neurol, 15*:327, 1955.

Blackman, N.: Group therapy with aphasics. *J Nerv Ment Dis, 111*:154, 1950.

Blakemore, C. B. and Falconer, M. A.: Long-term effects of anterior temporal lobectomy on certain cognitive functions. *J Neurol Neurosurg Psychiatry, 30*:364, 1967.

Blanchard, E. B. and Young, L. D.: Clinical applications of biofeedback training: A review of evidence. *Arch Gen Psychiatry, 30*:573, 1974.

Blasubramanian, V. and Ramamurthi, B.: Stereotaxic amygdalotomy in behavior disorder. *Confin Neurol, 32*:367, 1970.

Blau, T. H. and Schaffer, R. E.: The Spiral Aftereffect Test (SAET) as a predictor of normal and abnormal electroencephalographic records in children. *J Cons Psychol, 24*:35, 1960.

Blessed, G., Tomlinson, B. E., and Roth, M.: The association between quantitative measures of dementia and the senile change in the cerebral gray matter of elderly subjects. *Br J Psychiatry, 114:*979, 1968.

Bodamer, J.: Die Prosop-Agnosie. *Arch Psychiat Nerven Krankh, 118:*6, 1947.

Boll, T. J.: Psychological differentiation of patients with schizophrenia versus lateralized cerebrovascular, neoplastic or traumatic brain damage. *J Abnorm Psychol, 83:*456, 1974a.

Boll, T. J.: Behavioral correlates of cerebral damage in children aged 9 through 14. In Reitan, R. M. & Davison, L. A. (Eds.): *Clinical Neuropsychology: Current Status and Applications.* Washington, Winston, 1974b.

Boll, T. J.: *The Effect of Age at Onset of Brain Damage on Adaptive Abilities in Children.* Submitted for publication, 1976.

Boll, T. J. and Reitan, R. M.: Psychological test results of subjects with known cerebral lesions and Parkinson's disease as compared to controls. *Percept Mot Skills, 31:*824, 1970.

Boll, T. J. and Reitan, R. M.: Motor and tactile-perceptual deficits in brain damaged children. *Percept Mot Skills, 34:*343, 1972.

Boll, T. J. and Reitan, R. M.: Effect of age on performance of the Trail Making Test. *Percept Mot Skills, 36:*691, 1973.

Boller, F.: Latent aphasia: Right and left "non-aphasic" brain damaged patients compared. *Cortex, 4:*245, 1968.

Boller, F.: Destruction of Wernicke's area without language disturbance. *Neuropsychologia, 11:*243, 1973.

Boone, D. R.: A plan for rehabilitation of aphasic patients. *Arch Phys Med Rehabil, 48:*410, 1967.

Borkowski, J. G., Benton, A. L., and Spreen, O.: Word fluency and brain damage. *Neuropsychologia, 5:*135, 1967.

Bornstein, B. and Kidron, D. P.: Prosopagnosia. *J Neurol Neurosurg Psychiatry, 22:*124, 1959.

Bortner, M. and Birch, H. G.: Perceptual and perceptual-motor dissociation in brain damaged patients. *J Nerv Ment Dis, 130:*49, 1960.

Botez, M. I. and Wertheim, N.: Expressive aphasia and amusia following right frontal lesion in a right-handed man. *Brain, 82:*186, 1959.

Bourestom, N. C. and Howard, M. T.: Behavioral correlates of recovery of self-care in hemiplegic patients. *Arch Phys Med Rehabil, 49:*449, 1968.

Bowen, F. P., Hoehn, M. M. and Yahr, M. D.: Parkinsonism: Alterations in spatial orientation as determined by a route-walking test. *Neuropsychologia, 3:*355, 1972.

Bowley, A.: Reading difficulty with minor neurological dysfunction. *Dev Med Child Neurol, 11:*493, 1969.

Boyle, R. W. and Scalzitti, P. D.: A study of 480 consecutive cases of cerebral vascular accident. *Arch Phys Med Rehabil, 44:*19, 1963.

Brain, W. R.: Visual disorientation with special reference to lesions of the right cerebral hemisphere. *Brain, 64:*244, 1941.

Brain, W. R.: Henry Head: The man and his ideas. *Brain, 84:*561, 1961.

Brewer, W. F., Visual memory, verbal encoding and hemisphere localization. *Cortex,* 5:145, 1969.

Brilliant, P. J. and Gynther, M. D.: Relationships between performance on three tests for organicity and selected patient variables. *J Consult Psychol,* 27:474, 1963.

Broadbent, D. E.: The role of auditory localization in attention and memory span. *J Exp Psychol,* 47:191, 1954.

Broca, P.: Perte de la parole. *Bull Soc Anthropol,* 2:1, 1861.

Brodmann, K.: *Vergleichende Lokalisationstehre der Grosshirnrinde in ihren Prinzipien dargestellt auf Grund des Zellenbaues.* Leipzig, Barth, 1909.

Brooks, D. N.: Memory and head injury. *J Nerv Ment Dis,* 155:350, 1972.

Brooks, D. N.: Recognition memory and head injury. *J Neurol Neurosurg Psychiatry,* 37:794, 1974.

Brooks, D. N.: Wechsler Memory Scale performance and its relationship to brain damage after severe closed head injury. *J Neurol Neurosurg Psychiatry,* 39:593, 1976.

Brown, E. C., Casey, A., Fisch, R. I., and Neuringer, C.: Trail Making Test as a screening device for the detection of brain damage. *J Consult Psychol,* 22:469, 1958.

Bruell, J. H. and Albee, G. W.: Higher intellectual functions in a patient with hemispherectomy for tumors. *J Consult Psychol,* 26:90, 1962.

Bruell, J. H. and Simon, J. I.: Development of objective predictors of recovery in hemiplegic patients. *Arch Phys Med Rehabil,* 41:564, 1960.

Bruhn, A. R. and Reid, M. R.: Simulation of brain damage on the Bender-Gestalt test by college subjects. *J Pers Assess,* 39:244, 1975.

Burns, G. W. and Watson, B. L.: Factor analysis of the revised ITPA with underachieving children. *J Learn Disabil,* 6:371, 1973.

Butters, N. and Brody, B. A.: The role of the left parietal lobe in the mediation of intra- and cross-modal associations. *Cortex,* 4:328, 1969.

Canter, A. H.: Direct and indirect measures of psychological deficit in multiple sclerosis. Part II. *J Gen Psychol,* 44:27, 1951.

Canter, A. H.: A background interference procedure to increase sensitivity of the Bender-Gestalt test to organic brain disorder. *J Consult Psychol,* 30:91, 1966.

Canter A. H.: BIP Bender test for the detection of organic brain disorder: Modified scoring method and replication. *J Consult Clin Psychol,* 32: 522, 1968.

Canter, A. H.: A comparison of the background interference procedure effect in schizophrenic, non-schizophrenic and organic patients. *J Clin Psychol,* 27:473, 1971.

Canter, A. H.: *The Canter Background Interference Procedure for the Bender-Gestalt Test.* Nashville, Counselor Recordings, 1976.

Caplan, D., Kellar, L., and Locke, S.: Inflection of neologisms in aphasia. *Brain, 95*:169, 1972.

Carmon, A.: Sequenced motor performance in patients with unilateral cerebral lesions. *Neuropsychologia, 9*:445, 1971.

Carmon, A.: Impaired memory for duration of time intervals in patients with cerebral damage. *Eur Neurol, 7*:339, 1972.

Carmon, A. and Bechtoldt, H. P.: Dominance of the right cerebral hemisphere for stereopsis. *Neuropsychologia, 7*:29, 1969.

Carmon, A. and Nachson, I.: Effect of unilateral brain damage on perception of temporal order. *Cortex, 8*:410, 1972.

Casey, T. and Ettlinger, G.: The occasional "independence" of dyslexia and dysgraphia from dysphasia. *J Neurol Neurosurg Psychiatry, 23*:228, 1960.

Cermak, L. S., Butters, N., and Goodglass, A.: The extent of memory loss in Korsakoff patients. *Neuropsychologia, 9*:307, 1971.

Chandler, B. C., Vega, A., and Parsons, O. A.: Dichotic listening in alcoholics with and without a history of possible brain damage. *Q J Stud Alcohol, 34*:1099, 1973.

Chapman, L. F. and Wolff, H.: The cerebral hemispheres and the highest integrative functions of man. *Arch Neurol, 1*:357, 1959.

Chapmann, L. F. and Wolff, H.: The human brain—one organ or many. *Arch Neurol, 5*:463, 1961.

Chedru, F., Leblanc, M., and Lhermitte, F.: Visual searching in normal and brain damaged subjects: Contribution to study of unilateral inattention. *Cortex, 9*:94, 1973.

Chorost, S. B., Spivack, G., and Levine, M.: Bender-Gestalt rotations and EEG abnormalities in children. *J Consult Psychol, 23*:559, 1959.

Christensen, A. L.: *Luria's Neuropsychological Investigation,* New York, Spectrum, 1975a.

Christensen, A. L.: *Luria's Neuropsychological Investigation; Text Cards.* New York, Spectrum, 1975b.

Christensen, A. L.: *Luria's Neuropsychological Investigation. Manual.* New York, Spectrum, 1975c.

Chusid, J.: *Correlative Neuroanatomy and Functional Neurology,* 14th ed. Los Altos, Lange, 1970.

Cleeland, C. S.: Behavioral technics in the modification of spasmodic torticollis. *Neurology, 23*:1241, 1973.

Cleeland, C. S., Matthews, C. G., and Hopper, C. L.: MMPI profiles in exacerbation and remission of multiple sclerosis. *Psychol Rep, 27*:373, 1970.

Clements, S. D.: *Minimal Brain Dysfunction in Children: Terminology and*

Identification. Phase One of a Three Phase Project. Washington, U.S. Public Health Service, 1966.

Coheen, J. J.: Disturbances in time discrimination in organic brain disease. *J Nerv Ment Dis, 112:*121, 1950.

Cohn, R.: Delayed acquisition of reading and writing abilities in children. *Arch Neurol, 4:*153, 1961a.

Cohn, R.: Dyscalculia. *Arch Neurol, 4:*301, 1961b.

Cole, M. and Kraft, M. B.: Specific learning disability. *Cortex, 1:*302, 1964.

Colligan, R. C.: Psychometric deficits related to perinatal stress. *J Learn Disabil, 7:*154, 1974.

Colonna, A. and Faglioni, P.: The performance of hemisphere damaged patients on spatial intelligence tests. *Cortex, 2:*293, 1966.

Connolly, C. J.: *External Morphology of the Primate Brain.* Springfield, Thomas, 1950.

Constantindis, J., Richard, J., and Tissot, R.: Pick's disease. *Eur Neurol, 11:* 208, 1974.

Corkin, S.: Tactually guided maze learning in man. Effects of unilateral cortical excisions and bilateral hippocampal lesions. *Neuropsychologia, 3:*339, 1965.

Corkin, S.: Serial ordering deficits in inferior readers. *Neuropsychologia, 12:* 347, 1974.

Corkin, S., Milner, B., and Rasmussen, T.: Somatosensory thresholds contrasting effects of post central gyrus and posterior parietal lobe excisions. *Arch Neurol, 23:*41, 1970.

Corkin, S., Milner, B., and Taylor, L.: Bilateral sensory loss after unilateral cerebral lesion in man. *Trans Am Neurol Assoc, 98:*118, 1973.

Costa, L. D.: Interset variability on the Raven Coloured Progressive Matrices as an indicator of specific ability deficit in brain lesioned patients. *Cortex, 12:*31, 1976.

Costa, L. D., Scarola, L. M., and Rapin, I.: Purdue Pegboard scores for normal grammar school children. *Percept Mot Skills, 18:*748, 1964.

Costa, L. D. and Vaughan, H.: Performance of patients with lateralized cerebral lesions. I. Verbal and perceptual tests. *J Nerv Ment Dis, 134:* 162, 1962.

Costa, L. D., Vaughan, H. G., Horwitz, M., and Ritter, W.: Patterns of behavioral deficit associated with visual spatial neglect. *Cortex, 5:*242, 1969.

Costa, L. D., Vaughan, H. G., Levita, E., and Farber, N.: Purdue Pegboard as a predictor of the presence and laterality of cerebral lesions. *J Consult Psychol, 27:*133, 1963.

Courville, C. B.: Coup-countrecoup mechanism of craniocerebral injuries. *Arch Surg, 45:*19, 1942.

Crinella, F. M.: Identification of brain dysfunction syndromes in children through profile analysis. *J Abnorm Psychol, 82:*33, 1973.

Critchley, M.: *The Parietal Lobes.* Baltimore, Williams & Wilkins, 1953.

Critchley, M.: Head's contribution to aphasia. *Brain, 84*:551, 1961.

Critchley, M.: The enigma of Gerstmann's syndrome. *Brain, 89*:183, 1966.

Crookes, T. G.: Wechsler's deterioration ratio in clinical practice. *J Consult Psychol, 25*:234, 1961.

Crookes, T. G. and Coleman, J. A.: The Minnesota Percepto-Diagnostic in adult psychiatric practice. *J Clin Psychol, 29*:204, 1973.

Crovitz, H. F. and Zener, K.: A group test for assessing hand and eye dominance. *Am J Psychol, 75*:271, 1962.

Crown, S.; Psychological changes following operations on the human frontal lobe. *J Consult Psychol, 17*:92, 1953.

Cumming, W. J. K., Hurwitz, L. J., and Perl, N. T.: A study of a patient who had alexia without agraphia. *J Neurol Neurosurg Psychiatry, 33*: 34, 1970.

Dailey, C. A.: Psychological findings 5 years after head injury. *J Clin Psychol, 12*:349, 1956.

Darley, F. L.: Treatment of acquired aphasia. *Adv Neurol, 7*:111, 1975.

Daube, J. R.: Sensory precipitated seizures: A review. *J Nerv Ment Dis, 141*:524, 1965.

Davids, A., Goldenberg, L., and Laufer, M. W.: The relation of the Archimedes Spiral Aftereffect and the Trail Making Test to brain damage in children. *J Consult Psychol, 21*:429, 1957.

Davies, A. D. M.: The influence of age on Trail Making Test performance. *J Clin Psychol, 24*:96, 1968.

Davison, L. A.: Introduction. In Reitan, R. M. & Davison, L. A. (Eds.): *Clinical Neuropsychology: Current Status and Applications.* Washington, Winston, 1974.

Day, R. H.: The aftereffect of seen movement and brain damage. *J Consult Psychol, 24*:311, 1960.

Dee, H. L. and Van Allen, M. W.: Simple and choice reaction time and motor strength in unilateral cerebral disease. *Acta Psychiat Scand, 47*:315, 1971.

Dee, H. L. and Van Allen, M. W.: Psychomotor testing as an aid in the recognition of cerebral lesions. *Neurology, 22*:845, 1972.

DeJong, R. N., Itabashi, H. H., and Olson, J. R.: Memory loss due to hippocampal lesions: Report of a case. *Arch Neurol, 20*:339, 1969.

Denckla, M. B. and Bowen, F. B.: Dyslexia after left occipitotemporal lobectomy: A case report. *Cortex, 9*:321, 1973.

Denhoff, E.: The best management of learning disabilities calls for pediatric skills of a special sort. But it takes more than six easy lessons to do the job. *Clin Pediatr, 12*:427, 1973.

Denhoff, E., Hainsworth, P. K., and Hainsworth, M. L.: The child at risk for learning disorder. Can he be identified during the first year of life? *Clin Pediatr, 11*:164, 1972.

Dennerll, R. D.: Cognitive deficits and lateral brain dysfunction in temporal lobe epilepsy. *Epilepsia*, 5:177, 1964a.

Dennerll, P. D.: Prediction of unilateral brain dysfunction using Wechsler test scores. *J Consult Psychol, 28*:278, 1964b.

Denny-Brown, D.: Disintegration of motor function resulting from cerebral lesion. *J Nerv Ment Dis, 112*:1, 1950.

DeRenzi, E. and Faglioni, P.: The relationship between visuo-spatial impairment and constructional apraxia. *Cortex, 3*:327, 1967.

DeRenzi, E., Faglioni, P., and Scotti, G.: Tactile spatial impairment and unilateral cerebral damage. *J Nerv Ment Dis, 146*:468, 1968.

DeRenzi, E., Faglioni, P., and Scotti, G.: Hemispheric contribution to exploration of space through the visual and tactile modalities. *Cortex, 6*: 191, 1970.

DeRenzi, E., Faglioni, P., and Scotti, G.: Judgement of spatial orientation in patients with focal brain damage. *J Neurol Neurosurg Psychiatry, 34*:489, 1971.

DeRenzi, E., Faglioni, P., Scotti, G., and Spinnler, H.: Impairment in associating colour to form, concommitant with aphasia. *Brain, 95*:293, 1972.

DeRenzi, E., Pieczuro, A., Savoiardo, M., and Vignolo, L. A.: The influence of aphasia and of the hemisphere side of the cerebral lesion on abstract thinking. *Cortex, 2*:399, 1966.

DeRenzi, E., Pieczuro, A., and Vignolo, L. A.: Ideational apraxia: A quantitative study. *Neuropsychologia, 6*:41, 1968.

DeRenzi, E. and Piercy, M.: The Fourteenth International Symposium of Neuropsychology. *Neuropsychologia, 7*:583, 1969.

DeRenzi, E. and Spinnler, H.: Facial recognition in brain damaged patients: An experimental approach. *Neurology, 16*:145, 1966a.

DeRenzi, E. and Spinnler, H.: Visual recognition in patients with unilateral cerebral disease. *J Nerv Ment Dis, 142*:515, 1966b.

DeRenzi, E. and Spinnler, H.: Impaired performance on color tasks in patients with hemispheric damage. *Cortex, 3*:194, 1967.

DeRenzi, E. and Vignolo, L. A.: The Token Test: A sensitive test to detect receptive disturbances in aphasics. *Brain, 85*:665, 1962.

DeS Hamsher, K. and Benton, A. L.: *Interactive Effects of Age and Brain Disease on Test Performance.* Paper presented at the eighty-fourth Annual Convention of the American Psychological Association, Washington, 1976.

DeWolfe, A. S.: Differentiation of schizophrenia and brain damage with the WAIS. *J Clin Psychol, 27*:209, 1971.

DeWolfe, A. S., Barrell, R. P., Becker, B. C., and Spaner, F. E.: Intellectual deficit in chronic schizophrenia and brain damage. *J Consult Clin Psychol, 36*:197, 1971.

Dikmen, S., Matthews, C. G., and Harley, J. P.: The effect of early versus late onset of major motor epilepsy upon cognitive-intellectual performance. *Epilepsia, 16:*73, 1975.

Dikmen, S. and Reitan, R. M.: Minnesota Multiphasic Personality Inventory correlates of dysphasic language disturbances. *J Abnorm Psychol, 83:*675, 1974.

Diller, L.: A model for cognitive retraining in rehabilitation. *Clin Psychologist, 6:*13, 1976.

Diller, L., Ben-Yishay, Y., Gerstman, L. J., Goodkin, R., Gordon, W., and Weinberger, J.: *Studies on Cognition and Rehabilitation in Hemiplegia.* New York, Behavioral Science Institute of Rehabilitation Medicine, 1974.

Dimond, J. and Beaumont, J. G.: *Hemisphere Function in the Brain.* New York, Wiley, 1974.

Dodrill, C. and Wilkus, R. J.: EEG epileptiform activity and neurophychological performance. Presented at the eighty-fourth annual convention of the American Psychological Association, Washington, 1976.

Doehring, D. G. and Reitan, R. M.: MMPI performance of aphasic and non-aphasic brain-damaged patients. *J Clin Psychol, 16:*307, 1960.

Doehring, D. G., Reitan, R. M., and Klove, H.: Changes in patterns of intelligence test performance associated with homonymous visual field defects. *J Nerv Ment Dis, 132:*227, 1961.

Donnelly, E. F., Dent, J. K., Murphy, D. L., and Mignone, R. J.: Comparison of temporal lobe epileptics and affective disorders on the Halstead-Reitan Test Battery. *J Clin Psychol, 28:*61, 1972.

Douglas, R. J. and Pribram, K. H.: Learning aids and limbic lesions. *Neuropsychologia, 4:*197, 1966.

Drachman, D. A. and Arbit, J.: Memory and the hippocampal complex, *Arch Neurol, 15:*52, 1966.

Drachman, D. A. and Ommaya, A. K.: Memory and the hippocampal complex. *Arch Neurol, 10:*411, 1964.

Drewe, E. A.: The effect of type and area of brain lesion on Wisconsin Card Sorting Test performance. *Cortex, 10:*159, 1974.

Drewe, E. A., Ettlinger, G., Milner, A. D., and Passingham, A.: A comparative review of the results of neuropsychological research on man and monkey. *Cortex, 6:*129, 1970.

Dunn, L. M. and Markwardt, F. C.: *Manual. Peabody Individual Achievement Test.* Circle Pines, Minnesota, Guidance, 1970.

Durnford, M.: Visual field differences in visual-spatial perception. Unpublished dissertation, University of Western Ontario, 1971.

Durnford, M. and Kimura, D.: Right hemisphere specialization for depth perception reflected in visual field differences. *Nature, 231:*394, 1971.

Duvoisin, R.: Parkinsonism. *Ciba Found Symp, 28:*1, 1976.

Eagleson, H. M., Vaughn, G. R., and Knudson, A. B. C.: Hand signals for dysphasia. *Arch Phys Ment Rehabil, 51:*111, 1970.

Earle, K. M.: Metastatic brain tumors. *Dis Nerv Syst, 16:*86, 1955.

Eckhardt, W.: Piotrowski's signs: Organic or functional? *J Clin Psychol, 17:* 36, 1961.

Eisenson, J.: Developmental aphasia (dyslogia): A postulation of a unitary concept of the disorder. *Cortex, 4:*184, 1968.

Elithorn, A.: A preliminary report on perceptual maze test sensitive to brain damage. *J Neurol Neurosurg Psychiatry, 18:*287, 1955.

Elithorn, A., Piercy, M., and Crosskey, M. A.: Some mechanisms of tactile localization revealed by a study of lobotomized patients. *J Neurol Neurosurg Psychiatry, 15:*272, 1952.

Ettlinger, G.: Sensory deficits in visual agnosia. *J Neurol Neurosurg Psychiatry, 19:*297, 1956.

Ettlinger, G., Blakemore, C. B., Milner, A. D., and Wilson, J.: Agenesis of the corpus callosum: A further behavioral investigation. *Brain, 97:*225, 1974.

Ettlinger, G. and Moffett, A. M.: Learning in dysphasia. *Neuropsychologia,* 8:465, 1970.

Ettlinger, G., Warrington, E., and Zangwill, O. L.: A further study of visual spatial agnosia. *Brain, 80:*335, 1957.

Faglioni, P., Scotti, G., and Spinnler, H.: The performance of brain damaged patients in spatial localization of visual and tactile stimuli. *Brain, 94:*443, 1971.

Fedio, P. and Mirsky, A. F.: Selective intellectual deficits in children with temporal lobe or centrencephalic epilepsy. *Neuropsychologia, 7:*287, 1969.

Feldman, M. H. and Sahrmann, S.: The decerebrate state in the primate. II. Studies in man. *Arch Neurol, 25:*517, 1971.

Fernald, L. D., Fernald, P. S., and Rines, W. B.: Purdue Pegboard and differential diagnosis. *J Consult Psychol, 30:*279, 1966.

Fields, F. R. J. and Whitmyre, J. W.: Verbal and performance relationships with respect to laterality of cerebral involvement. *Dis Nerv Syst, 30:* 177, 1969.

Filskov, S. B. and Goldstein, S. G.: Diagnostic validity of the Halstead-Reitan Neuropsychological Battery. *J Consult Clin Psychol, 42:*382, 1974.

Fisher, G. M.: The efficiency of the Hewson Ratios in diagnosing cerebral pathology. *J Nerv Ment Dis, 134:*80, 1962.

Fisher, G. M. and Parsons, P. A.: The effect of intellectual level on the rate of false positive organic diagnosis from the Hewson and adolescent ratios. *J Clin Psychol, 18:*125, 1962.

Fisher, M.: Left hemiplegia and motor impersistence. *J Nerv Ment Dis, 123:*201, 1956.

Fitzhugh, K. B. and Fitzhugh, L. C.: WAIS results for S's with longstanding, chronic, lateralized and diffuse cerebral dysfunction. *Percept Mot Skills, 19:*735, 1964.

Fitzhugh, K. B. and Fitzhugh, L. C.: Effects of early and later onset of cerebral dysfunction upon psychological test performance. *Percept Mot Skills, 20:*1099, 1965.

Fitzhugh, K. B., Fitzhugh, L. C., and Reitan, R. M.: Relation of acuteness of organic brain dysfunction to Trail Making Test performance. *Percept Mot Skills, 15:*399, 1962.

Fitzhugh, K. B., Fitzhugh, L. C., and Reitan, R. M.: Wechsler-Bellevue comparisons in groups with "chronic" and "current" lateralized and diffuse brain lesions. *J Consult Psychol, 26:*306, 1962.

Fitzhugh, L. C. and Fitzhugh, K. B.: Relationships between Wechsler Bellevue Form I and WAIS performance of subjects with longstanding cerebral dysfunction. *Percept Mot Skills, 19:*539, 1964.

Fitzhugh, L. C., Fitzhugh, K. B., and Reitan, R. M.: Sensorimotor deficits of brain damaged S's in relation to intellectual level. *Percept Mot Skills, 15:*603, 1962.

Fleming, G. W.: The Shipley-Hartford Retreat Scale for measuring intellectual impairment. A preliminary communication. *J Ment Sci, 89:*64, 1943.

Flowers, C. R.: Proactive interference in short term recall by aphasic, brain damaged non-aphasic and normal subjects. *Neuropsychologia, 13:*59, 1975.

Fogel, M. L. and Rosillo, R. H.: Correlation of psychological variables and progress in physical rehabilitation. *Dis Nerv Syst, 30:*593, 1969.

Fogel, M. L. and Rosillo, R. H.: Motor impersistence in physical rehabilitation. *Confin Neurol, 33:*309, 1971a.

Fogel, M. L. and Rosillo, R. H.: Correlation of psychological variables and progress in physical rehabilitation. II. Ego functions and defensive and adaptive mechanisms. *Arch Phys Med Rehabil, 52:*15, 1971b.

Fontenot, D. J. and Benton, A. L.: Perception of direction in the right and left visual fields. *Neuropsychologia, 10:*447, 1972.

Forster, F. M., Booker, H. E., and Gascon, G.: Conditioning in musicogenic epilepsy. *Trans Am Neurol Assoc, 92:*236, 1967.

Forster, F. M. and Campos, G. B.: Conditioning factors in stroboscopic induced seizures. *Epilepsia, 5:*156, 1964.

Forster, F. M., Hansotia, P., Cleeland, C. S., and Ludwig, A.: A case of voice-induced epilepsy treated by conditioning. *Neurology, 19:*325, 1969.

Forster, F. M., Klove, H., Peterson, W. G., and Bengzon, A. R. A.: Modification of musicogenic epilepsy by extinction technique. *Trans Am Neurol Assoc, 110:*179, 1965.

Fox, J. C. and German, W. J.: Observations following left (dominant) temporal lobectomy. *Arch Neurol Psychiatry, 33:*791, 1935.

Foxx, R. M. and Azrin, W. H.: Restitution: A method of eliminating aggressive-disruptive behavior of retarded and brain damaged patients. *Behav Res Ther, 10*:15, 1972.

Frantz, K. E.: Amnesia for left limbs and loss of interest and attention in left fields of vision. *J Nerv Ment Dis, 112*:240, 1950.

French, J. D., Amerongen, F. K. V., and Magoun, H. W.: An activating system in the brain of the monkey. *Arch Neurol Psychiatry, 68*:577, 1952.

Friedman, J., Strochak, R. D., Gitlin, S., and Gottsagen, M. L.: Koppitz Bender scoring system and brain damage in children. *J Clin Psychol, 23*:179, 1967.

Friedrich, D. and Fuller, G. B.: Visual-motor performance: Delineation of the "perceptual deficit" hypothesis. *J Clin Psychol, 29*:207, 1973.

Friedrich, D. and Fuller, G. B.: Visual-motor performance: Additional delineation of the "perceptual deficit" hypothesis. *J Clin Psychol, 30*:30, 1974.

Fritsch, G. and Hitzig, E.: Über die elecktrische Erregbarkeit des Groshirns. *Arch Anat Physiol Wisse Med, 37*:1, 1870.

Frostig, M., Lefever, D. W., and Whittlesey, J.: A developmental test of visual perception for evaluating normal and neurologically handicapped children. *Percept Mot Skills, 12*:383, 1961.

Fuller, G. and Friedrich, D.: A diagnostic approach to differentiate brain damaged from non-brain damaged adolescents. *J Clin Psychol, 30*:361, 1974.

Fuller, G. B. and Laird, J. T.: The Minnesota Percepto-Diagnostic Test. *J Clin Psychol, 19*:3, 1963.

Fuller, G. B., Sharp, H., and Hawkins, W. F.: Minnesota Percepto-Diagnostic Test (MPD): Age norms and IQ adjustments. *J Clin Psychol, 23*: 456, 1967.

Gaddes, W. H.: A neuropsychological approach to learning disorders. *J Learn Disabil, 1*:523, 1968.

Gaddes, W. H.: Developmental aspects of learning. *Br Columbia Med J, 11*:401, 1969.

Gaddes, W. H. and Crockett, D. J.: *The Spreen-Benton Aphasia Tests: Normative Data as a Measure of Normal Language Development.* Victoria, British Columbia, University of Victoria Neuropsychology Laboratory, 1973.

Gainotti, G.: A quantitative study of the closing-in symptom in normal children and in brain damaged patients. *Neuropsychologia, 10*:429, 1972a.

Gainotti, G.: Emotional behavior and hemispheric side of lesion. *Cortex, 8*: 41, 1972b.

Gainotti, G., Cianchetti, C., and Tiacci, C.: The influence of the hemispheric side of lesion on non-verbal tasks of finger localization. *Cortex, 8*:364, 1972.

Gainotti, G., Messerli, P., and Tissot, R.: Qualitative analysis of unilateral spatial neglect in relation to laterality of cerebral lesions. *J Neurol Neurosurg Psychiatry, 35*:545, 1972.

Gainotti, G. and Tiacci, C.: Patterns of drawing disability in right and left hemisphere patients. *Neuropsychologia, 8*:379, 1970.

Gainotti, G. and Tiacci, C.: The relationships between disorders of visual perception and unilateral spatial neglect. *Neuropsychologia, 9*:451, 1971.

Gainotti, G. and Tiacci, C.: The unilateral forms of finger agnosia. *Confin Neurol, 35*:271, 1973.

Garfield, J. C.: Motor impersistence in normal and brain damaged children. *Neurology, 14*:623, 1964.

Garfield, J. C., Benton, A. L., and MacQueen, J. C.: Motor impersistence in brain damaged and cultural familial defectives. *J Nerv Ment Dis, 142*:434, 1966.

Garfield, S. L. and Fey, W. F.: A comparison of the Wechsler-Bellevue and Shipley Hartford Scales as measures of mental impairment. *J Consult Psychol, 12*:259, 1948.

Garrett, E. S., Price, A. C., and Deabler, H. L.: Diagnostic testing for cortical brain impairment. *Arch Neurol Psychiatry, 77*:223, 1957.

Garvin, J. S.: Psychomotor epilepsy: A clinicoencephalographic syndrome. *J Nerv Ment Dis, 117*:1, 1953.

Gascon, G. and Gilles, F.: Limbic dementia. *J Neurol Neurosurg Psychiatry, 36*:421, 1973.

Gassel, M. M. and Williams, D.: Visual function in patients with homonymous hemianopia. Part II. Oculomotor mechanisms. *Brain, 86*:1, 1963.

Gastaut, H.: The role of the reticular formation in establishing conditioned reactions. In Jasper, K. H., Proctor, L. D., Knighton, R. S., Noshay, W. C., and Costello, R. C. (Eds.): *Reticular Formation of the Brain.* Boston, Little, 1958.

Gawler, J., Bull, J. W. D., DuBoulay, G. H., and Marshall, J.: Computerized axial tomography: The normal EMI scan. *J Neurol Neurosurg Psychiatry, 38*:935, 1975.

Gazzaniga, M. S.: Interhemispheric communication of visual learning. *Neuropsychologia, 4*:183, 1966.

Gazzaniga, M. S.: Determinants of cerebral recovery. In Stein, D. G., Rosen, J. R., and Butters, N.: *Plasticity and Recovery of Function in the Central Nervous System.* New York, Acad Pr, 1974.

Gazzaniga, M. S., Bogen, J. E., and Sperry, R. W.: Dyspraxia following division of the cerebral commissures. *Arch Neurol, 16*:606, 1967.

Gazzaniga, M. S., Glass, A. V., Sarno, M. T., and Posner, J. B.: Pure word deafness and hemispheric dynamics: A case history. *Cortex, 9*:136, 1973.

Gazzaniga, M. S. and Hillyard, S. A.: Language and speech capacity of the right hemisphere. *Neuropsychologia*, 9:273, 1971.

Gazzaniga, M. S. and Sperry, R. W.: Language after section of the cerebral commissures. *Brain*, 90:131, 1967.

George, J.: Differentiating clinical groups by means of the Minnesota Percepto-Diagnostic Test. *J Clin Psychol*, 29:210, 1973.

German, W. J. and Fox, J. C.: Observations following unilateral lobectomy. *Res Publ Assoc Res Nerv Ment Dis*, 13:378, 1934.

Gerstmann, J.: On the symptomatology of cerebral lesions on the transitional area of the lower parietal and middle occipital convolutions. *Arch Neurol*, 24:476, 1971.

Gerstmann, J.: On the symptomatology of cerebral lesions in the transition-of aphasia. *Cortex*, 1:214, 1964.

Geschwind, N.: Disconnexion syndromes in animals and man. *Brain*, 88: 237, 1965.

Geschwind, N.: Wernicke's contribution to the study of aphasia. *Cortex, 3:* 449, 1967.

Geschwind, N.: Language and the brain. *Sci Am*, 226:76, 1972.

Geschwind, N.: The anatomical basis of hemispheric differentiation. In Dimond, J. and Beaumont, J. G. (Eds.): *Hemisphere Function in the Brain*. New York, Wiley, 1974.

Geschwind, N.: Late changes in the nervous system: An overview. In Stein, D. G., Ross, J. R., and Butters, N. (Eds.): *Plasticity and Recovery of Function in the Central Nervous System*. New York, Acad Pr, 1974.

Giebink, J. W. and Birch, R.: The Bender-Gestalt Test as an ineffective predictor of reading achievement. *J Clin Psychol*, 26:484, 1970.

Glaser, G. H.: Limbic epilepsy in childhood. *J Nerv Ment Dis*, 144:391, 1967.

Glaser, G. H. and Pincus, J. H.: Limbic encephalitis. *J Nerv Ment Dis, 149:* 59, 1969.

Glass, A. V., Gazzaniga, M. S., and Premack, D.: Artificial language training in global aphasics. *Neuropsychologia*, 11:95, 1973.

Glowinski, H.: Cognitive deficits in temporal lobe epilepsy. *J Nerv Ment Dis, 157:*129, 1973.

Goldberg, L. R.: The effectiveness of clinicians' judgements: The diagnosis of organic brain damage from the Bender-Gestalt Test. *J Consult Psychol*, 23:25, 1959.

Goldberg, L. R.: Objective diagnostic tests and measures. *Ann Rev Psychol*, 25:343, 1974.

Golden, C. J.: A group version of the Stroop Color and Word Test. *J Pers Assess*, 39:386, 1975.

Golden, C. J.: The identification of brain damage by an abbreviated form of the Halstead-Reitan Neuropsychological Battery. *J Clin Psychol, 32:* 821, 1976a.

Golden, C. J.: Identification of brain disorders by the Stroop Color and Word Test. *J Clin Psychol, 32:*621, 1976b.

Golden, C. J.: Neurotherapy for the brain injured child. *Acad Ther,* 1977, in press.

Golden, C. J.: The validity of the Halstead-Reitan Neuropsychological Battery in a mixed psychiatric and brain damaged population. *J Consult Clin Psychol,* in press.

Goldman, R., Fristoe, M., and Woodcock, R. W.: *GFW Diagnostic Auditory Discrimination Test.* Circle Pines, Minnesota, Guidance, 1974.

Goldstein, G.: The use of clinical neuropsychological methods in the lateralization of brain lesions. In Dimond, J. and Beaumont, J. G. (Eds.): *Hemisphere Function in the Brain.* New York, Wiley, 1974.

Goldstein, G., Neuringer, C., and Olson, J.: Impairment of abstract reasoning in the brain damaged: Qualitative or quantitative. *Cortex, 4:*372, 1968.

Goldstein, G. and Shelly, C. H.: Statistical and normative studies of the Halstead Neuropsychological Test Battery relevant to a neuropsychiatric hospital setting. *Percept Mot Skills, 34:*603, 1972.

Goldstein, G. and Shelly, C. H.: Univariate vs. multivariate analysis in neuropsychological test assessment of lateralized brain damage. *Cortex, 9:*204, 1973.

Goldstein, G. and Shelly, C. H.: Neuropsychological diagnosis of multiple sclerosis in a neuropsychiatric setting. *J Nerv Ment Dis, 158:*280, 1974.

Goldstein, K.: Die Lokalisation in der Grosshirnrinde. In Bethe, A. (Ed.): *Handbuch der Normalen und Pathologischen Physiologie.* Berlin, Springer, 1927.

Goldstein, K.: *The Organism.* New York, American, 1939.

Goldstein, K.: The two ways of adjustment of the organism to cerebral defects. *J Mt Sinai Hosp, 9:*504, 1942.

Goldstein, K.: The mental changes due to frontal lobe damage. *J Psychol, 17:*1, 1944.

Goldstein, K.: *Language and Language Disorders.* New York, Grune, 1948.

Goldstein, K.: Frontal lobotomy and impairment of abstract attitude. *J Nerv Ment Dis, 110:*93, 1949.

Goldstein, K. and Scheerer, M.: Abstract and concrete behavior: An experimental study with special tests. *Psychol Monogr, 53:* No. 239, 1941.

Goldstein, K. and Scheerer, M.: Tests of abstract and concrete behavior. In Weider, A. (Ed.): *Contributions to Medical Psychology.* New York, Ronald, 1953, Vol. II.

Goldstein, S. G., Deysack, R. E., and Kleinknecht, R. A.: Effect of experience and amount of information on identification of cerebral impairment. *J Consult Clin Psychol, 41:*30, 1973.

Gonen, J. Y.: The use of Wechsler's deterioration quotient in cases of diffuse and symmetrical cerebral atrophy. *J Clin Psychol, 26*:174, 1970.

Gonen, J. Y. and Brown, L.: Role of vocabulary in deterioration and restitution of mental functioning. *Proceedings of the Seventy-Sixth Annual Convention of the American Psychological Association, 3*:30, 1968.

Gooddy, W.: Cerebral representation. *Brain, 79*:167, 1956.

Gooddy, W. and Reinhold, M.: The function of the cerebral cortex. *Brain,* 77:416, 1954.

Goodglass, H. and Quadfasel, F. A.: Language laterality in left-handed aphasics. *Brain, 77*:521, 1954.

Gordon, H. W. and Bogen, J. E.: Hemispheric lateralization of singing after intracarotid sodium amylobarbitone. *J Neurol Neurosurg Psychiatry, 37*: 727, 1974.

Gordon, N. G.: The Trail Making Test in neuropsychological diagnosis. *J Clin Psychol, 28*:167, 1972.

Gosling, R. H.: The association of dementia with radiological demonstrated cerebral atrophy. *J Neurol Neurosurg Psychiatry, 18*:129, 1955.

Gott, P. S.: Cognitive abilities following right and left hemispherectomy. *Cortex, 9*:266, 1973.

Gottlieb, A. L. and Parsons, O. A.: A coaction compass evaluation of Rorschach determinants in brain damaged individuals. *J Consult Psychol, 24*:54, 1960.

Goul, W. R. and Brown, M.: Effects of age and intelligence on Trail Making Test performance and validity. *Percept Mot Skills, 30*:319, 1970.

Graham, F. R. and Kendall, B. S.: Memory for designs test: Revised general manual. *Percept Mot Skills, 11*:147, 1960.

Grant, D. A. and Berg, E. A.: A behavioral analysis of degree of reinforcement and ease of shifting to new responses in a Weigl-type card sorting problem. *J Exp Psychol, 38*:404, 1948.

Grassi, J. R.: *The Grassi Block Substitution Test for Measuring Organic Brain Pathology.* Springfield, Thomas, 1953.

Greenblatt, S. A.: Alexia without agraphia or hemianopsia: Anatomical analysis of an autopsied case. *Brain, 96*:307, 1973.

Grundvig, J. L., Ajax, E. T., and Needham, W. E.: Screening organic brain impairment with the Memory for Designs Test. Validation of comparison of different scoring systems and exposure times. *J Clin Psychol, 29*: 350, 1973.

Grundvig, J. L., Needham, W. E., and Ajax, E. T.: Comparison of different scoring and administration procedures for the Memory for Designs Test. *J Clin Psychol, 26*:353, 1970.

Grundvig, J. L., Needham, W. E., Ajax, E. T., and Beck, E. C.: The use of the sensory-perceptual examination in diagnosis of degree of impairment of higher cerebral functions. *J Nerv Ment Dis, 151*:114, 1970.

Gubbay, S. S., Ellis, E., Walton, J. N., and Court, S. D. M.: Clumsy children—A study of apraxic and agnosis deficits in 21 children. *Brain, 88:* 295, 1965.

Gudeman, H. E. and Craine, J. F.: Principles and techniques of neurotraining. Unpublished paper, Honolulu, 1976.

Gudeman, H., Golden, C. J., and Craine, J. F.: A program of neurotraining. Submitted for publication, 1977.

Hain, J. D.: The Bender-Gestalt Test: A scoring method for identifying brain damage. *J Consult Psychol, 28:*34, 1964.

Halberstam, J. L., Zaretsky, H. H., Brucker, B. S., and Guttman, A. R.: Avoidance conditioning of motor responses in elderly brain damaged patients. *Arch Phys Med Rehabil, 52:*318, 1971.

Hallahan, D. P., and Cruickshank, W. M.: *Psychoeducational Foundations of Learning Disabilities.* Englewood Cliffs, P-H, 1973.

Halstead, W. C.: *Brain and Intelligence.* Chicago, U Chicago Pr, 1947.

Halstead, W. C. and Wepman, J. M.: The Halstead-Wepman Aphasia Screening Test. *J Speech Hear Disord, 14:*9, 1949.

Hamlin, R. M.: Intellectual functions 14 years after frontal lobe surgery. *Cortex, 6:*299, 1970.

Hammill, D. D., Colarusso, J. L., and Wiederholt, J. L.: Diagnostic value of the Frostig Test: A factor analytic approach. *J Special Ed, 4:*279, 1970.

Hansotia, P. and Wadia, N. H.: Temporal lobe epilepsy with absences. *Dis Nerv Syst, 32:*316, 1971.

Hanvik, L. J. and Andersen, A. L.: The effect of focal brain lesions on recall and on the production of rotations in the Bender-Gestalt test. *J Consult Psychol, 14:*197, 1950.

Harlow, H. F.: Functional organization of the brain in relation to mentation and behavior. In Milbank Memorial Fund (Ed.): *The Biology of Mental Health and Disease.* New York, Hoeber, 1952.

Hartje, W., Kerschensteiner, M., Poeck, K., and Orgass, B.: A cross validation study on the Token Test. *Neuropsychologia, 11:*119, 1973.

Hartlage, L.: Common psychological tests applied to the assessment of brain damage. *J Proj Tech Pers Assess, 30:*319, 1966.

Hartlage, L. C.: Diagnostic profiles of four types of learning disabled children. *J Clin Psychol, 29:*458, 1973.

Hartlage, L. C. and Green, J. B.: EEG abnormalities and WISC subtest differences. *J Clin Psychol, 28:*170, 1972.

Head, H.: *Aphasia and Kindred Disorders of Speech.* Cambridge, England, Cambridge U Pr, 1926.

Heath, R. G.: Brain function and behavior. *J Nerv Ment Dis, 160:*159, 1975.

Heaton, R. K.: The validity of neuropsychological evaluations in psychiatric settings. *Clin Psychologist, 6:*10, 1976.

Hebb, D. O.: The effect of early and late brain injury upon test scores and the nature of normal adult intelligence. *Proc Am Philos Soc, 85*:275, 1942.

Hebb, D. O.: Man's frontal lobes. *Arch Neurol Psychiatry, 54*:10, 1945.

Hebb, D. O.: Intelligence, brain function and the theory of mind. *Brain, 82*: 260, 1959.

Hebb, D. O. and Penfield, W.: Human behavior after extensive bilateral removal from the frontal lobes. *Arch Neurol Psychiatry, 44*:421, 1940.

Hecaen, H., Ajuriaguerra, J., and Massonnet, J.: Les troubles visuels constructifs par lesion parieto-occipitale droite. *L'Encephale, 40*:122, 1951.

Hecaen, H. and Angelergues, R.: Agnosia for faces (prosopagnosia). *Arch Neurol, 7*:92, 1962.

Hecaen, H. and Assal, G.: A comparison of constructive deficits following right and left hemisphere lesions. *Neuropsychologia, 8*:289, 1970.

Hecaen, H., Penfield, W., Bertrand, C., and Malmo, R.: The syndrome of apractagnosia due to lesions of the minor cerebral hemisphere. *Arch Neurol Psychiatry, 75*:400, 1956.

Hecaen, H., Wyke, M., and DeRenzi, E.: The Sixteenth International Symposium of Neuropsychology. *Neuropsychologia, 10*:253, 1972.

Heilbrun, A. B.: Lateralization of cerebral lesion and performance on spatial-temporal tasks. *Arch Neurol, 1*:282, 1959.

Heimburger, R. F., Demyer, W., and Reitan, R. M.: Implications of Gerstmann's syndrome. *J Neurol Neurosurg Psychiatry, 27*:52, 1964.

Heimburger, R. F. and Reitan, R. M.: Easily administered written test for lateralizing brain lesions. *J Neurosurg, 18*:301, 1961.

Henschen, S. E.: On the function of the right hemisphere of the brain in relation to the left in speech, music, and calculation. *Brain, 49*:110, 1926.

Henson, R. A.: Henry Head's work on sensation. *Brain, 84*:535, 1961.

Hertzig, M. F., Bortner, M., and Birch, H. G.: Neurologic finding in children educationally designated as "brain damaged." *Am J Orthopsychiatry, 39*:437, 1969.

Hewson, L. R.: The Wechsler-Bellevue Scale and the substitution test as aids in neuropsychiatric diagnosis. Part II. *J Nerv Ment Dis, 109*:246, 1949.

Hilliard, R. D.: Hemispheric laterality effects on a facial recognition task in normal subjects. *Cortex, 9*:246, 1973.

Hines, D. and Satz, P.: Superiority of right visual half-fields in right-handers for recall of digits presented at varying rates. *Neuropsychologia, 9*:21, 1971.

Hinton, C. G. and Knights, R. M.: Children with learning problems: Academic history, academic prediction, and adjustment three years after assessment. *Except Child, 37*:513, 1971.

Hirschenfang, S., Shulman, L., and Benton, J. G.: Psychological factors influencing the rehabilitation of hemiplegic patients. *Dis Nerv Syst, 29:* 373, 1968.

Hirt, M.: An evaluation of the Grassi Test for organic involvement. *J Clin Psychol, 14:*48, 1958.

Holland, T. R.: Wechsler Memory Scale paired associate learning in discrimination of brain damaged and non-brain damaged psychiatric patients. *Percept Mot Skills, 39:*227, 1974.

Holland, T. R., Lowenfeld, J., and Wadsworth, H. M.: MMPI indices in the discrimination of brain damaged and schizophrenic groups. *J Consult Clin Psychol, 43:*426, 1975.

Holland, T. R., Wadsworth, H. M., and Royer, F. L.: The performance of brain damaged and schizophrenic patients on the Minnesota Percepto-Diagnostic test under standard and BIP conditions of administration. *J Clin Psychol, 31:*21, 1975.

Hollon, T.: Behavior modification in a community hospital rehabilitation unit. *Arch Phys Med Rehabil, 54:*65, 1973.

Holroyd, J. and Wright, F.: Neurological implications of WISC verbal performance discrepancies in a psychiatric setting. *J Consult Psychol, 29:* 206, 1965.

Hovey, H. B.: Brain lesions and five MMPI items. *J Consult Psychol, 28:* 78, 1964.

Howard, A. R.: Diagnostic value of the Wechsler Memory Scale with selected groups of brain damaged patients. *J Consult Psychol, 14:*395, 1950.

Hughes, H. E.: Norms developed at the University of Chicago for the neuropsychological evaluation of children. *J Pediatr Psychol, 1*(3):11, 1976.

Hunt, W. L.: The relative rates of decline of Wechsler-Bellevue "hold" and "don't hold" tests. *J Consult Psychol, 13:*440, 1949.

Hurlburt, R. T.: *Self observation and self control.* Unpublished dissertation, University of South Dakota, 1975.

Hutt, M.: *The Hutt Adaptation of the Bender-Gestalt Test, 2nd ed.* New York, Grune, 1969.

Hyman, M. D.: Social psychological determinants of patients performance in stroke rehabilitation. *Arch Phys Med Rehabil, 53:*217, 1972.

Ince, L. P.: Escape and avoidance conditioning of responses in the plegic arm of stroke patients: A preliminary study. *Psychonom Sci, 16:*49, 1969.

Ingham, S.: Cerebral localization of psychological processes occurring during a two-minute experience. *J Nerv Ment Dis, 107:*388, 1948.

Isaacson, R.: When brains are damaged. *Psychol Today, 3:*38, 1970.

Isaacson, R.: Hippocampal destruction in man and other animals. *Neuropsychologia, 10:*47, 1972.

Jastak, J. F. and Jastak, S. R.: *The Wide Range Achievement Test.* Wilmington, Guidance, 1965.

Jerger, J., Lovering, L., and Wertz, M.: Auditory disorder following bilateral temporal lobe insult: report of a case. *J Speech Hear Disord*, 37: 523, 1972.

Johnson, J. E., Hellkamp, D. T., and Lottman, T. J.: The relationship between intelligence, brain damage, and Hutt-Briskin errors on the Bender-Gestalt. *J Clin Psychol*, 27:84, 1971.

Johnson, R. and Meyer, R. G.: Phased biofeedback approach for epileptic seizure control. *J Behav Ther Exp Psychiatry*, 5:185, 1974.

Joynt, R. J.: Paul Pierre Broca: His contribution to the knowledge of aphasia. *Cortex*, 1:206, 1964.

Joynt, R. J., Benton, A. L., and Fogel, M. L.: Behavioral and pathological correlates of motor impersistence. *Neurology*, 12:876, 1962.

Joynt, R. J. and Goldstein, M. N.: Minor cerebral hemisphere. *Adv Neurol*, 7:147, 1975.

Jurko, M. F. and Andy, O. J.: Psychological changes correlated with thalamotomy site. *J Neurol Neurosurg Psychiatry*, 36:846, 1973.

Kahn, R. L., Pollack, M., and Fink, M.: Figure-ground discrimination after induced altered brain function. *Arch Neurol*, 2:547, 1960.

Kamin, S. H., Llewelleyn, C. J., and Sledge, W. L.: Group dynamics in the treatment of epilepsy. *J Pediatr*, 53:410, 1958.

Karp, E., Belmont, I., and Birch, H.: Unilateral hearing loss in hemiplegic patients. *J Nerv Ment Dis*, 148:83, 1969.

Kaszniak, A. W.: Organic brain syndromes. In Reiss, S., Peterson, R. A., Eron, L. D., and Reiss, M. (Eds.): *Experimental and Clinical Approaches to Abnormality*. New York, Macmillan, 1977.

Kaszniak, A. W., Garron, D. C., Fox, J. H., Huckman, M. S., and Ramsey, R. G.: Relation between psychometric assessment of dementia and computerized tomogram measures of cerebral atrophy. *Neurology*, 25:387, 1975. (abstract)

Kaufman, A.: A substitution test: A survey of studies on organic mental impairment and the role of learning and motor factors in test performance. *Cortex*, 4:47, 1968.

Keenan, J. S. and Brassell, E. G.: A study of factors related to prognosis for individual aphasic patients. *J Speech Hear Disord*, 39:257, 1974.

Kenny, T. J.: Background interference procedure: A means of assessing neurologic dysfunction in school age children. *J Consult Clin Psychol*, 37:44, 1971.

Kershner, J. R. and King, A. J.: Laterality of cognitive functions in achieving hemiplegic children. *Percept Mot Skills*, 39:1283, 1974.

Kiernan, R. J. and Matthews, C. G.: Impairment index versus T-score averaging in neuropsychological assessment. *J Consult Clin Psychol*, 44: 951, 1976.

Kiev, A., Chapman, L. F., Guthrie, T. C., and Wolff, H. G.: The highest integrative functions and diffuse cerebral atrophy. Neurology, 12:385, 1962.

Kilpatrick, D. L. and Spreen, O.: A revision of the Halstead Category test for children aged 9 to 15. Psychol Schools, 10:101, 1973.

Kimura, D.: Cerebral dominance and the perception of verbal stimuli. Can J Psychol, 15:166, 1961a.

Kimura, D.: Some effects of temporal lobe damage on auditory perception. Can J Psychol, 15:156, 1961b.

Kimura, D.: Right temporal lobe damage. Arch Neurol, 8:264, 1963.

Kimura, D.: Functional asymmetry of the brain in dichotic listening. Cortex, 3:163, 1967.

Kimura, D.: Spatial localization in left and right visual fields. Can J Psychol, 23:445, 1969.

Kimura, D. and Archibald, Y.: Motor functions of the left hemisphere. Brain, 97:337, 1974.

Kimura, J.: Effect of hemispheral lesions on the contralateral blink reflex. Neurology, 24:168, 1974.

King, E.: The nature of visual field defects. Brain, 90:647, 1967.

Kinsbourne, M.: The minor cerebral hemisphere as a source of aphasic speech. Arch Neurol, 25:302, 1971.

Kinsbourne, M. and Warrington, E. K.: A disorder of simultaneous form perception. Brain, 85:461, 1962a.

Kinsbourne, M. and Warrington, E. K.: A study of finger agnosia. Brain, 85:47, 1962b.

Kinsbourne, M. and Warrington, E. K.: The developmental Gerstmann syndrome. Arch Neurol, 8:490, 1963a.

Kinsbourne, M. and Warrington, E. K.: Jargon aphasia. Neuropsychologia, 1:27, 1963b.

Kinsbourne, M. and Warrington, E. K.: Disorders of spelling. J Neurol Neurosurg Psychiatry, 27:224, 1964.

Kirk, S. A., McCarthy, J. J., and Kirk, W. D.: Illinois Test of Psycholinguistic Abilities, exp. ed. Urbana, U of Ill Pr, 1961.

Kirk, S. A., McCarthy, J. J., and Kirk, W. D.: Illinois Test of Psycholinguistic Abilities, rev. ed. Urbana, U of Ill Pr, 1968.

Kleist, K.: Gehirnpathologie. Leipzig, Barth, 1933.

Kljajic, I.: Wechsler Memory Scale indices of brain pathology. J Clin Psychol, 31:698, 1975.

Klonoff, H., Fibiger, C. H., and Hutton, G. H.: Neuropsychological patterns in chronic schizophrenia. J Nerv Ment Dis, 150:291, 1970.

Klonoff, H. and Low, M.: Disordered brain function in young children and early adolescents: Neuropsychological and electroencephalographic correlates. In Reitan, R. M. and Davison, L. A. (Eds.): Clinical Neuropsychology: Current Status and Applications. Washington, Winston, 1974.

Klonoff, H. and Paris, R.: Immediate, short term and residual effects of acute head injuries in children: Neuropsychological and neurological correlates. In Reitan, R. M. and Davison, L. A. (Eds.): *Clinical Neuropsychology: Current Status and Applications.* Washington, Winston, 1974.

Klonoff, H., Robinson, G. C., and Thompson, G.: Acute and chronic brain syndromes in children. *Dev Med Child Neurol, 11:*198, 1969.

Klove, H.: Relationship of differential electroencephalographic patterns to distribution of Wechsler-Bellevue Scores. *Neurology, 9:*871, 1959.

Klove, H.: Validation studies in adult clinical neuropsychology. In Reitan, R. M. and Davison, L. A. (Eds.): *Clinical Neuropsychology: Current Status and Applications.* Washington, Winston, 1974.

Klove, H. and Matthews, C. G.: Psychometric and adaptive abilities in epilepsy. *Epilepsia, 7:*330, 1966.

Klove, H. and Matthews, C. G.: Neuropsychological evaluation of the epileptic patient. *Wis Med J, 68:*296, 1969.

Klove, H. and Matthews, C. G.: Neuropsychological studies of patients with epilepsy. In Reitan, R. M. and Davison, L. A. (Eds.): *Clinical Neuropsychology: Current Status and Applications.* Washington, Winston, 1974.

Klove, H. and Reitan, R. M.: Effects of dysphasia and spatial distortion on Wechsler-Bellevue results. *Arch Neurol Psychiatry, 80:*708, 1958.

Klüver, H. and Bucy, P. C.: Preliminary analysis of the temporal lobe functions in the monkey. *Arch Neurol Psychiatry, 42:*979, 1939.

Knights, R. M. and Watson, P.: The use of computerized test profiles in neuropsychological assessment. *J Learning Disabilities, 1:*696, 1968.

Kohn, B. and Dennis, M.: Selective impairment of visuo-spatial abilities in infantile hemiplegia after right cerebral hemidecortication. *Neuropsychologia, 12:*505, 1974a.

Kohn, B. and Dennis, M.: Somatosensory functions after cerebral hemidecortication for infantile hemiplegia. *Neuropsychologia, 12:*119, 1974b.

Koppitz, E. M.: The Bender-Gestalt Test and learning disturbances in young children. *J Clin Psychol, 14:*292, 1958.

Koppitz, E. M.: Diagnosing brain damage in young children with the Bender-Gestalt Test. *J Consult Psychol, 26:*541, 1962.

Koppitz, E. M.: *The Bender-Gestalt Test for Young Children.* New York, Grune and Stratton, 1964.

Kramer, H. C.: Some observations on post-lobotomy patients. *J Nerv Ment Dis, 122:*89, 1955.

Kraus, J. and Selecki, B. R.: Assessment of laterality in diffuse cerebral atrophy using the WAIS. *J Clin Psychol, 23:*91, 1967.

Krech, D.: Cortical localization of function. In Postman, L. (Ed.): *Psychology in the Making.* New York, Knopf, 1962.

Kreuter, C., Kinsbourne, M. and Trevarthen, C.: Are deconnected cerebral hemispheres independent channels? A preliminary study of the effect of unilateral loading on bilateral finger tapping. *Neuropsychologia, 10:* 453, 1972.

Kutner, B.: Rehabilitation: Whose goals? Whose priorities? *Arch Phys Med Rehabil,* 52:284, 1971.

L'Abate, L.: The clinical usefulness of the Minnesota Percepto-Diagnostic Test with children. *J Clin Psychol,* 22:298, 1966.

L'Abate, L., Boelling, G. M., Hutton, R. D., and Matthews, D. L.: The diagnostic usefulness of four potential tests of brain damage. *J Consult Psychol,* 26:479, 1962.

L'Abate, L., Friedman, W. H., Volger, R. E., and Chused, T. M.: The diagnostic usefulness of two tests of brain damage. *J Clin Psychol,* 19:87, 1963.

Lackner, J. R. and Teuber, H. L.: Alterations in auditory fusion thresholds after cerebral injury in man. *Neuropsychologia,* 11:409, 1973.

Lacks, P. B.: Revised interpretation of Benton visual retention scores. *J Clin Psychol,* 27:481, 1971.

Lacks, P. B., Harrow, M., Colbert, J., and Levine, J.: Further evidence concerning the diagnostic accuracy of the Halstead organic test battery. *J Clin Psychol,* 26:480, 1970.

Lair, C. V. and Trapp, E. P.: The differential diagnostic value of MMPI with somatically disturbed patients. *J Clin Psychol,* 18:146, 1962.

Lansdell, H.: Verbal and nonverbal factors in right hemisphere speech: relation to early neurological history. *J Comp Physiol Psychol,* 69:734, 1969.

Lansdell, H.: Relation of extent of temporal removals to closure and visuomotor factors. *Percept Mot Skills,* 31:491, 1970.

Lashley, K. S.: *Brain Mechanisms and Intelligence.* Chicago, U of Chicago Pr, 1929.

Lashley, K. S.: Functional determinants of cerebral localization. *Arch Neurol Psychiatry,* 38:371, 1937.

Lehmann, J. F., DeLateur, B. J., Fowler, R. S., and Warren, C. G.: Stroke: Does rehabilitation affect outcome? *Arch Phys Med Rehabil,* 56:375, 1975a.

Lehmann, J. F., DeLateur, B. J., Fowler, R. S., and Warren, C. G.: Stroke rehabilitation: Outcome and prediction. *Arch Phys Med Rehabil,* 56: 383, 1975b.

Leuthold, C. A., Bergs, L. P., Matthews, C. G., and Harley, J. P.: Neuropsychological test performance in an older VA patient. *VA Res Bull,* 15: 373, 1975.

Levin, H. S.: Motor impersistence in patients with unilateral cerebral disease: A cross validational study. *J Consult Clin Psychol,* 41:287, 1973.

Levin, H. S. and Benton, A. L.: Temporal orientation in patients with brain disease. *Appl Neurophysiol,* 38:56, 1975.

Levin, H. S., deS Hamsher, K., and Benton, A. L.: A short form of the test of facial recognition for clinical use. *J Psychol, 91*:223, 1975.

Levin, M.: Reflex action in the highest cerebral centers: A tribute to Hughlings Jackson. *J Nerv Ment Dis, 118*:481, 1953.

Levine, J. and Feirstein, A.: Differences in test performance between brain-damaged, schizophrenic, and medical patients. *J Consult Clin Psychol, 39*:508, 1972.

Levita, E., Riklan, M., and Cooper, I. S.: Cognitive and perceptual performance in Parkinsonism as a function of age and neurological impairment. *J Nerv Ment Dis, 139*:516, 1964.

Levita, E., Riklan, M., and Cooper, I. S.: Psychological comparison of unilateral and bilateral thalamic surgery: A preliminary report. *J Ab Psychol, 72*:251, 1967.

Levy, J.: Psychobiological implications of bilateral asymmetry. In Dimond, S. and Beaumont, J. G .(Eds.): *Hemisphere Function in the Human Brain.* New York, Wiley, 1974.

Levy, J., Nebes, R. D., and Sperry, R. W.: Expressive language in the surgically separated minor hemisphere. *Cortex, 7*:49, 1971.

Levy-Agresti, J. and Sperry, R. W.: Differential perceptual capacities in major and minor hemispheres. *Proc Natl Acad Sci, 61*:1151, 1968.

Lewinsohn, P. M.: *Psychological Assessment of Patients with Brain Injury.* Report to Division of Research, Health, Education and Welfare, 1973.

Lezak, M. D.: *Neuropsychological Assessment.* New York, Oxford U Pr, 1976.

Lhermitte, F. and Beauvois, M. F.: A visual speech disconnection syndrome. *Brain, 96*:695, 1973.

Lilliston, L.: Tests of cerebral damage and the process-reactive dimension. *J Clin Psychol, 26*:180, 1970.

Lilliston, L.: Schizophrenic symptomatology as a function of probability of cerebral damage. *J Abnorm Psychol, 82*:377, 1973.

Lin, Y. and Rennick, P. M.: Correlations between performance on the Category test and the Wechsler Adult Intelligence Scale in an epileptic sample. *J Clin Psychol, 30*:62, 1974.

Lindsley, D. B.: The reticular system and perceptual discrimination. In Jasper, K. H., Proctor, L. D., Knighton, R. S., Noshay, W. C., and Costello, R. C. (Eds.): *Reticular Formation of the Brain.* Boston, Little, 1958.

Loeser, J. D. and Alvord, E. C.: Agenesis of the corpus callosum. *Brain, 91*: 553, 1968.

Logue, P. E. and Allen, K.: WAIS predicted Category Test score with the Halstead Neuropsychological Battery. *Percept Mot Skills, 33*:1095, 1971.

Luria, A. R.: Brain disorders and language analysis. *Lang Speech, 1*:1, 1958.

Luria, A. R.: *Restoration of Function after Brain Injury.* New York, Macmillan, 1963.

Luria, A. R.: Neuropsychology in the local diagnosis of brain injury. *Cortex, 1:3,* 1964.

Luria, A. R.: Two kinds of motor perseveration in massive injury of the frontal lobes. *Brain, 88:1,* 1965a.

Luria, A. R.: L. S. Vygotsky and the problem of localization of function. *Neuropsychologia, 3:387,* 1965b.

Luria, A. R.: *Higher Cortical Functions in Man.* New York, Basic, 1966.

Luria, A. R.: *Traumatic Aphasia: Its Syndromes, Psychology and Treatment.* The Hague, Mouton, 1970.

Luria, A. R.: Memory disturbances in local brain lesions. *Neuropsychologia, 9:367,* 1971.

Luria, A. R.: Aphasia reconsidered. *Cortex, 8:34,* 1972.

Luria, A. R.: *The Working Brain.* New York, Basic, 1973.

Luria, A. R.: Towards the mechanisms of naming disturbance. *Neuropsychologia, 11:417,* 1973.

Luria, A. R., Homskaya, E. D., Blinkov, S. M., and Critchley, M.: Impaired selectivity of mental processes in association with a lesion of the frontal lobes. *Neuropsychologia, 5:105,* 1967.

Luria, A. R. and Karassev, A.: Disturbances of auditory speech memory in focal lesions of the deep regions of the left temporal lobe. *Neuropsychologia, 6:97,* 1968.

Luria, A. R., Pribram, H., and Homskaya, E. D.: An experimental analysis of the behavioral disturbance produced by a left frontal arachnoidal endothelioma (meningioma). *Neuropsychologia, 2:257,* 1964.

Luria, A. R., Simernitskaya, E. G., and Tubylevich, B.: The structure of psychological processes in relation to cerebral organization. *Neuropsychologia, 8:13,* 1970.

Luria, A. R., Sokolov, E. N., and Klimkowski, M.: Towards a neurodynamic analysis of memory disturbances with lesions of the left temporal lobe. *Neuropsychologia, 5:1,* 1967.

Luria, A. R. and Tsvetkova, L. S.: The programming of constructive activity in local brain injuries. *Neuropsychologia, 2:95,* 1964.

McCloskey, D. I.: Position sense after surgical deconnection of the cerebral hemispheres in man. *Brain, 96:269,* 1973.

McConnell, O. L.: Koppitz's Bender-Gestalt Scores in relation to organic and emotional problems in children. *J Clin Psychol, 23:370,* 1967.

McDonald, R. D.: Effect of brain damage on adaptability. *J Nerv Ment Dis, 138:241,* 1964.

McDonald, R. D. and Burns, S. B.: Visual vigilance and brain damage: An empirical study. *J Neurol Neurosurg Psychiatry, 27:206,* 1964.

McFie, J.: Cerebral dominance in cases of reading disability. *J Neurol Neurosurg Psychiatry, 15:194,* 1952.

McFie, J.: Psychological testing in clinical neurology. *J Nerv Ment Dis,* *131:*383, 1960.

McFie, J.: The effects of hemispherectomy on intellectual functioning in cases of infantile hemiplegia. *J Neurol Neurosurg Psychiatry,* 24:20, 1961a.

McFie, J.: Intellectual impairment in children with localized post-infantile cerebral lesions. *J Neurol Neurosurg Psychiatry,* 24:361, 1961a.

McFie, J.: The diagnostic significance of disorders of higher nervous activity. In Vinken, P. J. and Bruyn, G. W. (Eds.): *Handbook of Clinical Neurology.* New York, Wiley, 1969, Vol. III.

McFie, J.: The other side of the brain. *Dev Med Child Neurol,* 12:514, 1970.

McFie, J.: *Assessment of Organic Intellectual Impairment.* New York, Acad Pr, 1975.

McFie, J. and Piercy, M. F.: Intellectual impairment with localized cerebral lesions. *Brain,* 75:292, 1952.

McFie, J., Piercy, M. F., and Zangwill, O. L.: Visual-spatial agnosia associated with lesions of the right cerebral hemisphere. *Brain,* 73:167, 1950.

McFie, J. and Zangwill, O. L.: Visual-constructive disabilities associated with lesions of the left cerebral hemisphere. *Brain,* 83:243, 1960.

McGuire, F. L.: A comparison of the Bender-Gestalt and flicker fusion as indicators of CNS involvement. *J Clin Psychol,* 16:276, 1960.

McIver, D., McLaren, S. A., and Phillip, A. E.: Inter-rater agreement on memory for designs test. *Br J Soc Clin Psychol,* 12:194, 1973.

McKeever, W. F.: The validity of Hewson ratios: A critique of Wolff's study. *J Nerv Ment Dis, 132:*417, 1961.

McKeever, W. F. and Gerstein, A. I.: Validity of the Hewson ratios: Investigation of a fundamental methodological consideration. *J Consult Psychol, 22:*150, 1958.

McKeever, W. F. and Huling, M. D.: Lateral dominance in tachistoscope word recognition performances obtained with simultaneous bilateral input. *Neuropsychologia,* 9:15, 1971.

McLardy, T.: Memory function in hippocampal gyri but not in hippocampi. *Int J Neurosci,* 1:113, 1970.

McLean, O.: The limbic system with respect to two life principles. In *Second Macy Conference: The Central Nervous System and Behavior.* Bethesda, National Institutes of Health, 1959.

McManis, D. M.: Memory for Designs performance of brain damaged and non-brain damaged psychiatric patients. *Percept Mot Skills, 38:*47, 1974.

McManis, D. L. and Roth, G.: Performance of brain damaged and non-brain damaged retardates on the memory for designs. *Percept Mot Skills, 38:*583, 1974.

Macrae, D. and Trolle, E.: The defect of function in visual agnosia. *Brain,* 79:94, 1956.

Magaret, A. and Simpson, M.: A comparison of two measures of deterioration in psychotic patients. *J Consult Psychol, 12:*265, 1948.

Mahan, H.: Sensitivity of WAIS tests to focal lobe damage. Privately mimeographed, 1976.

Malamud, R. F.: Validity of the Hunt-Minnesota Test for organic brain damage. *J Appl Psychol, 30:*271, 1946.

Malmo, H. P.: On frontal lobe functions: Psychiatric patient controls. *Cortex, 10:*231, 1974.

Manson, M. P. and Grayson, H. M.: The Shipley-Hartford Retreat Scale as a measure of intellectual impairment for military prisoners. *J Appl Psychol, 31:*67, 1947.

Marie, P.: The third left frontal convolution plays no special role in the function of language. *Sem Med, 26:*241, 1906.

Markwell, E. D., Wheeler, W. M., and Kitzinger, H.: Changes in Wechsler-Bellevue Test performance following prefrontal lobotomy. *J Consult Psychol, 17:*229, 1953.

Marsh, G. G. and Kravitz, E. A.: Increase in fine motor control in Parkinson patients following Levodopa. *Percept Mot Skills, 33:*211, 1971.

Masland, R. L.: Higher cerebral functions. *Ann Rev Physiol, 20:*533, 1958.

Maslow, P., Frostig, M., Lefever, D. W., and Whittlesley, J. R. B.: The Marianne Frostig Developmental Test of Visual Perception, 1963 standardization. *Percept Mot Skills, 19:*463, 1964.

Matthews, C. G.: Applications of neuropsychological test methods in mentally retarded subjects. In Reitan, R. M. and Davison, L. A.: *Clinical Neuropsychology: Current Status and Applications.* Washington, Winston, 1974.

Matthews, C. G. and Booker, H. E.: Pneumoencephalographic measurements and neuropsychological test performance in human adults. *Cortex, 8:*69, 1972.

Matthews, C. G., Cleeland, C. S., and Hopper, C. L.: Neuropsychological patterns in multiple sclerosis. *Dis Nerv Syst, 31:*161, 1970.

Matthews, C. G., Guertin, W. H., and Reitan, R. M.: Wechsler-Bellevue subtest mean rank orders in diverse diagnostic groups. *Psychol Rep, 11:*3, 1962.

Matthews, C. G. and Klove, H.: Differential psychological performances in major motor, psychomotor, and mixed classifications of known and unknown etiology. *Epilepsia, 8:*117, 1967.

Matthews, C. G. and Reitan, R. M.: Correlations of Wechsler rank orders of subtest means in lateralized and non-lateralized brain damaged groups. *Percept Mot Skills, 19:*391, 1964.

Matthews, C. G., Shaw, D. J., and Klove, H.: Psychological test performance in neurologic and pseudo-neurologic subjects. *Cortex, 2:*244, 1966.

Mayo Clinic: *Clinical Examinations in Neurology.* Philadelphia, Saunders, 1976.

Medina, J. L., Rubino, F. A., and Ross, E.: Agitated delirium caused by infarctions of the hippocampal formation and fusiform and lingual gyri: A case report. *Neurol, 24:*1181, 1974.

Meehl, P.: Schizotaxia, schizotypy, schizophrenia. In Buss, A. H. and Buss, E. H. (Eds.): *Theories of Schizophrenia.* New York, Atherton, 1969.

Meehl, P. E. and Jeffery, M.: The Hunt-Minnesota test for organic brain damage in cases of functional depression. *J Appl Psychol, 30:*276, 1946.

Meier, M. J.: Some challenges for clinical neuropsychology. In Reitan, R. M. and Davison, L. A. (Eds.): *Clinical Neuropsychology: Current Status and Applications.* Washington, Winston, 1974.

Meier, M. J. and French, L. A.: Some personality correlates of unilateral and bilateral EEG abnormalities in psychomotor epileptics. *J Clin Psychol, 21:*3, 1965.

Meier, M. J. and French, L. A.: Lateralized deficits in complex visual discrimination and bilateral transfer of reminisence following unilateral temporal lobotomy. *Neuropsychologia, 3:*261, 1965.

Meier, M. J. and French, L. A.: Longitudinal assessment of intellectual function following unilateral temporal lobectomy. *J Clin Psychol, 22:*22, 1966.

Meissner, W. W.: Memory function in the Korsakoff syndrome. *J Nerv Ment Dis, 145:*106, 1967.

Menolascino, F. J. and Eaton, O. L.: Comprehensive treatment for the child with cerebral dysfunction. *Am J Orthopsychiatry, 37:*347, 1967.

Merskey, H. and Woodforde, J. M.: Psychiatric sequelae of minor head injury. *Brain, 95:*521, 1972.

Meyer, V.: Cognitive changes following temporal lobectomy for relief of temporal lobe epilepsy. *Arch Neurol Psychiatry, 81:*299, 1959.

Meyer, V. and Jones, H. G.: Patterns of cognitive test performance as functions of the lateral localization of cerebral abnormalities in the temporal lobe. *J Ment Sci, 103:*758, 1957.

Meyer, V. and Yates, A. J.: Intellectual changes following temporal lobectomy for psychomotor epilepsy. *J Neurol Neurosurg Psychiatry, 18:*44, 1955.

Miller, E.: Short and long term memory in patients with presenile dementia. *Psychol Med, 3:*221, 1973.

Milner, B.: Psychological defects produced by temporal lobe excision. In Solomon, H. C., Cobb, S., and Penfield, W. (Eds.): *The Brain and Human Behavior.* Baltimore, Williams & Wilkins, 1958.

Milner, B.: Laterality effects in audition. In Mountcaste, V. B. (Ed.): *Inter-*

hemispheric Relations and Cerebral Dominance. Baltimore, Hopkins, 1962.

Milner, B.: Effects of different brain lesions on card sorting. *Arch Neurol,* 9:90, 1963.

Milner, B.: Some effects of frontal lobectomy in man. In Warren, J. M. and Akert, K. (Eds.): *The Frontal Granular Cortex and Behavior.* New York, McGraw, 1964.

Milner, B.: Visually guided maze learning in man: Effects of bilateral hippocampal, bilateral frontal and unilateral cerebral lesions. *Neuropsychologia,* 3:317, 1965.

Milner, B.: Visual recognition and recall after right temporal lobe excision in man. *Neuropsychologia,* 6:191, 1968.

Milner, B.: Interhemispheric difference in the localization of psychological processes in man. *Br Med Bull,* 27:272, 1971.

Milner, B.: Disorders of learning and memory after temporal lobe lesions in man. *Clin Neurosurg,* 19:421, 1972.

Milner, B.: Sparing of language function after early unilateral brain damage. *Neurosci Res Prog Bull,* 12:213, 1974.

Milner, B.: Psychological aspects of focal epilepsy and its neurosurgical management. *Adv Neurol,* 8:299, 1975.

Milner, B., Hecaen, H., and Jung, R.: The Twelfth International Symposium of Neuropsychology. *Neuropsychologia,* 5:191, 1967.

Milner, B. and Taylor, L.: Right hemisphere superiority in tactile pattern recognition after cerebral commissurotomy: Evidence for non-verbal memory. *Neuropsychologia,* 10:1, 1972.

Milner, B. and Teuber, H.-L.: Alteration of perception and memory in man: Reflections on method. In Weiskrantz, L. (Ed.): *Analysis of Behavior in the Child.* New York, Har-Row, 1968.

Mishkin, M.: Visual discrimination performance following partial ablation of the temporal lobe. *J Comp Physiol Psychol,* 47:14, 1954.

Mishkin, M.: Effects of small frontal lesions on delayed alternation in monkeys. *J Neurophysiol,* 20:615, 1957.

Mishkin, M. and Pribram, K.: Visual discrimination performance following partial ablations of the temporal lobe. *J Comp Physiol Psychol,* 48:1, 1954.

Mitsuyama, Y. and Takamatsu, I.: An autopsied unusual case of Pick's disease. *Folia Psychiatr Neurol,* 25:141, 1971.

Mohan, K. J., Salo, M. W., and Nagaswami, S.: A case of limbic system dysfunction with hypersexuality and fugue states. *Dis Nerv Syst,* 36: 621, 1975.

Monakow, C.: *Die Lokalisation in Grosshirn.* Wiesbaden, Bergman, 1914.

Monakow, C. and Morgue, R.: *Introduction biologique a l'étude de la neurologie et de la psychopathologie.* Paris, Alcan, 1928.

Mones, R. J., Christoff, N., and Bender, M. B.: Posterior cerebral artery occlusion. *Arch Neurol,* 5:68, 1961.

Money, J.: Two cytogenetic syndromes: Psychologic comparisons: I. Intelligence and specific factor quotients. *J Psychiatric Res,* 2:223, 1964.

Money, J.: Turner's syndrome and parietal lobe function. *Cortex,* 9:387, 1973.

Money, J., Alexander, D., and Erhardt, A.: Visual constructional deficit in Turners syndrome. *J Pediat,* 69:126, 1966.

Money, J. and Granoff, D.: IQ and the somatic stigmata of Turner's syndrome. *Am J Ment Defic,* 70:68, 1965.

Moore, J. C.: Behavior bias and the limbic system. *Am J Occup Ther,* 30: 11, 1976.

Morant, R. B. and Efstathiou, A.: The Archimedes spiral and diagnosis of brain damage. *Percept Mot Skills,* 22:391, 1966.

Morrow, R. S. and Mark, J. C.: The correlation of intelligence and neurological findings on twenty-two patients autopsied for brain damage. *J Consult Psychol,* 19:283, 1955.

Mosher, D. L. and Smith, J. P.: The usefulness of two scoring systems for the Bender-Gestalt Test for identifying brain damage. *J Consult Psychol,* 29:530, 1965.

Motto, J. J.: The MMPI performance of veterans with organic and psychiatric disabilities. *J Consult Psychol,* 22:304, 1958.

Mullan, S. and Penfield, W.: Illusions of comparative interpretation and emotion. *Arch Neurol Psychiatry,* 81:269, 1959.

Myers, R. E.: Localization of function in the corpus callosum. *Arch Neurol,* 1:74, 1959.

Nebes, R. D.: Superiority of the minor hemisphere in commissurotimized man for the perception of part-whole relations. *Cortex,* 7:333, 1971.

Nebes, R. D.: Perception of spatial relationships by the right and left hemispheres in commissurotimized man. *Neuropsychologia,* 11:285, 1973.

Nebes, R. D. and Sperry, R. W.: Hemispheric deconnection syndrome with cerebral birth injury in the dominant arm area. *Neuropsychologia,* 9: 247, 1971.

Neff, W. D. and Goldberg, J. M.: Higher functions of the central nervous system. *Ann Rev Psychol,* 22:499, 1960.

Nemiah, J. C.: Common emotional reactions of patients to injury. *Arch Phys Med Rehabil,* 45:621, 1964.

Netley, C.: Colour aphasia: A case report. *Cortex,* 10:388, 1974.

Neuringer, C., Dombrowski, P. S., and Goldstein, G.: Cross validation of an MMPI scale of differential diagnosis of brain damage from schizophrenia. *J Clin Psychol,* 31:268, 1975.

New, P. J. and Scott, W. R.: *Computed Tomography of the Brain and Orbit.* Baltimore, Williams & Wilkins, 1975.

Newcombe, F.: *Missile Wounds of the Brain*. London, Oxford U Pr, 1969.

Newcombe, F. and Marshall, J. C.: Immediate recall of "sentences" by subjects with unilateral cerebral lesions. *Neuropsychologia, 5:*329, 1967.

Nielsen, J. M.: *Agnosia, Apraxia, Aphasia*. New York, Hoeber, 1946.

Noback, C. R. and Demarest, R. J.: *The Human Nervous System*. New York, McGraw, 1975.

Norman, R. D.: A revised deterioration formula for the Wechsler Adult Intelligence Scale. *J Clin Psychol, 22:*287, 1966.

Norton, J. C. and Matthews, C. G.: Psychological test performance in patients with subtentorial versus supratentorial CNS disease. *Dis Nerv Syst, 33:*312, 1972.

Nyberg-Hansen, R.: Functional aspects of cerebellar signs in clinical neurology. *Acta Neurol Scand, 51:*219, 1972.

Ojemann, G. A.: Alteration in nonverbal short term memory with stimulation in the region of the mammillothalamic tract in man. *Neuropsychologia, 9:*195, 1971.

Ojemann, G. A. and Ward, A. A.: Speech representation in the ventrolateral thalamus. *Brain, 94:*669, 1971.

Olbrich, R.: Reaction time in brain damaged and normal subjects to variable preparatory intervals. *J Nerv Ment Dis, 155:*356, 1972.

Oldfield, R. C.: The assessment and analysis of handedness: The Edinburgh inventory. *Neuropsychologia, 9:*97, 1971.

Orgass, B. and Poeck, K.: Clinical validation of a new test for aphasia: An experimental study on the Token Test. *Cortex, 2:*222, 1966.

Orgel, S. A. and McDonald, R. D.: An evaluation of the Trail Making Test. *J Consult Psychol, 31:*77, 1967.

Orme, J. E.: Bender design recall and brain damage. *Dis Nerv Syst, 23:* 329, 1962.

Oxbury, J. M., Campbell, D. C., and Oxbury, S. M.: Unilateral spatial neglect and impairments of spatial analysis and visual perception. *Brain, 97:*551, 1974.

Oxbury, J. M., Oxbury, S. M., and Humphrey, N.: Varieties of color anomia. *Brain, 92:*847, 1969.

Page, R. D. and Linden, J. D.: "Reversible" organic brain syndrome in alcoholics. *Q J Stud Alcohol, 35:*98, 1974.

Paolino, A. F. and Friedman, I.: Intellectual changes following frontal lobe procainization. *J Clin Psychol, 15:*437, 1959.

Papez, J. W.: Path for projections of non-specific diffuse impulses to the cortex. *Dis Nerv Syst, 17:*103, 1956.

Papez, J. W.: Visceral brain, its component parts and their connections. *J Nerv Ment Dis, 126:*40, 1958.

Parker, J. W.: The validity of some current tests for organicity. *J Consult Psychol, 21:*425, 1957.

Parkinson, J.: An essay on the shaking palsy. *Arch Neurol, 20:*441, 1969.

Parsons, O. A., Vega, A., and Burn, J.: Different psychological effects of lateralized brain damage. *J Consult Clin Psychol, 33:*551, 1969.

Pascal, G. R. and Suttell, B.: *The Bender-Gestalt Test: Quantification and Validity for Adults.* New York, Grune, 1951.

Paul, N., Fitzgerald, E., and Greenblatt, M.: Bimedial lobotomy: five-year evaluation. *J Nerv Ment Dis, 124:*49, 1956.

Penfield, W.: Mechanisms of voluntary movement. *Brain, 77:*1, 1954.

Penfield, W.: Conditioning the uncommitted cortex for language learning. *Brain, 88:*787, 1965.

Penfield, W. and Evans, J.: The frontal lobe in man: A clinical study of maximum removals. *Brain, 58:*115, 1935.

Penfield, W. and Mathieson, G.: Memory. *Arch Neurol, 31:*145, 1974.

Penfield, W. and Milner, B.: Memory deficit produced by bilateral lesions in the hippocampal zone. *Arch Neurol Psychiatry, 79:*475, 1958.

Pennington, H., Galliani, C., and Voegele, G.: Unilateral electroencephalographic dysrhythmia and children's intelligence. *Child Dev, 36:*539, 1965.

Perez, F. I., Rivera, V. M., Meyer, J. S., Gay, J. R., Taylor, R. L., and Mathew, N. T.: Analysis of intellectual and cognitive performance in patients with multi-infarct dementia, vertebrobasilar insufficiency with dementia and Alzheimer's disease. *J Neurol Neurosurg Psychiatry, 38:* 533, 1975.

Perret, E.: The left frontal lobe of man and the suppression of habitual responses in verbal categorical behavior. *Neuropsychologia, 12:*323, 1974.

Piercy, M. and Smyth, V. O. G.: Right hemisphere dominance for certain non-verbal intellectual skills. *Brain, 85:*225, 1962.

Pihl, R. O.: The degree of verbal-performance discrepancy on the WISC and the WAIS and severity of EEG abnormality in epileptics. *J Clin Psychol, 24:*418, 1968.

Piotrowski, Z.: The Rorschach Inkblot Method in organic disturbances of the central nervous system. *J Nerv Ment Dis, 86:*525, 1937.

Plutchik, R. and DiScipio, W. J.: Personality patterns in chronic alcoholism (Korsakoff's syndrome), chronic schizophrenia, and geriatric patients with chronic brain syndrome. *J Am Geriat Soc, 22:*514, 1974.

Poeck, K. and Orgass, B.: A qualitative study on Token Test performance in aphasic and non-aphasic brain damaged patients. *Neuropsychologia, 12:*49, 1974.

Pontius, A. A.: Dysfunction patterns analogous to frontal lobe system and caudate nucleus syndrome in some groups of minimal dysfunction. *J Am Med Wom Assoc, 28:*285, 1973.

Pool, D. and Brown, R.: The Peabody Picture Vocabulary Test as a measure of general adult intelligence. *J Consult Clin Psychol, 34:*8, 1970.

Pronovost, W. and Dumbleton, C.: A picture type speech sound discrimination test. *J Speech Hear Disord, 18:*258, 1953.

Ptacek, J. and Young, F. M.: Comparison of the Grassi Block Substitution Test with the Wechsler-Bellevue in the diagnosis of organic brain damage. *J Clin Psychol, 10:*375, 1954.

Quadfasel, F. A.: Aspects of the work and life of Kurt Goldstein. *Cortex, 4:* 113, 1968.

Quattlebaum, L. F.: A brief note on the relationship between two psychomotor tests. *J Clin Psychol, 24:*198, 1968.

Rabinowitz, H. S.: Motivation for recovery: Four social psychologic aspects. *Arch Phys Med Rehabil, 42:*799, 1961.

Ramier, A. M. and Hecaen, H.: Rôle réspectif des atteintes frontales et de la latéralisation lesionnelle dans les déficits de la "fluence verbale." *Rev Neurol, 123:*17, 1970.

Rapaport, D., Gill, M. M. and Schafer, R.: *Diagnostic Psychological Testing.* New York, Intl Univs Pr, 1968.

Rapin, I., Tourk, L. M., and Costa, L. D.: Evaluation of the Purdue Pegboard as a screening test for brain damage. *Dev Med Child Neurol, 8:* 45, 1966.

Ratcliff, G. and Newcombe, F.: Spatial orientation in man: Effects of left, right, and bilateral posterior cerebral lesions. *J Neurol Neurosurg Psychiatry, 36:*448, 1973.

Raven, J. C.: *Guide to the Standard Progressive Matrices.* London, Lewis, 1960.

Reed, H. B. and Fitzhugh, K. B.: Patterns of deficits in relation to severity of cerebral dysfunction in children and adults. *J Consult Psychol, 30:* 98, 1966.

Reed, J. C. and Reitan, R. M.: Verbal and performance differences among brain injured children with lateralized motor deficits. *Percept Mot Skills, 29:*747, 1969.

Reed, H. B., Reitan, R. M., and Klove, H.: Influence of cerebral lesions on psychological test performance of older children. *J Consult Psychol, 29:* 247, 1965.

Reitan, R. M.: *Neuropsychological Methods of Inferring Brain Damage in Adults and Children.* Unpublished manuscript, undated.

Reitan, R. M.: Affective disturbances in brain damaged patients. *Arch Neurol Psychiatry, 73:*530, 1955a.

Reitan, R. M.: The distribution according to age of a psychologic measure dependent upon organic brain functions. *J Gerontol, 10:*338, 1955b.

Reitan, R. M.: Investigation of the validity of Halstead's measure of biological intelligence. *Arch Neurol Psychiatry, 73:*28, 1955c.

Reitan, R. M.: The relation of the Trail Making Test to organic brain damage. *J Consult Psychol, 19:*393, 1955d.

Reitan, R. M.: Validity of the Trail Making Test as an indicator of organic brain damage. *Percept Mot Skills, 8:*271, 1958.

Reitan, R. M.: Correlations between the Trail Making Test and the Wechsler-Bellevue Scale. *Percept Mot Skills, 9:*127, 1959a.

Reitan, R. M.: The comparative effects of brain damage on the Halstead Impairment Index and the Wechsler-Bellevue Scale. *J Clin Psychol, 15:* 281, 1959b.

Reitan, R. M.: *Manual for Administration of Neuropsychological Test Batteries for Adults and Children.* Indianapolis, privately mimeographed, 1959c.

Reitan, R. M.: The effect of brain lesions on adaptive abilities in human beings. Unpublished manuscript, 1959d.

Reitan, R. M.: The significance of dysphasia for intelligence and adaptive abilities. *J Psychol, 50:*355, 1960.

Reitan, R. M.: Relationship of differential abstraction ability levels to psychological test performances in mentally retarded subjects. *Am J Ment Defic, 68:*235, 1963.

Reitan, R. M.: Psychological deficits resulting from cerebral lesions in man. In Warren, J. M. and Akert, K. A. (Eds.): *The Frontal Granular Cortex and Behavior.* New York, McGraw, 1964.

Reitan, R. M.: Problems and prospects in studying the psychological correlates of brain lesions. *Cortex, 2:*127, 1966.

Reitan, R. M.: *Examples of Children with Brain Lesions and Children with Neuropsychological Diagnostic Problems.* Privately mimeographed manuscript, 1969.

Reitan, R. M.: Trail Making Test results for normal and brain-damaged children. *Percept Mot Skills, 33:*575, 1971.

Reitan, R. M.: Verbal problem solving as related to cerebral damage. *Percept Mot Skills, 34:*515, 1972.

Reitan, R. M.: Methodological problems in clinical neuropsychology. In Reitan, R. M. and Davison, L. A. (Eds.): *Clinical Neuropsychology: Current Status and Applications.* Washington, Winston, 1974a.

Reitan, R. M.: Psychological effects of cerebral lesions in children of early school age. In Reitan, R. M. and Davison, L. A. (Eds.): *Clinical Neuropsychology: Current Status and Applications.* Washington, Winston, 1974b.

Reitan, R. M.: Neuropsychology: The vulgarization Luria always wanted. *Contemp Psychol, 21:*737, 1976.

Reitan, R. M. and Boll, T. J.: Intellectual and cognitive functions in Parkinson's disease. *J Consult Clin Psychol, 37:*364, 1971.

Reitan, R. M. and Boll, T. J.: Neuropsychological correlates of minimal brain dysfunction. *Ann NY Acad Sci, 205:*65, 1973.

Reitan, R. M. and Davison, L. A.: *Clinical Neuropsychology: Current Status and Applications.* Washington, Winston, 1974.

Reitan, R. M. and Fitzhugh, K. B.: Behavioral deficits in groups with cerebrovascular lesions. *J Consult Clin Psychol, 37:*215, 1971.

Reitan, R. M. and Klove, H.: *Hypothesis Supported by Clinical Evidence That Are Under Current Investigation.* Unpublished manuscript, undated.

Reitan, R. M., Reed, J. C., and Dyken, M. L.: Cognitive, psychomotor and motor correlates of multiple sclerosis. *J Nerv Ment Dis, 153:* 218, 1971.

Reitan, R. M. and Tarshes, E. L.: Differential effects of lateralized brain lesions on the Trail Making Test. *J Nerv Ment Dis, 129:*257, 1959.

Rey, A.: *L'examen Clinique et Psychologie.* Paris, Presses Universitaires, 1964.

Riese, W.: Hughlings Jackson's doctrine of consciousness. *J Nerv Ment Dis, 120:*330, 1954.

Riese, W.: Semantic aphasia. *J Nerv Ment Dis, 123:*18, 1956a.

Riese, W.: The sources of Jacksonian neurology. *J Nerv Ment Dis, 124:* 125, 1956b.

Riese, W.: The source of Hughling Jackson's views on aphasia, *Brain,* 88:811, 1965.

Riklan, M. and Levita, E.: Psychological studies of thalamic lesions in humans. *J Nerv Ment Dis, 150:*251, 1970.

Riseman, J., Eagle, M. N., Benjamin, H. J., and Bernstein, L. J.: Short-term recall in left hemiplegic patients. *Arch Phys Med Rehabil, 52:* 118, 1971.

Robbins, S. L.: *Pathologic Basis of Disease.* Philadelphia, Saunders, 1974.

Roberts, D. R.: Catatonia in the brain: A localization study. *Int J Neuropsychiatry, 1:*395, 1965.

Rochford, G. and Williams, M.: Studies in the development and breakdown of the use of names. I. *J Neurol Neurosurg Psychiatry, 25:*222, 1962.

Roeser, R. J. and Daly, D. D.: Auditory cortex deconnection associated with thalamic tumor. *Neurology, 24:*555, 1974.

Roland, P. E.: Astereognosis. *Arch Neurol, 33:*543, 1976.

Roland, P. E. and Larsen, B.: Focal increase of cerebral blood flow during stereognostic testing in man. *Arch Neurol, 33:*551, 1976.

Roofe, P. G.: Some letters from the Herrick-Lashley correspondence. *Neuropsychologia, 8:*3, 1970.

Rosecrans, C. J. and Schaffer, H. B.: Bender-Gestalt time and score differences between matched groups of hospitalized psychiatric and brain damaged patients. *J Clin Psychol, 25:*409, 1969.

Rosenblum, J. A.: Human sexuality and cerebral cortex. *Dis Nerv Syst,* 35:268, 1974.

Rosenstock, H. A.: Alzheimer's presenile dementia. *Dis Nerv Syst, 31:* 826, 1970.

Rosillo, R. H. and Fogel, M. L.: Correlation of psychologic variables and progress in physical rehabilitation. I. Degree of disability and denial of illness. *Arch Phys Med Rehabil, 51:*227, 1970.

Rosillo, R. H. and Fogel, M. L.: Correlation of psychologic variables and progress in physical rehabilitation. IV. The relation of body image to success in physical rehabilitation. *Arch Phys Med Rehabil,* 52:182, 1971.

Ross, A. O.: *Psychological Aspects of Learning Disabilities and Reading Disorders.* New York, McGraw, 1976.

Ross, W. D. and McNaughton, F. L.: Head injury: A study of patients with chronic post-traumatic complaints. *Arch Neurol Psychiatry, 52:* 255, 1944.

Rourke, B. P.: Brain-behavior relationships in children with learning disabilities: A research program. *Am Psychol,* 30:911, 1975.

Rourke, B. P., Dietrich, D. M., and Young, G. C.: Significance of WISC verbal-performance discrepancies for younger children with learning disabilities. *Percept Mot Skills, 36:*275, 1973.

Rourke, B. P. and Telegdy, G. A.: Lateralizing significance of WISC verbal-performance discrepancies for older children with learning disabilities. *Percept Mot Skills,* 33:875, 1971.

Rourke, B. P., Yanni, D. W., MacDonald, G. W., and Young, G. C.: Neuropsychological significance of lateralized deficits on the grooved pegboard test for older children with learning disabilities. *J Consul Clin Psychol, 41:*128, 1973.

Rourke, B. P., Young, G. C., and Flewelling, R. W.: The relationship between WISC verbal performance discrepancies and selected verbal, auditory-perceptual, visual-perceptual, and problem-solving abilities in children with learning disabilities. *J Clin Psychol, 27:*475, 1971.

Rubens, A. B. and Benson, D. F.: Associative visual agnosia. *Arch Neurol, 24:*305, 1971.

Rubino, C. A.: Hemispheric lateralization of visual perception. *Cortex,* 6:102, 1970.

Rudel, R. G. and Denckla, M. B.: Relation of forward to backward digit repetition to neurological impairment in children with learning disabilities. *Neuropsychologia, 12:*109, 1974.

Russell, E. W.: WAIS factor analysis with brain damaged subjects using criterion measures. *J Consult Clin Psychol,* 39:133, 1972.

Russell, E. W.: Validation of a brain damage vs. schizophrenia MMPI key. *J Clin Psychol, 31:*659, 1975.

Russell, E. W., Neuringer, C., and Goldstein, G.: *Assessment of Brain Damage—A Neuropsychological Key Approach.* New York, Wiley, 1970.

Russell, W. R. and Espir, M. L. E.: *Traumatic Aphasia.* London, Oxford U Pr, 1961.

Sanides, F.: Structure and function of the human frontal lobe. *Neuropsychologia, 2:*209, 1964.

Sarno, M. T. and Levita, E.: Natural course of recovery in severe aphasia. *Arch Phys Med Rehabil, 52:*175, 1971.

Sauguet, J., Benton, A. L., and Hecaen, H.: Disturbances of the body schema in relation to language impairment and hemispheric locus of lesion. *J Neurol Neurosurg Psychiatry, 34:*496, 1971.

Saunders, T. R.: Toward a distinctive role for the psychologist in neurodiagnostic decision making. *Prof Psychol, 6:*161, 1975.

Scherer, I. W., Winne, J. F., and Baker, R. W.: Psychological changes over a three-year period following bilateral prefrontal lobotomy. *J Consult Psychol, 19:*291, 1955.

Schiller, F.: Aphasia studied in patients with missile wounds. *J Neurol Neurosurg Psychiatry, 10:*183, 1947.

Schreiber, D. J., Goldman, H., Kleinman, K. M., Goldfader, P. R., and Snow, M. Y.: The relationship between independent neuropsychological and neurological detection and localization of cerebral impairment. *J Nerv Ment Dis, 162:*360, 1976.

Schwartz, M.: Separate versus full MMPI method: Reliability of the pseudoneurologic scale. *J Clin Psychol, 30:*79, 1974.

Science Research Associates: *Purdue Pegboard.* Chicago, Science Research Associates, 1948.

Scotti, G. and Spinnler, H.: Colour imperception in unilateral hemisphere damaged patients. *J Neurol Neurosurg Psychiatry, 33:*22, 1970.

Scoville, W. B. and Milner, B.: Loss of recent memory after bilateral hippocampal lesions. *J Neurol Neurosurg Psychiatry, 20:*11, 1957.

Shaffer, D.: Psychiatric aspects of brain injury in childhood: a review. *Dev Med Child Neurol, 15:*211, 1973.

Shaffer, D., Chadwick, D., and Rutter, M.: Psychiatric outcome of localized head injury in childhood. In CIBA Foundation (Ed.): *Outcome of Severe Damage to the Central Nervous System (Ciba Found Symp 34).* New York, Elsevier, 1975.

Shalman, D. C.: The diagnostic use of the McGill Picture Anomaly Test in temporal lobe epilepsy. *J Neurol Neurosurg Psychiatry, 24:*220, 1961.

Shankweiler, D.: Effects of temporal lobe damage on perception of dichotically presented melodies. *J Comp Physiol Psychol, 62:*115, 1966.

Shaw, D. J.: The reliability and the validity of the Halstead Category Test. *J Clin Psychol, 22:*176, 1966.

Shaw, M. C. and Cruickshank, W. M.: The use of the Bender-Gestalt Test with epileptic children. *J Clin Psychol, 12:*192, 1956.

Shaw, D. J. and Matthews, C. G.: Differential MMPI performance of brain damaged vs. pseudo-neurologic groups. *J Clin Psychol, 21:*405, 1965.

Shaw, D. J., Matthews, C. G., and Klove, H.: The equivalence of WISC and PPVT IQ's. *Am J Ment Defic, 70:*601, 1966.

Shearn, C. R., Berry, D. F., and Fitzgibbons, B.: Usefulness of the Memory for Designs Test in assessing mild organic complications in psychiatric patients. *Percept Mot Skills, 38:*1099, 1974.

Shipley, W. C.: A self-administering scale for measuring intellectual impairment and deterioration. *J Psychol, 9:*371, 1940.

Shipley, W. C.: *Institute of Living Scale.* Los Angeles, Western, 1946.

Sidman, M.: *Tactics of Scientific Research.* New York, Basic, 1960.

Silverstein, A. and Hollin, S.: Internal carotid versus middle cerebral artery occlusions. *Arch Neurol, 12:*468, 1965.

Sim, M. and Sussman, I.: Alzheimer's disease: Its natural history and differential diagnosis. *J Nerv Ment Dis, 135:*489, 1962.

Simard, T. G. and Ladd, H. W.: differential control of muscle segments by quadriplegic patients: An electromyographic procedural investigation. *Arch Phys Med Rehabil, 52:*447, 1971.

Simernitskaya, E. G.: On two forms of writing defect following local brain lesions. In Dimond, J. and Beaumont, J. G. (Eds.): *Hemisphere Function in the Brain.* New York, Wiley, 1974.

Simpson, C. D. and Vega, A.: Unilateral brain damage and patterns of age corrected WAIS subtest scores. *J Clin Psychol, 27:*204, 1971.

Small, I. F., Small, J. G., Milstein, V., and Moore, J. E.: Neuropsychological observations with psychosis and somatic treatment. *J Nerv Ment Dis, 155:*6, 1972.

Smith, A.: Psychodiagnosis of patients with brain tumors. *J Nerv Ment Dis, 135:*513, 1962.

Smith, A.: Changing effects of frontal lesions in man. *J Neurol Neurosurg Psychiatry, 27:*511, 1964.

Smith, A.: Verbal and nonverbal test performances of patients with "acute" lateralized brain injuries (tumors). *J Nerv Ment Dis, 141:*517, 1965.

Smith, A.: Certain hypothesized hemisphere differences in language and visual functions in human adults. *Cortex, 2:*109, 1966.

Smith, A.: Intellectual functions in patients with lateralized frontal tumours. *J Neurol Neurosurg Psychiatry, 29:*52, 1966.

Smith, A.: The Symbol-Digits Modality Test: A new psychologic test for economic screening of learning and other cerebral disorders. *J Learning Disabilities, 3:83,* 1968.

Smith, A.: Objective indices of severity of chronic aphasia in stroke patients. *J Speech Hear Disord, 36:167,* 1971.

Smith, A.: Neuropsychological testing in neurological disorders. *Adv Neurol, 7:49,* 1975.

Smith, A.: *Differing Effects of Hemispherectomy in Children and Adults.* Paper presented to the Eighty-fourth Annual Convention of the American Psychological Association, Washington, 1976.

Smith, C. E. and Keogh, B. K.: A group Bender-Gestalt as a reading readiness screening instrument. *Percept Mot Skills, 15:639,* 1962.

Smith, T. E.: Relation of the Trail Making Test to mental retardation. *Percept Mot Skills, 17:719,* 1963.

Snyder, R. and Snyder, P.: Maturational changes in visual motor perception: An item analysis of Bender-Gestalt errors from ages 6 to 11. *Percept Mot Skills, 38:51,* 1974.

Solursh, L. P., Margulies, A. I., Ashem, B., and Stasiak, E. A.: The relationship of the agenesis of the corpus callosum to perception and learning. *J Nerv Ment Dis, 141:180,* 1965.

Somasundaram, O.: Alzheimer's disease. *J Indian Med Assoc, 63:66,* 1974.

Song, A. Y. and Song, R. H.: The Bender-Gestalt Test with background interference procedure in mental retardates. *J Clin Psychol, 25:69,* 1969.

Spalding, J. M. K.: Wounds of the visual pathway. *J Neurol Neurosurg Psychiatry, 15:99,* 1952.

Sparks, R., Helm, N., and Albert, M.: Aphasia rehabilitation resulting from melodic intonation therapy. *Cortex, 10:303,* 1974.

Spellacy, F. J. and Spreen, O.: A short form of the Token Test. *Cortex, 5:390,* 1969.

Spiegel, E. A. and Wycis, A. T.: Multiplicity of subcortical localization of various functions. *J Nerv Ment Dis, 147:45,* 1968.

Spreen, O. and Benton, A. L.: Comparative studies of psychological tests for cerebral damage. *J Nerv Ment Dis, 140:323,* 1965.

Spreen, O. and Benton, A. L.: *Neurosensory Center Comprehensive Examination for Aphasia.* Victoria, British Columbia, U of Victoria Pr, 1969.

Spreen, O. and Gaddes, W. H.: Developmental norms for 15 neuropsychological tests ages 6 to 15. *Cortex, 5:170,* 1969.

Stepien, L. and Sherpinski, S.: Impairment of recent memory after temporal lobe injuries in man. *Neuropsychologia, 2:291,* 1964.

Sterling, H. M.: Pediatric rehabilitation. *Arch Phys Med Rehabil, 48:* 474, 1967.

Sterman, M. B., MacDonald, L. R., and Stone, R. K.: Biofeedback training of the sensorimotor electroencephalogram rhythm in man: Effects on epilepsy. *Epilepsia, 15:*395, 1974.

Sterne, D. M.: The Benton, Porteus and WAIS Digit Span Tests with normal and brain injured subjects. *J Clin Psychol, 25:*173, 1969.

Sterne, D. M.: The Hooper Visual Organization Test and the Trail Making Test as discriminants of brain damage. *J Clin Psychol, 29:*212, 1973.

Storms, L. H.: Relationships among patients' emotional problems, neurologists' judgements and psychological tests of brain dysfunction. *J Clin Psychol, 28:*54, 1972.

Stroop, J. R.: Studies of interference in serial verbal reactions. *J Exp Psychol, 18:*643, 1935.

Strub, R. and Geschwind, N.: Gerstmann's syndrome without aphasia. *Cortex, 10:*378, 1974.

Subirana, A.: The prognosis in aphasia in relation of cerebral dominance and handedness. *Brain, 81:*415, 1958.

Swiercinsky, D.: Clinical neuropsychological evaluation: A capsule description. Submitted for publication, 1976.

Swiercinsky, D. P. and Hallenbeck, C. E.: A factorial approach to neuropsychological assessment. *J Clin Psychol, 31:*610, 1975.

Swiercinsky, D. P. and Warnock, J. K.: Comparison of the neuropsychological key and discriminant analysis approach in predicting cerebral damage and localization. Submitted for publication, 1976.

Swisher, L. P.: Auditory intensity discrimination in patients with temporal lobe damage. *Cortex, 3:*179, 1967.

Swisher, L. P. and Sarno, M. T.: Token Test scores of three matched patient groups: Left brain damaged with aphasia, right brain damaged without aphasia, non-brain damaged. *Cortex, 5:*264, 1969.

Symonds, C.: Disorders of memory. *Brain, 89:*625, 1966.

Taft, L. T., Delagi, E. F., Wilkie, O. L. and Abramson, A. S.: Critique of rehabilitative technics in treatment of cerebral palsy. *Arch Phys Med Rehabil, 43:*238, 1962.

Talland, G. A.: Psychological studies of Korsakoff's psychosis. III. Concept formation. *J Nerv Ment Dis, 128:*214, 1959.

Talland, G. A.: Psychological studies of Korsakoff's psychosis. VI. Memory and learning. *J Nerv Ment Dis, 130:*366, 1960.

Tarter, R. E.: Intellectual and adaptive functioning in epilepsy. *Dis Nerv Syst, 33:*759, 1972.

Tarter, R. E.: An analysis of cognitive deficits in chronic alcoholics. *J Nerv Ment Dis, 157:*138, 1973.

Tarter, R. E.: Brain damage associated with chronic alcoholism. *Dis Nerv Syst, 36*:185, 1975.

Tarter, R. E. and Jones, B. M.: Motor impairment in chronic alcoholics. *Dis Nerv Syst, 32*:632, 1971.

Taylor, A. M. and Warrington, E. K.: Visual discrimination in patients with localized cerebral lesions. *Cortex, 9*:82, 1973.

Taylor, E. M.: *Psychological Appraisal of Children with Cerebral Defects.* Cambridge, Massachusetts, Harvard U Pr, 1959.

Terzian, H. and Dale, O. G.: Syndrome of Klüver and Bucy produced in man by bilateral removal of the temporal lobes. *J Neurol Neurosurg Psychiatry, 20*:11, 1957.

Teuber, H.-L.: Space perception and its disturbances after brain injury in man. *Neuropsychologia, 1*:47, 1963.

Teuber, H.-L.: Recovery of function after lesions of the central nervous system: History and prospects. *Neurosci Res Prog Bull, 12*:197, 1974.

Teuber, H.-L.: Recovery of function after brain injury in man. In CIBA Foundation (Ed.): *Outcome of Severe Damage to the Central Nervous System (Ciba symposium 34).* New York, Am Elsevier, 1975.

Teuber, H.-L., Battersby, W. S., and Bender, M. B.: Performance of complex visual tasks after cerebral lesions. *J Nerv Ment Dis, 114*:413, 1951.

Teuber, H.-L., Battersby, W. S., and Bender, M. B.: *Visual Field Defects After Penetrating Missile Wounds of the Brain.* Cambridge, Massachusetts, Harvard U Pr, 1960.

Teuber, H.-L. and Rudel, R. G.: Behavior after cerebral lesions in children and adults. *Dev Med Child Neurol, 4*:3, 1962.

Thomas, C. A.: An application of the Grassi Block Substitution Test in the determination of organicity. *J Clin Psychol, 19*:84, 1963.

Thomsen, I. V.: Evaluation of outcome of aphasia in patients with severe closed head trauma. *J Neurol Neurosurg Rehabil, 38*:713, 1975.

Thweatt, R. C.: Prediction of school learning disabilities through the use of the Bender-Gestalt test: A validation study of Koppitz's scoring technique. *J Clin Psychol, 19*:216, 1963.

Toglia, J. U.: The corpus callosum. *Dis Nerv Syst, 22*:428, 1961.

Tolor, A. and Schulberg, H.: *An Evaluation of the Bender-Gestalt.* Springfield, Thomas, 1963.

Tymchuk, A. J.: Comparison of the Bender error and time scores from groups of epileptic, retarded, and behavior problem children. *Percept Mot Skills, 38*:71, 1974.

Tymchuk, A. J., Knights, R. M., and Hinton, G. G.: The behavioral significance of differing EEG abnormalities in children with learning and/or behavioral problems. *J Learn Disabil, 3*:547, 1970.

Ullmann, L. P. and Krasner, L.: A *Psychological Approach to Abnormal Behavior*. Englewood Cliffs, P-H, 1967.

University of Wisconsin Neuropsychology Laboratory: *Experimental T-score Norms for Performance on the Wisconsin Neuropsychology Test Battery*. Privately published, undated.

Upper, D. and Seeman, W.: Brain damage, schizophrenia and five MMPI items. *J Clin Psychol, 24:*444, 1968.

Urmer, A. H., Morris, A. B., and Wendland, L. V.: The effect of brain damage on Raven's Progressive Matrices. *J Clin Psychol, 16:*182, 1960.

Vega, A.: Use of Purdue Pegboard and finger tapping performance as a rapid screening test for brain damage. *J Clin Psychol, 25:*255, 1969.

Vega, A. and Parsons, O.: Cross-validation of the Halstead-Reitan Tests for brain damage. *J Consult Clin Psychol, 31:*619, 1967.

Vega, A. and Parsons, O.: Lateralized brain damage and differential psychological effects: Reply to Dr. Woo-Sam. *Percept Mot Skills, 33:*269, 1971.

Vignolo, L. A.: Evolution of aphasia and language rehabilitation: A retrospective exploratory study. *Cortex, 1:*344, 1964.

Vilkki, J and Laitinen, V.: Differential effects of left and right ventro-lateral thalamotomy on receptive and expressive verbal performances and face matching. *Neuropsychologia, 12:*11, 1974.

Vineberg, S. E. and Willems, E. P.: Observation and analysis of patient behavior in the rehabilitation hospital. *Arch Phys Med Rehabil, 52:*8, 1971.

Vitale, J. H., Pulos, S. M., Wollitzer, A. O., and Steinhelber, J. C.: Relationships of psychological dimensions to impairment in a population with cerebrovascular insufficiency. *J Nerv Ment Dis, 158:*456, 1974.

Vogel, W.: Some effects of brain lesions on MMPI profiles. *J Consult Psychol, 26:*412, 1962.

Vygotsky, L. S.: Psychology and localization of functions. *Neuropsychologia, 3:*381, 1965.

Wada, J. A., Clarke, R., and Hamm, A.: Cerebral hemispheric asymmetry in humans. *Arch Neurol, 32:*239, 1975.

Walker, M.: Perceptual coding, visuo-motor and spatial difficulties and their neurological correlates: A progress note. *Dev Med Child Neurol, 7:*543, 1965.

Wanderer, Z. W.: Therapy as learning: Behavior therapy. *Am J Occu Ther, 28:*207, 1974.

Wang, P., Kaplan, J., and Rogers, E.: Memory functioning in hemiplegics: A neuropsychological analysis of the Wechsler Memory Scale. *Arch Phys Med Rehabil,* 56:517, 1975.

Warrington, E. K. and James, M.: Disorders of visual perception in patients with localized cerebral lesions. *Neuropsychologia,* 5:253, 1967.

Warrington, E. K., James, M., and Kinsbourne, M.: Drawing disability in relation to laterality of cerebral lesion. *Brain,* 89:53, 1966.

Warrington, E. K., Logue, V., and Pratt, R. T. C.: The anatomical localization of selective impairment of auditory short term memory. *Neuropsychologia,* 9:377, 1971.

Warrington, E. K. and Pratt, R. T. C.: Language laterality in left-handers assessed by unilateral E.C.T. *Neuropsychologia,* 11:423, 1973.

Warrington, E. K. and Taylor, A. M.: The contribution of the right parietal lobe to object recognition. *Cortex,* 9:152, 1973.

Watson, C. G.: The separation of NP hospital organics from schizophrenics with three visual motor screening tests. *J Clin Psychol,* 24:412, 1968.

Watson, C. G.: An MMPI scale to separate brain damaged from schizophrenic men. *J Consult Clin Psychol,* 36:121, 1971.

Watson, C. G.: Cross validation of a sign developed to separate brain damaged from schizophrenic patients. *J Clin Psychol,* 28:66, 1972.

Watson, C. G.: Chronicity and the Halstead Battery in psychiatric hospitals: A reply to Levine and Feirstein. *J Consult Clin Psychol,* 42:136, 1974.

Watson, C. G. and Thomas, R. W.: MMPI profiles of brain damaged and schizophrenic patients. *Percept Mot Skills,* 27:567, 1968.

Watson, C. G., Thomas, R. W., Anderson, D., and Felling, J.: Differentiation of organics from schizophrenics at two chronicity levels by use of the Reitan-Halstead Organic Test Battery. *J Consult Clin Psychol,* 32:679, 1968.

Watson, C. G., Thomas, R. W., Felling, J., and Anderson, D.: Differentiation of organics from schizophrenics with Reitan's sensory perceptual disturbances test. *Percept Mot Skills,* 26:1191, 1968.

Watson, C. G., Thomas, R. W., Felling, J., and Anderson, D.: Differentiation of organics from schizophrenics with the Trail Making, dynamometer, critical flicker fusion, and light intensity matching tests. *J Clin Psychol,* 25:130, 1969.

Watson, C. G. and Uecker, A. E.: An attempted cross validation of the Minnesota Percepto-Diagnostic test. *J Consult Psychol,* 30:461, 1966.

Waugh, R. P.: The I.T.P.A.: Ballast or bonanza for the school psychologist. *J School Psychol,* 13:201, 1975.

Wechsler, D.: *The Measurement of Adult Intelligence.* Baltimore, Williams & Wilkins, 1944.

Wechsler, D.: A standardized memory scale for clinical use. *J Psychol,* *19*:87, 1945.

Wechsler, D.: *Wechsler Intelligence Scale for Children Manual.* New York, Psychol Corp, 1949.

Wechsler, D.: *WAIS Manual.* New York, Psychol Corp, 1955.

Wechsler, D.: *The Measurement and Appraisal of Adult Intelligence,* 4th ed. Baltimore, Williams & Wilkins, 1958.

Wechsler, D.: *WISC-R. Manual.* New York, Psychol Corp, 1974.

Weigl, E.: On the psychology of so-called processes of abstraction. *J Abnorm Soc Psychol, 36*:3, 1941.

Weil, A. A.: Ictal emotions occurring in temporal lobe dysfunction. *Arch Neurol, 1*:87, 1959.

Weinberg, J., Diller, L., Gerstman, L., and Schulman, P.: Digit span in right and left hemispherics. *J Clin Psychol, 28*:361, 1972.

Weinstein, E. A., Cole, M., Mitchell, M. S., and Lyerly, O. G.: Ansognosia and aphasia. *Arch Neurol, 10*:376, 1964.

Weisenburg, T. H. and McBride, K. E.: *Aphasia: A Clinical and Psychological Study.* New York, Commonwealth Fund, 1935.

Welcher, D. W., Wessel, K. W., Mellits, E. D. and Hardy, J. B.: The Bender-Gestalt Test as an indicator of neurological impairment in young, inner-city children. *Percept Mot Skills, 38*:899, 1974.

Wepman, J. M.: A conceptual model for the processes involved in recovery from aphasia. *J Speech Hear Disord, 18*:4, 1953.

Wernicke, C.: The aphasic symptom complex. *Arch Neurol, 22*:280, 1970.

Wetzel, K. H., Welcher, D. W., and Mellitis, E. D.: The possibility of overdiagnosing brain dysfunction from a single administration of the Bender-Gestalt Test. *Johns Hopkins Med J, 129*:6, 1971.

Wheeler, J. and Wilkins, W. L.: The validity of the Hewson ratios. *J Consult Psychol, 15*:163, 1951.

Wheeler, L.: Predictions of brain damage from an aphasia screening test, an application of discriminant functions and a comparison with a non-linear method of analysis. *Percept Mot Skills, 17*:63, 1963.

Wheeler, L., Burke, C. J., and Reitan, R. M.: An application of discriminant functions to the problem of predicting brain damage using behavioral variables. *Percept Mot Skills, 16*:417, 1963.

Wheeler, L. and Reitan, R. M.: Presence and laterality of brain damage predicted from responses to a short aphasia screening test. *Percept Mot Skills, 15*:783, 1962.

Wheeler, L. and Reitan, R. M.: Discriminant functions applied to the problem of predicting cerebral damage from behavioral tests: A cross validation study. *Percept Mot Skills, 16*:681, 1963.

Wilkins, R. H. and Brody, I. A.: Alzheimer's Disease. *Arch Neurol, 21:* 109, 1969.

Wilkins, R. H. and Brody, I. A.: Wernicke's sensory aphasia. *Arch Neurol,* 22:279, 1970.

Wilkins, R. H. and Brody, I. A.: Gerstmann's syndrome. *Arch Neurol,* 24:475, 1971.

Williams, D.: Man's temporal lobe. *Brain,* 91:639, 1968.

Williams, H. L.: The development of a caudality scale for the MMPI. *J Clin Psychol,* 8:293, 1952.

Williams, P. L. and Warwick, R.: *Functional Neuroanatomy of Man.* Philadelphia, Saunders, 1975.

Wolff, B. B.: The application of the Hewson ratios to the WAIS as an aid in the differential diagnosis of cerebral pathology. *J Nerv Ment Dis, 131:*98, 1960.

Woo-Sam, J.: Lateralized brain damage and differential psychological effects: Parsons, et al., re-examined. *Percept Mot Skills,* 33:259, 1971.

Woo-Sam, J., Zimmerman, I. L., and Rogal, R.: Location of injury and Wechsler indices of mental deterioration. *Percept Mot Skills,* 32: 407, 1971.

Wyke, M.: The effects of brain lesions on the performance of bilateral arm movements. *Neuropsychologia,* 9:33, 1971.

Wyke, M. and Holgate, D.: Colour naming defects in dysphasic patients. A qualitative analysis. *Neuropsychologia,* 4:451, 1973.

Yamadori, A.: Ideogram reading in alexia. *Brain,* 98:231, 1975.

Yamadori, A. and Albert, M. L.: Word category aphasia. *Cortex,* 9:112, 1973.

Yates, A. J.: The validity of some psychological tests of brain damage. *Psychol Bull,* 51:359, 1954.

Zaidel, D. and Sperry, R. W.: Performance on Raven's Colored Progressive Matrices Test by subjects with cerebral commissurotomy. *Cortex,* 9:34, 1973.

Zangwill, O. L.: Ninth International Neuropsychological Symposium. *Neuropsychologia, 1:*7, 1963.

Zangwill, O. L.: Psychological deficits associated with frontal lobe lesions. *Int J Neurol,* 5:395, 1966.

Zimet, C. and Fishman, D. B.: Psychological deficit in schizophrenia and brain damage. *Ann Rev Psychol,* 21:113, 1970.

Zimmerman, I. L.: Residual effects of brain damage and five MMPI items. *J Consult Psychol,* 29:394, 1965.

Zurif, E. B. and Ramier, A. M.: Some effects of unilateral brain damage on the perception of dichotically presented phoneme sequences and digits. *Neuropsychologia, 10:*103, 1972.

AUTHOR INDEX

SUBJECT INDEX

Date Due